To Joya

One of the [funniest]
friends I have.
great sense of humor
and a globe trotter like
me.

Ursula Borch

7/3/23
Sun City

THROUGH THE EYES
OF A GRINGA

Eight weeks in Peru & Ecuador

URSULA B. BORCK

authorHOUSE®

AuthorHouse™
1663 Liberty Drive, Suite 200
Bloomington, IN 47403
www.authorhouse.com
Phone: 1-800-839-8640

*This book is a work of non-fiction. Unless otherwise noted, the author
and the publisher make no explicit guarantees as to the accuracy of
the information contained in this book and in some cases, names of
people and places have been altered to protect their privacy.*

First published by AuthorHouse 4/14/2009

ISBN: 978-1-4389-5832-3 (sc)

Printed in the United States of America
Bloomington, Indiana

This book is printed on acid-free paper.

This book is dedicated to my dear and long-time friend Angela Vega Nazur, who opened a whole new world for me, enriching my life and making many of my dreams come true. May she stay healthy so we can travel many more miles together.

This is also for my beloved granddaughters Hailey and Stella hoping it will make them wish to explore the world for themselves in time, to discover and behold the wonders awaiting them and help them to think for themselves rather than accept outdated doctrines without question.

PROLOGUE

Ever since I was a very young girl, I was fascinated by far away countries and places wondering what it would be like to live there or at least to visit. Of course, at that time after the war it was an impossible dream and I could only read about other people's travels and experiences, never thinking that the world would open up to me one day also. I always had a particular interest in the Americas, their cultures and people before the Europeans arrived, reading their histories awakening my desire to visit these countries even more.

Now many years and miles later I've been fortunate to travel extensively and seen most the places I wanted to see, gathering experiences and comparisons along the way as only travelers can. It's been an eye opener because I've come to realize how beautiful the world is and how all people and cultures contribute.

Traveling frequently to South America in the past twenty years or so, this book is about my experiences in particular in Ecuador and Peru with tidbits of other trips as they pop into my mind. In recent years, I've been traveling by bus to see even more of the countries of South America which I crisscrossed by plane many times before.

My friend Angela has a tourist center in Milagro, a town near Guayaquil at the Rio Guayas close to the ocean. The first part of the book takes place mostly at 'La Granja' as the tourist center is referred to by us and the people we encounter there. In the second part we travel more and I talk about our experiences of what we see, my walkabouts in Guayaquil and daily life. Throughout the entire book I mention views and happenings I read in the newspaper or news shown on TV to inform on life in this part of the world compared to here and how other people see us and what they think. In our ever shrinking world it becomes more and more important for our common future that we develop understanding, tolerance and fairness to our fellow men so as to bring us closer and avoid more wars and destruction. The book should be interesting to people who traveled there and can relate to the happenings as well as to people who haven't been there and would like to know more. Since it takes place mostly with the same people, it's also a human interest story as seen 'Through the Eyes of a Gringa.' I hope you find it interesting, entertaining and thought provoking. To me my memories are priceless.

Friday, 10/18/02

"**P**eruvians love to eat!" I have been informed more than once by my wonderful friends in Lima, Peru, as we are eating a big breakfast. Many good things are on the table like avocado, tuna salad, cheese, cold cuts, marmalade, fruit salad, delicious fresh rolls, freshly squeezed juices from fruits I hardly know and fresh coffee. Maria is encouraging me all the time to try this and that.

"No puedo," I tell Maria pushing my plate away. "I'll have some more coffee."

She says her older daughter will come home early this afternoon to take us out to eat *ceviche de conchas negras* which I was introduced to this time and just love. I like almost any seafood. Peru, like most Latin countries, prepares wonderful seafood dishes so that, when in this part of the world, I usually eat seafood.

I go upstairs to pack my suitcase which is much easier now than it was at home where I had to decide what to take. I'm done in no time at all hoping that my suitcase would not be quite as full having handed out all the gifts. No such luck! I can never leave here without receiving gifts as well. The native arts and crafts markets in Lima have a magnetic attraction for me. I have bought many wonderful arts in the past but my house is full now. Woolen blankets, wall hangings with intricate designs, bags, clothes, leather goods, paintings, furniture, silver jewelry and more are bargains and a feast for the eyes but still lighten the wallet. I concentrate on a few pieces of silver jewelry needing less space.

Finished with packing, I go downstairs when Maria's youngest daughter arrives with her baby daughter of one year. After the initial greeting, she goes straight into the kitchen.

"Vamos a tomar Pisco Sour," she calls out to me, handing me a glass of my favorite Peruvian drink as I walk in.

"A drink at this hour?" It's only one o'clock in the afternoon.

"Cómo no," she replies. "It's your last day with us."

Unfortunately this is true. I'm not looking forward to leaving although I am expected at my other friend's house in Guayaquil,

Ecuador, and am looking forward to seeing her, but a good-bye from good friends is always difficult for me.

"Salud," Maria and her daughter raise their glasses in my direction and we enjoy this Peruvian specialty made from the grape.

"Mira, mira!" somebody shouts at that moment pointing to the baby who is trying to take her first steps then looking up with a big smile on her face realizing she just accomplished something.

"Hola," my friend's oldest daughter comes in, "Cómo estás?" She joins us in a drink, but suggests we better leave soon as the reservation is for a certain time and this restaurant is always busy. We all get into the car and leave for the old historic part of town. Once there we have a hard time finding a parking spot in these narrow streets.

The restaurant is huge consisting of many individual rooms and patios without roofs. This is possible here as it never rains in Lima. We end up in a room where a giant umbrella tree serves as roof. To one side I see a small stove where certain dishes can be prepared for all to see. An old wall shields us from the outside on two sides. Happy people are talking and laughing enjoying the food and each other's company. Some sparrows are hopping around looking for whatever may have been dropped, chirping and pecking away. Nice background music enhances the atmosphere. My kind of place!

The waiter comes and we order first another Pisco Sour and then I get my *ceviche de conchas negras*, a large portion served in a bowl. Maria and her daughter also have seafood. We eat leisurely. I enjoy everything, company, food, setting and all. It's a perfect sunny day with a pleasant temperature. Upon leaving I suggest we go over to the wall on the other side of the street so I can catch one last glimpse and take another photo of this little harbor down below.

The Pacific Ocean is glistening silvery in the late afternoon sun. The boats are little dark specks far below on the water. The wide beach is largely empty only a few children play down there and brave the cool waves. My friends tell me during the season it's so crowded that people seem to be almost sitting on top of each other.

"You have taken so many photos of this spot already," says Maria. This is true but I simply love this cove always full of boats. Then we walk back to our car and slowly drive through beautiful Miraflores where all the elegant shops, hotels and restaurants are.

Artists exhibit their creations, hoping for sales. Last Saturday we saw a wonderful oil painting exhibit here and I saw many paintings I would have loved to buy but where to hang them?

Finally we are home again and now it's really time to leave. Maria takes me to the Ormeño bus station. I want to travel by bus to Ecuador to see more along the way. Ormeño is an international bus line which travels all over South America. I had flown into Lima but booked my return to the States from Guayaquil so the manner of travel from Lima to Guayaquil is open to me.

We wiggle our way through the heavy traffic and then through the crowded terminal. Across from us I see a young blonde woman. Maria wonders if perhaps she will be traveling with me. I speak to her and learn that she is with an American health team in Quito, the capitol of Ecuador, studying and working but right now on her way to Southern Peru to work in a health clinic there for ten days. We talk a little before I return to Maria. It doesn't take long before I have to say good-bye to Maria and remind her once again that I'm expecting her in my house soon. We have established next November for her visit with me.

My seat is the first one on top of the double-decker bus with windows all around and even curling up onto the roof. Too bad the bus leaves at night but Maria says there isn't that much to see along the coast but sand. The seats in these buses are wonderful. They are the size of first class seats on airplanes and can be lowered so far that one is actually lying flat. The other great feature I really appreciate is the leg support. This is a round-shaped support, starting from the end of the seat all the way down so that one's legs can rest most comfortably. I had experienced this for the first time on my trip from Buenos Aires, Argentina, to Bariloche a resort area in the Andes of Argentina. The buses in South America are mostly Mercedes buses, the likes of which I've never seen in the States.

Finally our bus pulls out into the heavy traffic of Lima on Friday night. We move slowly through the busy streets until we come to a complete stop. At the intersection in front of us the most unbelievable traffic congestion, with cars facing any which direction, completely stops all movement. The streets around also resemble parking lots as far as I can see.

Ursula B. Borck

"Goodness, how are we going to get past this?" I can't see how this can ever unravel. There is no room for any car to move. Standing there observing the scene I fear the trip will not even get started. Horns are sounding while people are leaving their cars to check the situation. I'm so glad that I'm not behind the wheel. Finally, after about 20 minutes, I see one man gesticulating with his arms trying to direct. Wonder oh wonder eventually one car moves, then another, and finally the knot unravels until all cars move including our bus. Hallelujah!

We arrive in the suburbs where people have set up little cooking stoves here and there to prepare simple meals like rice and beans, the all time staple of Latin America. Meat is not eaten as much but what is consumed in large quantities is fruit of first quality and mostly unadulterated. People are busy cooking, eating and talking and enjoying the end of the workday. Soon we are out of town and surrounded by darkness. I can see nothing but know that the Pacific has to be to the left and the coastal desert to the right as we are heading north.

A box dinner is being served with juice. Maria gave me some food to take as well. She was worried I might not have enough. Then they turn on the TV where some American cowboys are doing their stuff.

Looking up at the sky I see so many bright stars. The moon is almost full. I think of all the extraterrestrial flying saucers supposed to zoom around here in South America and wonder why I never see one. No matter how I scrutinize the sky I see nothing unusual. My mind wonders and I think of the reason I am here on this bus.

"It's all Teresa's fault!" When I flew down to Lima on American Airlines from Dallas/Fort Worth on October eighth I had two very nice travel companions. Lisa, a young American, was on her way to Lima to sponsor her fiancé for immigration into the States. She told us that she had met him when studying in Lima recently. They would have to get married within three months after his arrival in the States. She was worried and hoped all would go well when she had to appear at the American Embassy with him.

Then there was Teresa from Trujillo in Northern Peru in the window seat. She spoke no English and I got my Spanish practice before arriving in Lima. She was returning from the States after a

4

lengthy visit with her two married daughters. She said her luggage was so heavy because her daughters had sent gifts along for her and other family members.

"I had to buy another suitcase."

"Where are you going?" she asked me.

"I am going to see my friends in Lima. I haven't seen them in over three years or the new baby of my friend's youngest daughter."

"Oh, you have friends in Lima! That's very nice but you are not going to do any sight-seeing at all?"

"Well, I have seen quite a bit of Peru already. This is not my first trip here. I've been to Cuzco and Machu Picchu, down the coast south of Lima as far as Nazca and flown over the Nazca Lines. Last time we even went to Ayacucho high in the Andes where the Shining Path movement started. That was an interesting experience to which my friend refers to this day as *nuestra aventura* and an adventure it was."

"Oh! You have seen much already."

"Yes, I have been in Peru many times as I love to travel. Besides, Peru is such an interesting country full of history."

"Sí, but do you know Cajamarca or Trujillo in Northern Peru? Both are very interesting also with many archaeological sites of the Inca and Chimu cultures. This is where the famous Chan Chan ruins are."

Teresa didn't know she had said the magic words *archaeological sites.* I'm very interested in archaeology, in particular of the Americas, and have traveled many miles and distances to see one or the other site. I became immediately interested and asked her many questions.

We had a lively conversation before, during and after the meal which we enjoyed with some delicious Merlot American Airlines served us. The stewardess was obviously pleased when I commented on the much improved quality of the wine. Lisa and I even talked Teresa into having a glass of wine. Nobody noticed the movie they showed. We got on so well that none of us wanted to move to another row of seats even though there were some rows that had only one person in them.

"I'm very comfortable," Lisa said who was in the middle seat but is very slim. So we all stayed together and talked and talked until we finally dropped off to sleep or I should say I dozed because I don't ever remember having had a very sound sleep on a plane. Some people seem to sleep almost immediately and some even snore away but I'm not so lucky.

We arrived right on time in Lima just before midnight. We collected our luggage and were out of the plane and through Customs and Immigration in no time. "What improvement," I thought remembering the many times I had passed through here and was in line forever - or so it seemed - as there were only three counters or so. Now there were between eight and ten counters processing people quickly.

Teresa, Lisa and I said good-bye to each other. We wished Lisa well with the American Embassy. I hope she'll be happy. She would be picked up and Teresa also. Teresa has family here and would spend the night with them going to Trujillo tomorrow.

Walking through the Terminal towards the exit I saw Maria laughing and arms waving. It was a happy reunion with many hugs. Her oldest daughter was along also and the three of us drove home. Their house is quite some distance from the airport and by the time we arrived it was close to one in the morning but we continued talking until we finally went to bed by about three in the morning.

Now here I am on this bus and the visit to Lima I had so looked forward to, is already behind me. Too bad I didn't get Teresa's phone number; however, I was not at all sure then that I would take this trip. Only when Maria confirmed what Teresa had said that Cajamarca and Trujillo are well worth visiting did I decide to take this bus tour.

Saturday, 10/19/02

D awn is just breaking when I wake up. Looking out the window, I see a very different landscape. We are in a valley with high mountains rising steeply to the right whereas the side to the left of the road seems to be falling off just as steeply. A narrow and fast-moving creek is visible now and then as we come around curves. The bus is moving carefully on this road that is so narrow in places that we, or oncoming traffic, have to stop. There is only room for one vehicle to pass. I have a panoramic view of this beautiful part of the country and the winding road climbing steadily. I trust our driver thinking he knows this road inside out. My front seat, however, would not be for the fainthearted.

Now and then we encounter some Indians along the road walking or waiting for some transportation. In these areas the bus stops wherever there are people. The Indians are tightly wrapped in their serapes as it is very cold so early in the morning at this altitude. The bus comes to a sudden stop and then slowly moves through the middle of a small herd of cattle being driven to their grazing grounds by two Indian boys on horses.

It's about seven in the morning when we arrive in Cajamarca at the Bus Terminal. I find the washroom and wash my face, brush my teeth and comb my hair before going to the counter to buy my return ticket to Trujillo for that same evening and to leave my luggage with them. I thought one day was probably enough to look around here. Then I inquire how much the taxi should cost to the center of town and walk out to the street. All the other passengers have left already. I wave down a taxi and tell him the price I had been told. He is agreeable and takes me to the main plaza. He wants to know where I'm from and how long I'll stay and offers to tour and guide me to the bath of the last Inca and other sites for 'only' fifty dollars. I tell him that's much too high for me.

"I'll be inquiring for a tour and if you want to wait for me if your price is better, do so."

We arrive at the plaza. I pay and before I enter the tourist office I see the taxi speeding away. I find out the tour costs five American dollars and I pay with a bill. There is still time before the departure to have a cup of coffee. I find a little restaurant on the other side where a friendly lady serves me the coffee and a roll. From my chair I can see the plaza, watch the people go by and when done, leave to walk a little. There are two beautiful cathedrals at opposite sides on the plaza which consists of a well-maintained park, walks and benches to sit. As early as it is, just around eight in the morning, there are already many people out.

Cajamarca is where the last Inca ruler Atahualpa was killed by the Spaniards in 1533. It is the capital of the province by the same name in Northern Peru situated at an elevation of over 9,000 feet high in the Andes bordering on Ecuador. Looking through a pamphlet I see that they grow corn, wheat, barley and potatoes here. There is also dairy ranching, mining and not to forget, tourism. It is still an important trading center. The population appears to be mainly Indian to this day.

Our tour starts with a mini bus, definitely too small for this size group. We are sitting as tightly as sardines in a can. Then comes the next surprise my five dollar bill isn't good because it has a tiny rip on one side. I tell them that this is a sign it is definitely good - it has been around for a while and is not printed just now but they say the bank won't accept the bill and as we are not leaving either, I have to give them some other money. Unfortunately, it's too late to change buses as all the other tours have left. There are two main tours being offered and they leave at the same time in the morning and afternoon and they all go to one place in the morning and the other in the afternoon.

We start moving slowly up the rather steep streets with the overloaded bus. Right in the beginning we have to make a detour as it's a religious holiday and religious paintings are laid out in some streets, similar to the sand paintings of the Navajo, varying in size. One can't step on them nor can one drive over them. A neighborhood had decided to use their narrow street for a display so our bus has to back down and find a different route.

Ever so slowly we climb up higher and higher on steep cobblestoned streets. Once up, we all get out enjoying the view over the city and take photos. Then we travel further into the mountains. We leave the bus and are now walking slowly uphill all the time. The landscape is mostly green, rounded hills interrupted by rocks. Like bright flowers here and there we encounter the native Indian women in their colorful skirts and serapes wearing the typical hats of the area. They herd the sheep, spin wool, sit by the wayside or walk to whatever destination they have. I exchange a few words and take pictures. One or the other then sends a child to us to ask for money for the photo. Further down a man is getting off his wagon to walk across a meadow to catch a horse grazing peacefully.

Then we see them - interesting gray rock formations, some resembling people which immediately remind me of the Chiricahua National Monument in Southeastern Arizona. Our tour guide points out the particular rocks that seem to have human faces. Another rock formation looks like a giant castle. We walk on and come to an ancient aqueduct and springs of absolutely crystal clear water ending in a little pool eventually squeezing through rocks. All of a sudden it begins to rain, lightly at first getting heavier and then lighter again. At first we are not alarmed but the rain keeps falling and few of us carry an umbrella. We tell the tour guide we want to get back to the bus. He agrees because there isn't that much we can do in the rain. We do squeeze through a narrow rock formation and then head for the bus in a different location from where he dropped us off.

We drive back to town in quite heavy rain and arrive one half hour early. I can't believe the water in Cajamarca - the streets all resemble little rivers or currents gushing downhill. It's not easy to cross a street in ordinary shoes. I make my way across town by skipping and jumping as best I can but it doesn't take long and my feet are definitely wet. I find a large indoors market and buy some apples. Suddenly I have this craving for an apple. They look delicious and the young Indian girl tells me it's okay to eat them because they are clean. I believe her and devour two of them in no time at all, without bad after effects.

I spend the remaining time walking and looking around the city as far as possible because there are showers off and on. I look into one of the cathedrals and another church which is open and see a wedding party and a funeral procession. An open door of a hotel is inviting. I pass through the corridor into the inner courtyard which is very beautiful with its dark brown wooden staircases leading to the upper rooms, balconies and benches. I love these courtyards. Years ago in Lima I took a photo of a courtyard which turned out so nice that I enlarged and framed it for my dining room.

By late afternoon the sun is shining brightly and I need my sun glasses to protect my eyes from the glare. A wide stone staircase leading up the big hill to a chapel has interested me all day. It is very high and quite steep towards the top but I tackle it. As I climb little artist shops and boutiques on both sides are inviting and the storekeepers friendly so we have many nice little conversations. I had noticed earlier that, apart from knit sweaters and woolen serapes, they make beautiful masks here and metal objects. In the Mercado and in some shops I had seen huge round or rectangular blocks of chocolate. This is the chocolate of the Inca to make hot chocolate not to eat like that. It's also slightly spiced and tastes delicious. I had some in Lima. Maria's help is from Cuzco and her mother sends her these blocks of chocolate. Finally I arrive at the top and, turning around, I am immediately blinded by the city glistening in the late afternoon sun. Droplets of water hanging from trees, plants and roof tops, reflecting the bright light even stronger, are multiplying the brilliance. Putting my sunglasses on, I'm so glad I made the climb taking in the scene for a while before I start the descent.

The taxi driver, who takes me to the bus terminal later, tells me that this rain today was nothing. In the season the streets are often impassible and some of the houses get flooded or totally destroyed if not built well. The only good thing is that the water does run off eventually.

By now it's quite cold in Cajamarca. The terminal is not heated either and one manager there is determined to keep the door open at all times. The moment one person closes it he'll again open it upon his return. This way the wind is blowing throughout and I can hardly wait to get into the bus. By the time this happy moment arrives I am cold through and through.

We leave around eight in the evening. After a short while, they serve a box meal again with some hot coffee. The TV is on, another westerner I'm not watching. I have the front seat again but cannot see much anymore. How lucky I woke up this morning around six.

I think of my friends in Lima again feeling fortunate to know them. The entire family is so pleasant and spoils me whenever I visit. I accompanied Maria to a street market selling mostly vegetables, fruit and potatoes. If she didn't need much of a particular fruit she would ask the sellers anyway to give me one to taste on the spot telling me the names, etc. I must have had four or five different fruits right there and then with her and the vendors looking expectantly at me. "Te gusta?" they finally asked. Yes, I liked most of them. She has her special stands from which she buys and the women know her. Maria doesn't look like the typical Peruvian with her reddish hair, fair, freckled skin and tall stature. Her forefathers came from northern Europe generations ago. She is not easily overlooked in a crowd. Maria is also extremely funny. I remember the time when we both went to Nazca and found out it was hard to get on a plane to fly over the famous Nazca Lines properly visible from the air only. Maria, who was eating nuts at the time, did all the talking with the man arranging these flights. She would put one nut into her mouth and hand one to the man who took it. She continued this while telling him a funny story making him laugh. Next morning I flew over the Nazca Lines looking down and admiring the size of the different shapes of a monkey, humming bird, etc. thus fulfilling a dream I had ever since I was a teenager and wondering who put them there and why.

Maria took me to Miraflores and to Larco Mar a new shopping, eating and entertainment area sitting on top of the steep coast consisting of dark sand not rock. Larco Mar is a relatively new two-level development and contains something for the entire family with fancy boutiques, stores, expensive restaurants and fast-food places and daily entertainment. On that Saturday we went to Barranco afterwards, another area of Lima which has an artist market but much smaller. Naturally, we all found something we couldn't live without.

Sunday, 10/20/02

"Señora, Señora," I hear a voice calling, "estamos en Trujillo." Confused, I open my eyes, "Estamos en Trujillo," the stewardess says again.

I must have fallen into a deep sleep which is no surprise considering I didn't sleep much the night before. It takes a moment for me to be fully awake but then I get up immediately take my bag and step outside. Everyone around me is sleeping but once outside I see another person getting off also. The bus terminal is closed; everything is closed and I see no lights outside of the bus headlights and the moon above.

"Necessita un taxi," I tell them. Miraculously the bus driver brings back a taxi driver who takes my bags and off we go. The bus driver had told him a hotel nearby to which to take me. The streets are deserted. It is one-thirty in the morning. The taxi driver asks me the usual questions and then offers his services to take me to the ruins for a very high price. I tell him that the same thing had happened to me in Cajamarca, and I then had a tour for a fraction of the price and do not want to commit myself right now.

We arrive at the hotel. The taxi driver rings the bell and the night clerk lets me in saying their rate is thirty dollars for the night. That's fine with me. I am dead-tired and have only one desire right now - to make the most of what's left of the night.

The room is small but very nice with all the comforts, including color TV and bathroom with shower. It takes only a few minutes and I'm in bed. When I wake up it is eight in the morning. I shower and hurry down to breakfast included in the price. First I talk with the hotel manager about a tour. He tells me there are not many tours on Sunday and that it would be best to hire a taxi to take me around and he'll call somebody. Soon enough a taxi drives up and he goes out to talk with the driver. When he comes back in he says this man will take me around.

"Do you know him and is he a nice guy?" After all, I don't know where we have to go to see these Chan-Chan ruins.

"Sí, sí," he responds, "un buen hombre."

At that moment the taxi driver enters and I have to say I feel good about him. I like his face. That is very important to me as I go much by people's faces. He is middle-aged, medium build and slender. Stepping out into the street I don't feel so confident about the taxi which has certainly seen better days. The idea of being stuck somewhere out in nowhere in this banged-up taxi has no appeal and I ask him if his taxi is in good condition to travel outside of town.

"Sí," he replies with assurance, "the car has a new motor and it runs well." With these words he closes the door and we are on our way to see the Chimu ruins of Chan-Chan, the name of this archaeological site. The taxi rattles along on the cobble stones in Trujillo but once we are outside of town it's less noisy. We cross Trujillo and the Trans-America Highway which goes all the way from Alaska to Chile. The Chan-Chan complex is located close to the Pacific Ocean in the West and the Cordillera on the East.

Walter, the driver, informs me of all this. His Spanish is clear and I have no trouble understanding him. In fact he is a fountain of knowledge and I ask many questions, all of which he answers without hesitation. He informs me that the Chan-Chan complex consists of four main parts the first of which is the Museum giving the background information and displays items found, then Tchudi Palace the largest complex, next Dragon o Arco Iris, and La

Esmeralda. The name "Tchudi" seems strange to me for this part of the world and I comment on this. Walter tells me that the palace was named after the archaeologist who studied it.

"Well, it sounds Swiss or Italian to me."

"You know names and languages!"

"I'm no expert but interested in names, their origins and other cultures."

"Yes, I can see that. You also speak Spanish very well."

"Gracias."

At this point we are driving up to the museum where I have to buy my tickets for the four sites. Walter tells me he'll wait outside and just to take my time. Upon entering the first thing I see is a big plate showing the cultures and people in the valley of the Moche. The Chimu of the Chan-Chan site are believed to have been here from about 900 - 1400 AD it says. Then the Inca came. The Chimu probably co-existed with the Inca from then on. Before that the Wari people were there and the Moche, being older than any others, from about 450 - 700 AD.

There are more historical details which I read; some photos, some pottery and jewelry, but the museum is relatively small so that I finish pretty quickly. We drive a little further and arrive at Tchudi Palace, a busy place. Groups of tourists from all over the country and the world, even school children on a field trip are assembled. One can also buy some snacks and souvenirs. I give them one of my tickets and follow the clearly marked route.

The size of this complex almost takes my breath away the moment I come around a few corners and see the giant center plaza in front of me. Some of the decorated walls are still standing and show a fish and waterfowl design surrounded by waves showing a connection to the sea. Since Chan-Chan was built relatively close to the Pacific Ocean it's understandable that the sea played an important part in their culture. It's very hot here in the desert but the Chimu made sure they didn't run out of water as they had - in their time - four big lakes right on this site which is believed to have been their capital and cultural metropolis. Today there is still one big lake remaining on which there are some water fowl and two imported penguins whose well-being poses a concern as one of the guards tells me when I ask him.

As I slowly walk around this enormous complex which is considered the largest pre-Columbian metropolis in the Americas, I arrive at a tower with a viewing platform with many people up there and climb up as well. Everybody marvels at the size of this site as I hear from exclamations around me. It is truly overwhelming. Whenever I walk in these prehistoric sites I always wonder what the ancient people were like who lived there long before us, how their daily life went and what they thought. Were they happy and what was important to them? What did they believe, fear, avoid or wish for? Too bad we can't go back in time and watch - just a little bit. I walk around various plazas, palaces, walkways and to the one remaining lake, marveling at what I see. When I'm finally done I return to the taxi and express my admiration to Walter. He's obviously happy that I appreciate their history.

It's about lunch time. I invite Walter to have lunch with me and to find us a good restaurant. He is pleased and asks me what I like to eat.

"Mariscos," I respond, "I love seafood."

"Bueno," Walter answers, "so do I. I know a wonderful restaurant right by the sea but we have to travel a little further if you don't mind. It's in Huanchaco at the beach which is north of Trujillo."

Of course I don't mind. In fact I get a little extra sight-seeing this way. The restaurant *Lucho del Mar* is right on the beach, a big, beautiful beach curving to the north. We get a wonderful table upstairs on the balcony overlooking the promenade and entire playa below us. What a colorful scene! There are vendors selling ice cream, fruit, juices and souvenirs, people and tourists from everywhere and quite a few people at the beach swimming and sunbathing. A few reed boats are propped up for decoration. To the left of us a long pier extends out into the ocean. A large group of people at a table close to us enjoy their get-together and food.

Looking over the menu, I ask Walter what the specialty is. He recommends a certain fish dish which turns out to be a really excellent choice. While we sit there and eat we have a lively conversation going. I learn that he is 45 years old, has a wife who works also and two teenage children in college. They have a house of their own and apparently a nice lifestyle. He doesn't seem unhappy.

Walter mostly takes tourists like me around rather than providing the traditional taxi service.

We don't linger after lunch as there is much more to see, Walter reminds me. Next on our list is El Dragon o Arco Iris site. This consists of mostly a huge temple in pyramid form with extremely beautiful decorations. There are fourteen cubicles around the top platform which are believed to have been used for storage of food and other items for religious purposes. According to the pamphlet, this pyramid was probably constructed in the early period of the Chimu/end of Wari culture. The entire complex is small compared to Tchudi and surrounded by contemporary homes. It does, however, have some excellent relief work of animal, people and mythical figures. Walking on top of the wall, I look down on boys playing soccer right next to the temple.

Then we drive to La Esmeralda, a smaller place and go to Las *Huacas de Moche*. This site of the Moche people consists of the Huaca de la Luna mostly excavated and the Huaca del Sol still waiting to be uncovered. At least the Moon temple is the only one open to tourists.

I'm particularly interested in seeing this Moche site. I remember reading in our local paper about this older culture being discovered not that long ago. This new discovery fascinated me as I truly feel there are still many pieces missing in the anthropological as well as archaeological puzzle even though I am by no means an expert, just a person very interested in our past. This discovery again confirms my above belief.

The wind is blowing pretty strong but the sun is shining. Walter thinks I should take my jacket but I tell him I won't need it. I love the wind! Climbing up the long hill to the Moon Temple makes me warm already. On a platform a guide is telling a group of people that this particular temple varies from other constructions in that this building, as we see it today, is the result of various platforms and buildings built on top of each other. It is believed that it was built over a period of 600 years, in different epochs, for ceremonial purposes. So far they have discovered six different buildings on top of each other.

To my surprise there are various polychrome murals in very good condition. They depict a *Divinidad de la Montaña* - God of the

Mountain or *El Degollador.* I listen for a while to the guide before slowly going on my own discovery. It's a large complex and I find new rooms, doorways and decorations as I explore. From below, the size of this temple is not visible.

I see another doorway walk through it and turn around. Both sides are heavily decorated and in good condition. I take a photo and step back further out on another huge platform to get a better look at it. Upon turning around I'm facing a young Indian who greets me friendly telling me that he is working with the local archaeological team. He thinks it's a good idea I separated from the group to explore on my own. We talk a while about the temple. The Indian student points out the stylized serpent along the entire wall of this platform. I'm glad he is there so I can learn more details. At the far end of the platform which faces the Sun Temple opposite still largely covered, I see what is left of the city between the two temples where the ordinary people lived. I take a photo from up here this being the only way I can ever get anything of the city to show up because much of it is covered by sand over the eons of time.

Finally it's getting late and time to leave. Walter waited patiently for me everywhere and I'm so glad that I had him to drive me to all these sites. We discuss many things until we reach the hotel where I pay and thank him for all the information and the nice company he was. "De nada," he answers, "I see you are truly interested and that is gratifying to me."

"Gracias," I know that people here, like people everywhere, are proud of their past and happy when they see genuine interest.

Everybody in the hotel wants to know how my day went and I tell them how much I enjoyed it. That puts smiles on their faces. I thank the manager for having arranged for the taxi. He is pleased and wants to know what was all included, had I seen this and that, etc. Then, since it's only a little after five in the afternoon, I go for a walk in the city.

"La Plaza Mayor no es lejos," the manager tells me, adding "puedes caminar." Walter had told me already I could easily walk to the main plaza not forgetting the usual warning to be careful.

The street from the hotel leads directly to the plaza with many people out for a stroll but few stores open on Sunday, only the ones who have tourist items. The plaza is also crowded. Young and old is out walking, talking or taking a rest on a bench and watching the world go by. Children are playing noisily and vendors try to sell everything from cookies to fruit, juices or other items that can be loaded into a basket or put on a pushcart like ice cream and soft drinks. Not to forget the lottery ticket vendors - one sees them at all times everywhere. Chiclets, another popular item, is mostly sold by children. It's a very colorful scene. Then I walk along some nearby streets and take photos of the wonderful wooden, dark brown carved balconies from the colonial times everywhere - just like in Lima. The carved or lattice work in front allowed the people to see without being seen themselves.

After the walk I sit down on a bench to watch the people go by. A young couple joins me obviously eager to start a conversation. They are very young but tell me that they are engaged and want to get married next year. They are saving their money. Then they want to know where I come from and what life is like in Phoenix. After a while they tell me good-bye and "buen viaje" and leave. Finally I also get up and walk back to the hotel, it's getting darker and I feel hungry.

Walter had told me about a good restaurant very close to the hotel on the same side of the street. I ask about the restaurant in the hotel. The information is confirmed and I head out the door again seeing the restaurant almost immediately and entering, like what I see. Nice place, nice atmosphere and pleasant people. The food a fish dish - how could it be otherwise for me - is wonderful. I also have one more big tasty potato. The potatoes in Peru, where they originate, are by far the best I've ever eaten.

Later back at the hotel I sit down in the lobby and read the paper, talk with the people and watch the news on TV. They show Toledo, the Peruvian President, who has been under fire by his cabinet and was on the news every day I stayed with my friends in Lima due to a lawsuit regarding an illegitimate daughter he didn't want to acknowledge. He is shown with his wife and 'new' daughter, saying: Gané una hija!... She is a beautiful girl and said to be also very intelligent. Maria in Lima was so pleased when the announcement was made just before I left.

The Argentine couple comes in again and we greet each other with Buenas Noches. We had met in the morning at breakfast and started a little conversation about the usual things. They also complimented me on my good Spanish and wanted to know where I was from.

"Where do you think I'm from?"

"Brazil" they promptly replied.

I laughed out loud and told them, "No, I was born in Europe."

"Oh, we were also born in Europe, in Italy."

"In Italy," I said surprised, "I thought you were Argentineans because of the way you pronounce certain words, like playa *playsha* or lleno *sheno*."

I could see surprise on his face while his wife laughed out loud. He joined in but then asked me: "You can tell the difference?"

"I can tell the difference because it caused me quite a problem in Argentina when I visited there the first time and had no idea of this version of Spanish."

"Oh you have been to Argentina also!"

"Yes, on three different occasions. I love it there," asking, "do you know Bariloche?"

"No, we haven't been to Bariloche. Most of our trips were back to Italy. However we are thinking of going there soon."

They thought it most unusual that I, a foreigner, told them about Bariloche while they, living in Argentina, had never been there. Right now they were on their way to Ecuador as was I. When I mentioned to them no matter what they do to make sure they see Cuenca in the Andes they answered that it wasn't on their agenda. I suggested they squeeze it in if they have no time constraint. I know you'll not be sorry.

They had left their baggage in the hotel and came to pick it up. After exchanging our daily adventures we say our good-byes one more time and then they leave.

"Remember Cuenca," I call after them thinking what a nice couple they are and how, on all my travels, I encounter such wonderful people no matter where in the world I go. My fellow globetrotters everywhere always contribute so much to my travel experience.

Finally the time comes for me to go back to the Terminal and just before eleven in the evening we depart with Ormeño from Trujillo for Guayaquil, Ecuador.

This time I sit down below where there are two seats together on each side of the isle. The seats are just as wide but when the stewardess shows me mine it is next to an oversized man sprawled out over half of the other seat as well. He's in deep sleep. The expression on my face makes the stewardess suggest another seat right next to a very slender young girl.

"Much better," I tell her and ask that she please let me know when a seat upstairs becomes available in the morning. She says she will and I thank her.

Even though tired I can't sleep right away thinking how fortunate I am to see all the things I saw today and what a wonderful Sunday I had spent. Then last Sunday comes into my mind when Maria and I first drove to her youngest daughter's house and then together with her and her baby daughter to the beach south of Lima, La Playa Punto Hermoso, where her oldest daughter has had a beach house for some years and Maria now had one built also. Her house is basically finished except for some minor details and painting. It's beautiful and has a huge roof deck from which one can look down on the Pacific.

It was much warmer there than in Lima and we took a nice walk along the beach promenade. Many people were out, some sunbathing at the beach and children playing in the water. Surfers took advantage of the waves but the water was still cold. I tested it with my feet only. As I looked around I commented on how the area has grown - many more homes everywhere and some of considerable size. My friends confirm that many people from Lima have beach houses here for the summer because it's relatively close to Lima, thirty to forty minutes, and people come out here Friday after work and return Sunday night. It's convenient and the area picturesque.

The baby became acquainted with sand for the first time and didn't quite know what to make of it. The fine sand is dark in color in fact the entire coastline is dark sand - even the hills.

We sit down at the promenade and have some beer and the roasted corn nuts we all like so much. It was amazingly warm and we all tried to sit in the shade of the umbrella over the table watching the activities around us.

When we returned to Lima in the evening a message awaited Maria that one of her good, long-time friends succumbed to cancer after a long fight. She told me about her friend's suffering trying to fight this illness. Even though she knew this was happening she didn't expect it to happen so quickly. It was so final now to which I could relate very well because I also lost one of my best girlfriends to Cancer about nine years ago.

That same night the bombs went off in Bali - killing over two hundred people!

Later that evening we watched *El Clon* again, a TV series that has all of South America going. It shows every night for one hour and reminds me a little of *Peyton Place* such a long time ago.

While in Lima the birds and doves woke me up with their singing. Not that I got up so early but that was the first sound I heard every morning. After breakfast that day Maria and I drove to Callao, the port area of Lima, where their office is located. Her oldest daughter took us to lunch.

I had one less pleasant experience. When I wanted to buy my Ormeño ticket in Lima, I could neither pay with American Express nor with Citibank Mastercard. They wanted Visa. We didn't have enough cash between the two of us and tried to find Citibank. When we were finally successful they wanted my pin number which I didn't have as I never use the automatic teller. I showed them my Citibank Mastercard, driver's license and my passport, but to no avail. They mentioned another bank which would give me the money but by now it was too late and it was closed. We had no other choice but to drive back to the house where I took some of my cash I actually wanted to conserve and then we had to go out into the evening commute traffic again which was a nightmare.

That same night I called my friend Angela in Guayaquil to tell her I had bought the ticket and would arrive on Monday at two in the afternoon and would take a taxi to her house.

Monday, 10/21/02

I wake up early thinking we must be close to the border and, indeed, it doesn't take long before the bus stops in Tumbes, the northernmost city in Peru at the Pacific Ocean. We all have to get off, have our passports ready and fill in an entry permit before we pass by the immigration officers. One person is pulled aside; he doesn't seem to have the proper identification but the whole process is fast and we have only a little time left to buy some fruits and drinks before the bus snakes through the crowded streets of Tumbes with its *taxi chola* as Maria had called them in Ayacucho, a contraption on three wheels with a bike handlebar and a driver peddling away. Some people got off during the night and the stewardess takes me to a seat above close to the front.

Once in Ecuador, the road takes us along the Pacific for a while with partially pristine beaches, some rocky outcrops and a few huts and houses. Once in a while a small hotel is visible but the tourist industry is not the main business here – it's bananas and shrimp pools near Machala. We drive through banana plantations on both sides of the road for miles and miles which I remember from an earlier trip we took to Machala in southern Ecuador. Yes it all looks familiar - bananas everywhere. We travel from Machala to Naranjal, pass close to Milagro and finally are in Guayaquil. Approaching the city the area looks familiar but the new highway with a broad center divide planted with trees didn't exist when I was here last. It throws me off somewhat until we cross the bridges and I see the familiar outline of Guayaquil.

I ask some ladies traveling with me on the bus how much I should have to pay for a taxi to get to the center of town to my friends' house. They tell me three dollars. Ecuador, for about two years now, has dollar currency convenient for tourists.

A taxi pulls up and a young man gets out helping with my luggage asking where I want to go. I tell him and mention that I have been told the fare should be three dollars which he confirms saying with a smile he would accept more also. The usual conversation ensues where I'm from, how long I'll stay and how nice I have friends here. He tells me that he's a teacher and this is his second job to supplement his income. He also goes to school to learn English and he wants to speak English with me while I tell him I want to practice my Spanish.

"Okay," he says, "you speak Spanish to me and I speak English to you."

"That's good," I answer. "It's a good idea for you to know another language."

"Yes, I want to move to the United States because things are difficult here."

"It isn't easy to find work in the States either and many people are losing their jobs."

"But you see," he says, "I'm a teacher and the United States needs teachers now, especially teachers who can also speak Spanish."

"We do, however, we have many people who are bilingual, although I don't know if many of them are qualified teachers."

"Exactly; I've spoken with friends who assure me I shouldn't have difficulty obtaining employment but I want to improve my English first and then perhaps try in a year or two from now to get a visa. I'm twenty-six. I have time to improve my English before I go to the States."

"I've read in the papers in the States that the economy in Ecuador is moving up. Are you sure you want to leave?"

"It's getting better in some ways but the salaries are low and there is the corruption.

"I agree the corruption is a major problem in many of the countries here and is, of course, a direct result of the low salaries. People who cannot meet their expense will try to make money any way they can. On the other hand we have corruption in the States also, corruption of a different kind and on a larger scale. It's sad that people who have too much power have no social conscience."

"I still think life is better there."

"Tell that to the people who lose their jobs, their homes, have no healthcare and don't know how to carry on."

He is a good driver and wiggles his way easily through the traffic so that it takes no more than about ten minutes or so and we are at the Parque Centenario, the main plaza in Guayaquil, in front of the house. The young man takes my luggage out and I pay him and wish him good luck and he hopes I have a good time here.

Segundo, the indigenous vendor, is still there with his candy and newspaper stand. I walk over to him and request that he call Angela's mother upstairs. He complies immediately but I'm not sure he instantly recognizes me. He hangs up the receiver and tells me her help will come down.

Rosa greets me with a big smile. She is a very young and beautiful, slender girl of African descent who's Amelia's companion and cooks for her. I like her at once. She takes one of my suitcases and we go into the house. She opens the elevator for us and puts a key in a special lock so we can ascend. This is for security reasons and why I had to ask Segundo to call.

"Bienvenido Ursula, "Amelia greets me happily.

We hug and kiss on the cheek and I feel immediately at home. Amelia tells me that Angela and her son are still at *La Granja* as her tourist center is referred to. She says lunch is ready and we can eat in a few minutes after she also asks me about my son and my granddaughter whom she knew from a previous visit to my house.

"Can I please take a shower first," I ask, "I haven't had a shower since yesterday morning in the hotel in Trujillo and I feel dirty."

She asks Rosa to see that everything is in order and I take my shower, put clean clothes on and feel like a new person.

"Sientate, sientate," she says repeating in English," sit down you must be very hungry."

I can't deny that. The last real good meal I had the night before in Trujillo. Rosa serves us the soup, the salad and a delicious main course. I enjoy every bite and tell Rosa that she's a great cook. She smiles happily saying, "gracias."

"Hi Ursula, how are you," Angela greets me with a hug. "You look great!"

"Hello Angela, I'm fine and you look great, too."

"When did you arrive? I wanted to meet you at the Bus Terminal, but I couldn't get away on time."

"Not necessary at all. The bus came in early anyway. I took a taxi here."

"I was worried about you taking a taxi because we had a case not long ago where a taxi driver took some tourists to a lonely spot and then robbed and left them there."

"Oh really; I had such a nice young man, a teacher, who drives taxi as a second job. We had a great conversation."

"I'm so glad that you got here safely," Angela responds just as her son Ivan, whom I call Ivanovich, enters.

"Hi Ursula how are you? It's so nice to see you again!" I had seen him only two months ago in Arizona while he was visiting his oldest daughter and family. We had a few get-togethers and I drove him around the Phoenix area. He was so surprised about all the changes since he had been here thirty years ago or so.

We all talk for a long time exchanging news. A bed is set up for me in Angela's large air-conditioned bedroom which she keeps so cold that I refer to it as the *ice box* but she says she can't sleep otherwise. We talk some more then watch *El Clon* until we fall asleep.

Tuesday, 10/22/02

We are on the road again…on our way to *La Granja* driving the same divided highway I had come in yesterday, discussing the big improvement that took place here.

"It only exists for about a year," Angela says adding "the road in front of *La Granja* is also being turned into a four-lane highway which will make travel so much easier. Right now it's a big mess and I have to pay for some of the improvement."

Arriving at *La Granja* I see what she means. The road from the Guayaquil Highway to Milagro is in various stages of grading - also around her property. The entire road was widened from two lanes to four so Angela and all other people with walls or fences too close to the road, had to remove them and set them back to allow for the widening and for a ditch to be dug right outside their properties. The government took the wall down and dug the ditch for the new one but she had to buy all the material herself and pay for the work. I was surprised to hear that she won't be reimbursed for the cost but she said this is how it is.

Most the cement base and wall is up and so are the brick columns to hold the rest of the fence. Right now they are working at the gate column and entrance. Angela carefully maneuvers the old four-wheel-drive down from the road into the ditch and onto her property. She stops to talk with the people who all look at me curiously before we drive on towards the first set of buildings consisting of a restaurant/bar, a large separate kitchen building, another building with quarters for some of the workers, a kitchen, a museum and storage for the tools and then the house we live in.

Two women come out to greet us and she introduces Marta, the manager and Ida, Angela's personal help, to me. They both have big smiles on their faces and greet me friendly. I don't know them as both are very recent hires. In fact I don't know anyone anymore except for Pedro and I don't recognize him at first because he's put on quite a few pounds.

"Yo soy Ursula," I say to him thinking the face looks familiar.

"Yo soy Pedro," he responds with a big grin on his face.

"Pedro!" I shout, "My goodness I didn't recognize you at first. There is so much more of you now." hugging him affectionately.

"*Es muy gordo*," Marta throws in, "*come mucho*."

Pedro grins sheepishly and we all laugh. I tell him that I hope the T-Shirt I brought for him will fit because I remember him as very slender but after ten years of working here with more authority now as co-manager he doesn't have to work physically so hard anymore.

After talking for a while we go into the house where everything is as I remember it.

"I'm going to take a walk to have a look around," I tell Angela

"Sure, go ahead, Ursula. We'll eat at little later or are you hungry?"

"No, I am not hungry. I want to see how everything looks."

It's been almost three and a half years since my last visit and so I set out on my get-reacquainted walk. I love this place which is lush and green and well kept. It wasn't always like that. At one time it was a chicken farm but Angela turned it into a public recreation/tourist area for the people from Milagro, Guayaquil and tourists from different parts of the world. She had various groups from the United States over time she told me.

Stepping out of the house I turn left and follow a path which cuts through a grassy area shaded by tall trees until I come to a broad staircase which leads up to a huge stone-covered platform containing a large pool with waterfall, showers, tables and chairs. Behind all this the Club House with an open restaurant below out of which Pedro sells beer and soft drinks to the guests, rounds out this official area. Some more stairs lead to the Club House above with showers, saunas bar and social rooms. To the right there is a palm frond covered cabaña with hammocks, tables and chairs - my favorite place because it's the coolest and in great demand by all.

The previously water-filled ditch running through the property is now dry covered with all kinds of tropical plants. This is a big improvement. Without water there are hardly any mosquitoes. Pineapple are growing here, yucca and cacao beans and various bushes and trees with healing abilities as well as fruit trees like papaya and especially many mango trees full of green fruit resembling Easter Eggs strung from a tree. Two arched bridges cross over to a basket ball court and a soccer field.

Right now I walk past the Club House following the path leading past a building with toilets and changing rooms to another house at the far end of the walled-in property. This is a very beautiful house, quite large with many rooms, kitchen, showers and bathrooms. Angela told me this morning that she was expecting a group of *Gringos* the following week-end to whom she had rented this building.

In front of this house is a round duck pond with an island in the middle. This is the domain of a flock of ducks and geese eyeing me curiously, obviously mistrustful. I walk around the building to the far end of the wall and the wrought-iron gate, on the other side of which is nothing but jungle, the undeveloped part of Angela's land.

Morning doves in front of me take off as I approach. Pedro must have cut the grass earlier as it is lying there row after row. White egrets are busy feeding until I come closer and they fly away landing at a more distant spot. I continue along the other side of the wall where mango tree after mango tree is draped over the wall. Looking up I see a dark round something of enormous size in one tree which has to be a wasp nest.

The other building containing three side-by-side rooms with showers and TV is referred to as the *hotel* with beautiful tropical plants decorating the entrance.

Continuing on my walk, I now pass the huge *bodega*, the repair shop and tool storage. Then I slowly arrive at the front gate or, I should say, where it will be. Right now the entrance is wide open. The men working there shout a friendly *"Buenos días"* and we talk a little before I walk back to the houses where I find Angela busy discussing things with Marta and Ida.

"Okay, Ursula, let's eat; dinner is ready. I'm trying not to eat in the evening anymore but if you get hungry say something. That's how I lost pounds."

"That's fine with me. I could lose a pound or two also so let's see how it goes."

We have delicious soup, a wonderful salad and main course in the dining room overlooking the grassy area with the tall trees right up to the Club House in the back. The living and dining area has no glass in the windows only decorative wrought iron covered with screens to keep the bugs out. Everything is open and the singing of the birds can be heard all day long. It is truly a relaxing place, a peaceful retreat from the world, an oasis.

Wednesday, 10/23/02

We sleep longer these days. It's about eight-thirty in the morning when I wake up. After breakfast Angela and I are on our way again to *La Granja*. Having a divided new highway now the trip is so much faster. It used to be more like an obstacle course with parts of it covered with many potholes so that Angela used to drive like a drunken sailor trying to avoid most of them and I want to stress most because it wasn't always possible. In fact one time, right after my last visits here, she had a terrible accident that almost killed her. She was on her way back to Guayaquil at night and trying to escape one pothole she ended up in another, turning her car over and throwing her into the ditch. Luckily she is tough and thank God still around.

"They had to wire my ribs together. I feel this wire inside of me," she tells me.

"Well, the armor the knights wore on the outside you have on the inside now."

"Yeah," she says laughing.

We have to pass two toll booths, one where we pay and the other where we have to show the ticket that we have paid, when we use the highway under construction leading to Angela's property.

Once there we find that they have done some more grading to the road and the descent into the property is even steeper. I'm thinking that pretty soon we'll neither be getting in nor out anymore.

After my walk I head straight to the cabaña and my favorite hammock. It's much cooler there and I think a hammock is the most comfortable way to relax. Gently swinging back and forth I enjoy the breeze and watch the birds coming by looking for crumbs that guests drop. As a matter of fact I'm getting company from a young couple moving into the hammock next to me hugging and kissing. Yes, hammocks are also good for togetherness.

We drive back to Guayaquil that night again. Amelia and Rosa are in the kitchen. Amelia invites us at once to come and have something to eat with her; she always wants to feed the world. She has Rosa take down breakfast every morning to Segundo, the vendor in front of the building. She is the nicest, kindest lady I can think of. I love her dearly. At ninety-two she is still in good physical and excellent mental condition, although for the past eighteen years I remember her always telling me that she is not so good when I ask her how she is. She also lost quite a bit of weight, her face is not wrinkled and her very dark hair has only some gray strands. She walks without a cane and her mind is sharp. Her hearing is not good anymore. For the longest time I used to think she doesn't understand me because of my accent and limited Spanish but now I see that Angela and Ivanovich also have to repeat many times what they say in a loud voice.

As we sit and talk with Amelia, Ivanovich and his wife join us. They, with their children, have the entire floor below. We all talk for a long time about Ivan's visit in Arizona in August and life here. It's an animated conversation among good friends who have known each other for more than eighteen years and no need to pretend anything. I feel very comfortable here calling it my home away from home and feel like a member of the family being treated as such also.

Angela and I have been friends for more than twenty years by now. She has always said for me to come down to Ecuador and spend more time with them. She and I have had many fun times and trips together. Like her mother, she looks young. Her hair has its natural color without any gray. Her skin is smooth, she is slender and about my height. She speaks English with an accent but has a wonderful vocabulary. Angela has traveled the world and is largely responsible for my own globetrotting. I met Maria through her on a trip around South America opening up a whole new world for me when she invited me for the first time in 1985 to come and visit her in Ecuador. She took me to Quito, the capital founded in 1534, situated at over nine thousand feet close to the equator. We took part in the annual founding celebrations in early December and were dancing in the streets of Quito like everyone around us. I fell in love with Quito instantly. From Quito we went on to the high Andes and the colorful Indian market of Otavalo, a new experience for me and a feast for the eyes and the mind. It was in Otavalo that an Indian at one of the stands pointed to my diamond ring and suggested I turn the ring around to the inside of my hand and hold my handbag tight. I did as he said but that was also the last time I took any good jewelry along on a trip. I came to know artsy Cuenca in the Andes south of Quito and Salinas, the resort by the Pacific. In 1986 I traveled around South America with Angela for almost five weeks. She heard me say I was thinking of going to Australia.

"Australia, who do you know in Australia?"

"I know nobody!"

"Well, then you'd better come around South America with me. I have friends and family in many countries. We'll go to Peru and see my good friend Maria, to Chile, to Argentina and Brazil where I have relatives in Sao Paulo. We'll see Iguazu Falls and beautiful Rio de Janeiro. You'll love it I tell you."

"Rio de Janeiro! It was always a dream of mine to see Rio de Janeiro and all the other places. That would be so wonderful!"

"Okay, then we'll go."

That is how it all started so long ago and now here I am once more for a longer period of time than ever before.

Thursday, 10/24/02

Ivanovich has to take Amelia to the doctor and afterwards we all want to go to Milagro. Ida, Angela's help, also comes along. We pack some clothes because we plan to stay at *La Granja* for a few days. When Ivan comes back we leave immediately and arrive even quicker as he drives faster. Upon arriving he can't believe his eyes either when he has to somehow *maneuver* the car down. Angela is very upset and rightfully so. She speaks with the workers who inform her she needs to address her problem with the boss. Ida and I get out; Angela and Ivanovich leave with the worker to find the boss. Eventually they come back with him and he gives his people instructions to build a bit of a ramp. It's not much but at least the decline isn't as deep anymore.

We all leave again for Milagro when I mention the *conchas negras* I ate in Lima and Angela suggests we have some here because she likes them also.

Back at *La Granja* I relax in a hammock. My favorite one is taken but there is another one just waiting for me. I swing back and forth write my notes and watch the goings-on around me until Ivanovich comes back again bringing Amelia who'll stay with us for the next few days. His cousin Mario also came along for company.

Sitting around the dining table with the cool breeze of the evening passing through the house we have another lively conversation going. Ivanovich and Mario are both well educated and very much aware of what goes on in the world. They can and will talk about everything, one of the reasons I enjoy so much visiting there, the great conversations we have among other things. Both speak English very well also so that the conversation flows from one language into the other considering Amelia only speaks Spanish.

Finally it's time to retire for the night, Angela and I into her *ice box*. Yes, she has one here also, while Amelia prefers a room with normal temperature. This *ice box* here is even colder than the one in Guayaquil and I need another blanket.

Friday, 10/25/02

It's just before eight in the morning when I get up, take a hot shower and wash my hair. Afterwards I ask Angela to come walk around the property with me. We always used to do that but now she has some trouble with her legs and can't walk as well anymore. But today she joins me for a leisurely walk checking everything out, discussing this and that while looking around, accompanied by a symphony of birdsongs. The mornings are so wonderful here - nice and cool. Even the days are not as warm as I thought they'd be.

We have breakfast with Amelia who eats with gusto after which Amelia and I go outside and sit on the bench in front of the house. She asks me about her great-granddaughter and my son and my granddaughter.

Angela, Marta and Ida are busy getting the house ready for the *Gringos* she is expecting this week-end. We all march along carrying things back into the house and checking everything out. Then there is another problem, *la bomba* is still not working. I had heard about *la bomba,* one of the water pumps, the first day we went to *La Granja.* Angela has various people working for her including a mechanic, maestro Juan, who takes care of all sorts of plumbing and electrical problems and is also cutting and re-soldering the wrought iron gate for the main entrance. I like maestro Juan. Angela says he knows what he is doing. Ignoring the gate entirely, he's been working almost non-stop on *la bomba* but to no avail so far. Angela says it was in the shop for a long time and she paid a lot of money for it but it's still not working.

Saturday, 10/26/02

Today my little granddaughter Hailey-Schatzi celebrates her second birthday! Although not in person, in my mind I'm there often, birthday or not. Where ever I go I find things for her and she already has clothes and gifts from different continents. Wished I could be there, just for today, but she's still little and won't miss me.

During breakfast we discuss the arrival of the six *Gringos* today and the fact that *la bomba* is presently in Guayaquil being repaired once again. Ivanovich will bring it back here as soon as the job is done. Having no car right now, we have to go to town by taxi - three times - to do all the shopping.

Between our various trips I meet the lady of the *Gringos.* She's very nice. She and her pastor husband are part of a hands-on religious group that builds houses in Nicaragua for the poor people who lost their homes in this terrible tornado a few years ago. She tells me that they have so far constructed sixty-five homes but need one hundred and thirty. "It'll happen," she says confidently. They are from the United States but have been in Latin America for the past twenty years or so. The four men they expect are also from the States and spend their vacation coming here to build a youth center. They give their time and money to the project. I have instant respect for these people.

"Kids don't want to go to church so much these days," she says. "A youth center provides a place to get together and they are off the street."

"You are right this is a good thing for the young people. I admire your work and dedication."

Returning from our third trip to Milagro Ivan is back with the pump and brought one of his sons and Cousin Mario along. They want to get the one mechanic, Gutierrez, they trust the most. Angela, Ivanovich and I pile into the car and leave for Milagro. By now it's about seven-thirty in the evening on a Saturday night. I wonder aloud if he'll come at this hour.

"Sí, he'll come," says Angela.

When we arrive at the house, however, his wife tells us that her husband isn't home and not expected until much later. Now what? Angela says she knows more than one mechanic. Off we go again into the very crowded center of town where every single person seems to be congregating. After much maneuvering through the crowded streets with a carnival like atmosphere we arrive at the house of mechanic number two but he's not available either. We ask people sitting in front of the house if they know of another mechanic that might be available. Yes, it turns out they do. One of their sons joins us to direct us to his house.

Lucky us, he's home and willing to come along which gives us new hope again as soon as he starts working with Pedro.

We go inside to have a cup of coffee and a snack. Ida puts the tea pot on and sets the table. Suddenly the teapot starts whistling.

"*La vaca, la vaca,*" Ida shouts dashing to the stove.

Ivan looks at her - his whole face a question mark, "what cow?"

Ida takes the teapot in form of a cow's head, white with black spots, off the stove.

We all laugh as she pours hot water on the instant coffee. Ivanovich asks for milk and Ida pours something thick into his cup that goes blop, blop. I look at the thick globs floating in Ivan's coffee when I hear him say with a straight face à la Bob Hope, "*Pura mantequilla.*" It sure looks like butter. His cousin is trying to stifle a laugh but I can't contain myself any longer as I see humor in many things and when I have to laugh, I have to laugh. Everyone joins in.

Ivan tells us that they had a very strong wind in Guayaquil the night before. There is always a breeze in Guayaquil in the evening which makes it nice and cool and brings everybody outside to enjoy the evening air. This, however, was much more than a breeze. A strong wind made some overhead electrical wires close to the house touch which caused an explosion and put the entire house in darkness. Ivanovich didn't know at first what had happened and thought a bomb had gone off, the noise was so loud. After he recovered from the initial shock he went outside to investigate. People were assembling. Finally the city electricians came and took care of the problem, outside and inside the house, checking if all the wiring was safe before turning the lights on again. They had to replace all the fuses. Thank God it didn't cause a fire in the house.

One hour later Ivanovich goes to check on the progress of the water pump installation, but *la bomba* isn't working. Somehow the connection doesn't match the mechanic explains. Angela and Ivan don't believe him thinking he doesn't know what he's doing. Everybody is understandably upset when we take the mechanic back.

So, once more, we are back in the car and drive into town where we drop him off at his house, then go back to Gutierrez. By now it's ten-thirty at night on Saturday. Once more at his house, Angela calls out to him and knocks on the door until finally Gutierrez appears in person. I see them talking together then he accompanies Angela to our car.

"What's he wearing?" I wonder looking at him. "Looks like pajamas." There he is totally unperturbed about his appearance, shaking my hand, saying "Buenas noches," climbing into the car next to me.

Back at *La Granja* we all march to the house where the *Gringos* will be staying, at the other end of the property, to show Gutierrez that there's no water. The *Gringos* will be arriving after midnight. It is pitch-dark. We walk in file accompanied by Marta and Ida. I also see a guy toting a gun thinking this must be one of the guards Angela employs for the night watch but then recognize Pedro, the factotum for everything.

"Pedro, eres tú?"

"Sí,"answers Pedro while Marta adds laughing, "Pedro es nuestro Rambo. That's too funny - Pedro our Rambo - Marta has a great sense of humor I have noticed. Pedro, even toting the gun, looks nothing like Rambo. Here we are walking in goose file, at about eleven on a Saturday night in total darkness to the farthest corner of the property with Rambo and the mechanic dressed in his pajamas.

At the house, Gutierrez checks the switches on the outside shining the flash light here and there before we go inside checking the switches but no water anywhere. He looks again at the pump but cannot see enough in the dark and says he has to come back tomorrow morning to check it out. The *Gringos* will be arriving around midnight. Angela instructs Pedro to turn off the pool and use the pump for the house where the *Gringos* will be staying. Ivanovich takes Gutierrez back to town and I go to bed. It's midnight now.

Sunday, 10/27/02

I wake up at about two thirty in the morning and no Angela. I am worried thinking she has taken the guys back to Guayaquil and will come back alone. After all, it's quite a distance. All the roadwork makes it even more dangerous at night. Finally, to my relief, she comes into the room telling me that Mario had brought her back. Then we both fall asleep.

During a delicious breakfast, we discuss the goings-on of the past day and night.

"Why could the guys not stay here," I ask, saying that I was really worried about her.

"Ivan's wife called and said that she and their daughter were the only two in the big house. She was afraid so he had to go back," Angela informs me. Amelia is with us and Rosa, her help, had been given the week-end off.

While sitting at the breakfast table we see all the *Gringos* leaving, carrying photo equipment in true tourist fashion. They have to pass by our house to get to the road to catch a bus. The minister's wife had told me yesterday that they were planning some sightseeing for the men in Guayaquil today

Later outside Rambo comes by with a friendly "good morning." He passes frequently looking and smiling at me. It takes me a while to realize he's wearing the new T-shirt I brought for him. He wants to show me that it fits and I tell him it looks great on him.

We drive into Milagro again the pineapple capital of the world, Angela informs me.

"Then you are the pineapple queen of the world since you were born here."

"Yes," she says laughing out loud, "that's true and I love pineapple."

"So do I. By the way, I don't think we have any left."

"I'll buy some more."

We arrive at the Mercado. I love markets, all markets, although this one has a bit of an odor because they also sell meat here. The fruit and vegetables are wonderful and fresh. There are thousands and thousands of big, and I mean big, reddish-golden pineapple lying around. The size of the fruit is amazing compared to what we see mostly in the States. The pineapple are so fresh and juicy and the huge papayas, unbelievable. Avocados are the size of about three as we usually know them. Everything tastes so good and is not too expensive by our standards. Angela buys; Ida takes things back to the car while I observe the mostly indigenous vendors who bring the entire family, babies sleeping on blankets under the stands. Then we visit a few more people to whom she calls out from the street

Meanwhile, at *La Granja*, music is pouring from the loudspeakers. Quite a few people have arrived to spend Sunday at this wonderful place. They pay an entrance fee which is collected by Berta, a sister of a former employee of Angela's, who followed four sisters to Germany about a year ago. I find out that Europe is the destination of choice now for many people who want to earn more money. I knew her and ask Berta about her sister and how she likes life in Europe. She's doing well living with two sisters in Hamburg and has done some traveling. I'm happy for her. She plans on staying four more years before returning home while Berta is taking care of her young son who, at ten years, is the same age as her own son and the two boys get on very well. Her sister does miss her son but she's doing this mostly for him.

Gutierrez comes out to see what can be done about *la bomba*, why it isn't working. He says he can't find a problem and believes that the motor of the pump doesn't mix with the connection, the same thing the mechanic had said last night.

Angela and I go into town again to see if a mechanic shop is open but they are all closed. We go to visit with some family members of hers sitting outside their house, talking with friends who come by. We stay for a while and I find them to be extremely nice. All of Angela's relatives I've met so far are very nice

Back at *La Granja* Amelia calls for Ida to give her the medicine and some water. When Amelia goes to her room she says "Venga Zucchini" which strikes me as so funny because her poodle is like her shadow - where Amelia goes, the dog goes, often sitting in front of her and literally staring at her. He's getting blind poor thing. Zucchini otherwise is a very spoilt dog eating only meat, nothing else, so we have to watch Amelia that she doesn't feed her meat to the dog even though Angela tells her there is meat for the dog.

Right now Marta is calling Zucchini to come and eat his food outside. Ida answers and Angela and I break out laughing when we hear Marta replying to Ida, "I called the dog not you."

"This is like a comedy act," I say to Angela. "We should write a book about all this."

Monday 10/28/02

The new cook doesn't show up this morning. Neither does the replacement, probably because Angela had hired her for five days only expecting the new cook. Angela says she had heard that the expected cook was sleeping with one of her night guards and he probably didn't want her to come so early. That's a definite dilemma, because Angela provides meals for all the people working for her.

"Why can't Marta cook," I suggest.

"Yes, she can and I'll have to speak with her to help out until we have somebody else, but she doesn't really like to cook."

The *Gringos* come to mind and I ask how the water situation is working out. She says the switching of the pump from the pool to their house was working fine. The wife of the pastor does the cooking for the group and we don't have to worry about them.

Angela goes into town again to see about an engineer for *la bomba* which she needs so badly. This being Monday, the road work is also proceeding where they are unloading truck load after truck load of dirt which is then spread out and rolled. The cement foundation for the entrance is making progress but it's becoming increasingly more difficult again to get in and out by car.

There is also a leak under the kitchen sink and Pedro is trying to fix it. He has dug a big hole outside the house by the kitchen sink drain. Apparently a pipe is plugged up and needs to be replaced. Hope it works.

Amelia is calling for Ida to bring her the medicine but Ida has gone with Angela and I don't know what she needs to take and ask her to wait a little longer. Amelia tells me she would also like to go to Milagro. She and Angela's father had businesses here and lived in Milagro for very many years before they moved to Guayaquil. I assure her next time she'll go with Angela. We go outside to sit in the shade on the cement bench in front of the house.

Sitting there I see a familiar figure coming up the drive. Familiar from my last visit here more than three years ago.

"Eduardo, cómo estás?" I greet him. He remembers me also. Eduardo then was Angela's personal help. He must be about eighteen now but he still looks like a little boy being of a very slight stature. I always liked Eduardo and asked about him but was told something happened and he was let go. I was sorry to hear that. Now he is coming up the drive quite unexpectedly and after the initial greetings I ask what brings him here. He wants to speak to Marta and I direct him to the Club House.

Angela and Ida finally return saying she'll have to pick up the engineer at four thirty which means staying another day before returning to Guayaquil. After lunch I take my daily exercise walk around the huge property which I do twice daily.

Passing by the house presently occupied by the *Gringos* the lady comes out and we chat a little. She tells me she's cooking dinner for the men who are out working with her husband. They are all businessmen contributing financially and want to see what their money is being used for. She mentions that two of them had expressed their regrets that they didn't bring their wives because they would have loved it here

"How very nice; I'll tell Angela. It will make her happy. It's truly a beautiful place and you can tell the men that they can come back anytime. The other house over there has rooms with individual baths and TV. Now that they have been here and know Angela, all they have to do is call."

"I'll do that. We're having another hands-on workshop next March. We have already been discussing to come back here. The location is ideal for us with the youth center going up just a little down the road."

"That's great! I hope you know that you can swim in the pool anytime you want to."

"My husband was in already early in the morning."

"Early in the morning; it's cold then. The afternoon is better for swimming."

"I know, I wouldn't be going in, but he likes it."

I learn that she has four children and some grandchildren which is the reason she is ready to go back home after about twenty-eight years abroad. I understand what she is talking about. I miss my son and darling little granddaughter also. However, I also mention to her the many economic problems in the States, people being laid off left and right.

"Yes I know. My youngest son still hasn't found employment and that worries me very much. The entire situation is bad with the president wanting war and everybody afraid what that will all entail. I hope it won't come to a war, but it looks as if he is determined."

"Yes it looks bad. All my friends and people I talked with in Peru and here harbor the same fears. Nobody likes war; people want to live in peace."

We discuss the political and economic situation for quite a while. I always enjoy talking with people with extensive foreign experience, either by traveling or working abroad. They have an entirely different viewpoint and mindset. All of us who travel eventually realize that people around the globe have more in common than they are different. Whenever I hear of a disaster in a part of the world where I've been, I cannot help but think of the nice people I met there wondering how they are faring, if they are still alive, etc. To me it's not some place far away and meaningless. I've always said there should be a requirement that every young person during High School or College should have to spend at least one summer abroad to see different countries and become acquainted with other people and cultures to erase this automatic distrust of the *strange* felt by many people. The government could pay and consider it part of education and to promote peace and understanding in the world rather than sending our young people to fight, a much costlier and very destructive undertaking. After all, we are all in this together on this earth!

Well, that's a dream right now. The only way most of the young people get to travel is in uniform to kill somebody they've never seen in their lives before. Wearing this uniform, they are also automatically looked at as the *enemy* disliked and unwelcome - so different from when we tourists travel. Poor government that condemns somebody for having mistreated or killed their own people and then, without the blink of an eye, sends hundreds of thousands of young people into a war, the magnitude and repercussions of which are yet unknown!

Angela is happy hearing that the *Gringos* like it here and are thinking of returning next March.

"Most people who have come here are returning. We had various groups from the States before."

Then, all of a sudden, she says we're returning to Guayaquil because her mother wants to go home. I also know that Amelia doesn't want to stay here too long; she prefers to be in her own home in Guayaquil. She likes to come for an overnight but if it gets to be longer than that she becomes bored. We leave at about four in the afternoon which means no engineer. Many demands are made on Angela.

It's amazingly cool in Guayaquil so different from *La Granja*. No wonder Amelia wants to go home to enjoy the breeze downstairs which makes life in Guayaquil so pleasant by late afternoon.

I quickly buy a newspaper from Segundo before we head back to *La Granja* where I fix a *Cuba Libre* for Marta and myself. She likes this drink but the alcohol percentage of the rum here is lower than in the States. "Como agua," says Marta.

Tuesday, 10/29/02

The new cook still doesn't show and the door of Rafaela's house, the replacement, is locked. We hear her father has become ill and she has gone to take care of him. Marta has to keep cooking and does a much better job of it than the cook had. Besides, the cook never seemed really clean to me; I'm not sad at all that she isn't coming back.

Pedro finished the sink problem yesterday and is now 'playing' with the mowing tractor on which he's riding around without cutting the grass. He says it's not working right. Marta is looking for some spices she needs for cooking lunch and Stalin, a very young man, has returned to work after quitting abruptly and not showing up for a few days. Something or somebody had annoyed him. He's presently hacking away at some low-hanging branches of the mango tree next to the house. The birds Angela keeps in various cages outside the house are singing and the baby cats are soundly sleeping close together as usual.

"Todo es como siempre," I think. All is well.

The activities really begin around three-thirty in the afternoon with the road construction crew finally arriving to build a proper entrance/exit ramp for *La Granja* which has not been accessible by ordinary cars but can only be 'climbed' by a four-wheel drive. Angela had to buy, at her own expense, six huge cement sewer pipe sections which are now lowered into the ditch dug out by the crew with their modern heavy equipment and put into place by a large crane. Then dirt is put on and rolled and more dirt put on and rolled until it's high and solid enough.

We are all there watching this historic moment with great interest. I take some photos of these activities when the foreman walks over suggesting I needed a photo of myself as well so I stand there and he takes my photo.

Angela has Ida bring some fruit salad and Pedro has to bring some soft drinks for the construction crew. They gratefully accept.

While all this is going on heavy traffic passes by on the road outside with people craning their necks to see what's happening. A smaller truck stops outside and I see a group of men first staring then getting off and coming over to *La Granja*. Next, I see some heads popping up looking in over the wall. I think they look Anglo without putting two and two together until they start hoisting boxes and tools up on the wall before climbing it. Now it comes to me - they are our *Gringos* returning from work. Their faces show disbelief and surprise. I can't help laughing out loud.

"Aren't you glad you came?" I ask.

They look at me saying nothing at first and then some of them come over saying that this would never be possible in the States.

Perhaps not but on the other hand, what else to do? This is the final moment and everyone stands around watching. Angela comes over and apologizes to them for this inconvenience while I'm thinking how lucky the pastor's wife had stayed here cooking. I can't picture her climbing the wall. The thought alone puts a smile on my face. Angela tells me later she thought we were being invaded when the men came over the wall. We have a good laugh about all this.

At about six-thirty in the evening - they worked past their usual time – we now have a very nice ramp, one that a car can pass without fear of toppling over.

That night on television we hear 115 people have been gassed in a theatre in Russia. In the same newscast a commentator later refers to *the leaders of the USA, Israel and Russia as the despots whose new religion is anti-terrorism used by them as carta blanche to do whatever pleases them.*

Wednesday, 10/30/02

Still no cook and Stalin, only been rehired the day before, has not shown up either. Stalin is a very young, tall and slender man of about twenty with usually a stern face, hardly showing a smile. An angry look appears to be permanently engraved on his face.

"Where is Stalin today," I ask Angela.

"His father-in-law is in the hospital. He has to bring some food to him."

"Stalin is married?"

"Oh yes, he's married and has a little boy, a real cute little boy of about one year. They live with her parents which obligates him."

"Why is he called Stalin?"

"People give their children strange names. Some name them after car manufacturers."

"No."

"Would you believe I once had a Schubert working for me?"

Reading the paper I find out that our Stalin is not the only one. The name pops up now and then in the paper like in a funeral announcement of a Stalin. I learned something again.

We haven't heard from Ivanovich for a few days and Ida has not returned either. She should have come back yesterday morning from Guayaquil, where she went two days ago to attend to a school matter of her six-year old daughter. She's a single mother of about twenty-three with some college education but had to drop out to earn money. She and her daughter live with her mother and an aunt to share expense. The two women take care of the little girl when Ida is away from home. Her daughter is a very pretty child - she showed me some photos - and Ida, like any mother, is very proud of her. Ida herself is only about five feet tall and roly-poly. She laughs easily, can be very funny, but isn't the hardest working person in Angela's place.

Angela, who actually likes Ida, is upset that she hasn't come back. "You see how she is, unreliable and irresponsible."

By about eleven we drive to Guayaquil to find out what is going on. Angela drives like a maniac. We are flying along the new divided highway which is so wonderful to drive on.

Arriving at Parque Centenario in Guayaquil we find Amelia sitting by the news stand of Segundo watching the world go by. And a lot of world it is! This being the center of the city it's a very busy corner. She enjoys this diversion and having lived there for a long time people know and greet her, some stopping for a chat. She's well-liked and respected and truly a lady.

Amelia is happy to see us. When I ask her how she feels she says that she isn't so good. She always says that for as long as I can remember and who knows, at her advanced age, we may all not feel 'so good.' She complains that neither Rosa, her former maid, nor Ida had shown or Ivanovich, her grandson. By now Angela is even more upset and immediately calls an employment agency to find somebody for her mother. As it turns out, however, the only thing true is that Rosa hasn't returned but decided to go to Esmeraldas at the coast in the far North of the country.

Suddenly Ida shows up and is immediately confronted by Angela but Ida protests the accusations saying that she was with Amelia in the morning and returned home only to change clothes and check on her six-year old daughter. We both feel immediately that she's speaking the truth confirmed later by Ivanovich and Berto who have seen Ida here. Angela calms down considerably but makes clear to Ida that if she can't rely on her, she has no job with her. After taking some more clean clothes and vitamins we leave for *La Granja* again. It's quite warm today and I don't take the usual walk around the property but retire to my favorite hammock with the intention to wait out the heat.

"This hammock has my name on it," I tell Marta when she walks up to the cabaña. "I must have lived in the Latin world during a previous life."

"Sí," she answers laughing, "I'm going back to the house of the *Gringos;* you want to come with me?"

She is carrying a bucket full of leftovers from the kitchen to feed the geese and ducks in the pond. It's now late afternoon. One of the *Gringos* comes towards us saying, "There's a big iguana on the pool deck."

Angela told me about the many iguanas but no matter how hard I try to see one looking in all the places Marta told me, even in the *Iguana Hotel* as she refers to one bush by a little bridge leading over the now dry ditch, I saw nothing. I can't even see this one now from the distance until Marta points it out to me.

"You have eagle eyes," I say as we slowly walk closer and find that it has a beautiful greenish color, a very long skinny tail with yellow-greenish rings different from the grayish, dark looking iguanas of the Galápagos. Thinking of my first encounter with the iguanas of the Galápagos while looking for them in the distance I almost fell over a few right in front of my feet in the middle of the road. The iguanas of the Galápagos do not run away; they are protected and not afraid of people. This one here, a rather large specimen, keeps a watchful eye on us. When we come too close for his comfort, he takes off with amazing speed. Marta says they hide in the shrubbery and in the trees - yes they climb trees - coming out only in the sun.

Later back at the house I talk about the first iguana I saw. "I don't believe there are so many, because I look and look and see nothing."

"That's because Pedro has eaten them all which is the reason for his big tummy," throws in Marta. Everybody laughs including Pedro.

"Yes," I add, "I heard they are good to eat but one escaped and we encountered it just now." Poor Pedro, he's being teased quite a bit.

Angela tells me a story of her iguana experience which makes me laugh whenever I think of it. This is what happened: She had her friends for a big lunch to *La Granja*. Tables and chairs were set up under big mango trees by the house with nice table covers, china, silverware, etc. and while the ladies all sat there, talking, eating and drinking having a good time, reddish things kept falling down from the trees onto the tables, the food, into the drinks. Small and bigger pieces of the shed skins of the iguanas were coming down out of the trees.

"Can you imagine?" she asks.

"Yes," I answer laughing "I can imagine all these society ladies receiving a special gift from heaven!" I have this vivid imagination and having met many of the ladies, I have a perfect picture of the scene.

"Oh Angela, I know it wasn't pleasant at the time, but it's funny to me now."

Seeing me laugh like that she starts laughing also.

"You should have seen their faces," she continues, "I could have died! It was so embarrassing to me. We had to go and shoot as many as we could, about twenty of them, as it was like an infestation."

"An infestation; Angela, this sounds really bad."

"It was. You should have seen it."

I ponder the thought of iguanas shedding their skins and other animals changing into their winter or summer coats. Suddenly the thought pops into my mind that's nature's way of providing new clothes to the animals - also of a larger size..

Right now I hope I can take a few good photos of one or two specimen of this previous 'infestation.'

Angela walks up to the entrance to check on the night guards while I suddenly get the idea to take a swim. All these years I brought my bathing suit along without ever using it. The time has come to hop into the pool.

The guests have left, the entire pool is mine. At first the water feels quite cool but twice back and forth it's very refreshing and I enjoy the swim. Marta comes up and sits down at one of the tables reading the paper I always put out for them while I have a nice forty-five minute swim. I must do this more often.

Thursday, 10/31/02

Halloween! It's not celebrated in the way it is in the States. After breakfast I go on my morning walk with my camera hoping to see an iguana. Marta said they come out when the sun is shining which is when I don't want to walk around. Instead, I discover a few huge hornet nests in the mango trees and take a photo of one.

The road construction crew is back again working on the ditch in front of the property. They are dumping truck load after truck load of dirt from the ditch inside *La Granja* along the other wall which Angela needs to improve the road leading to the back of the property.

Pedro has finished cutting all the grass and Stalin is also back again working. I love the smell of fresh cut grass. Angela says it's good for one's nose. She, like most people here, is into all sorts of natural remedies.

The snow white egrets, attracted by the cut grass rows, apparently find all kinds of goodies there. The red birds, the size of starlets called hoyeros, are also busy in the newly cut grass. These birds are so beautiful and they are everywhere. They also have a very distinct call. On my last trip here I took a picture of one sitting on a wooden swing by an old wagon wheel leaning against a tree with the red brick wall in the background covered with bougainvilleas. I love it so much because it shows the peaceful ambiance of this oasis.

The baby cats also contribute to the peacefulness of the place. Angela told me the mother was killed outside her property and so she took the cats in. The baby cats love each other and sleep close together, almost in an embrace. They are very skinny. I always want to feed them but Angela says they are to catch mice.

"There are no mice here and that's why I have the cats."

They do get fed and I have fed them a few times with leftovers and now they come running to me the moment I step out of the house. These cats eat everything including lettuce, tomatoes, onions mixed with rice in comparison to the spoilt, often fat pets in the States.

I retreat to my hammock and read El UNIVERSO showing some beautiful photos of the Museum of Anthropology and Contemporary Art, which has been finished and handed over today to the regional direction of the Central Bank of Ecuador. The theatre holds four hundred people it says. Behind the building at the beginning of the Malecón 2000 shine the lights of el cerro Santa Ana. The mayor of Guayaquil also talks about the ongoing beautification of the city with the next project being the rejuvenation of el cerro del Carmen close to Santa Ana to make the city even more of a tourist attraction.

When I came downstairs this morning I ran straight into Berto. He has a shop in the building below and I see him quite often. He pointed out an article in the same paper talking about papaya being extremely good for the stomach and the digestion. Angela had told me that years ago but I still read the article with interest as it contained much valuable information, stressing that this fruit is most benevolent for good stomach health.

I'm finally successful snapping some photos of an iguana. Pedro pointed one out to me high in a tree where it lay totally still on a branch. I would never have seen it by myself. It was too high but there's another one sitting perfectly still on the high brick wall by the pool. I keep an eye on that one and run inside to get my camera. By the time I come out again it has already moved across a corner of the huge pool deck and is sitting on the stairs, ready to cross the grassy area to climb a tree. That is where I corner the iguana, approaching it from the grass so it can't run towards the trees. Totally surprised the iguana keeps completely still. We stare at each other for a moment.

"How beautiful it is with its green-yellow rings and what a long tail it has," I think.

I take one photo without flash but it's not a very bright day so I activate the flash. The first flash goes off with the iguana still suffering through this encounter. A second flash is decidedly too much. It turns around and runs straight back towards the bushes by the wall with lightening speed. However, once at safe distance, it turns around one more time looking at me before it disappears.

Suddenly, just before three in the afternoon, I see a horde of people coming in all dressed in business attire, followed by another large group and another. I wonder what's going on. Angela had said nothing about having a group here today. I go to ask her and find out that one department of a local company decided to have a dinner party here. She is to produce forty some meals just like that. They want chuletas and chicken. Now the rush begins.

Pedro, the man who wears many hats, turns on the music and opens the bar. Angela doesn't have enough meat at home for such a large group. We have to go into town to buy some pork chops and chicken and pick up Berta, the lady who helps out on week-ends, on the way back to help in the kitchen. Everybody works as fast as they can; even I get to peel the potatoes when I offer my help, but some time passes before we are ready to serve.

They become a little impatient. Every so often one or two will walk up and ask when they can expect the food as everybody is getting hungry. We make it clear to them that an advance notice would help greatly in order to have everything prepared on time rather than just blessing us with their presence by dropping in. Two of the young women laugh and say they told their boss to call but apparently he forgot. He grins while they tease him some more before walking off again.

In the end it all turns out well. They love the food. They also become a little drunk which becomes evident when I hear Angela announce over the loudspeaker that it is not permitted to jump into the pool with clothes and shoes on

At the same time we have also a small group of teenagers there. They take this time to climb up on the roof of the waterfall and jump into the pool. With Pedro busy inside selling beer and soft drinks, I walk over to them and in my very best Spanish tell the boys to stop this activity because we don't want for them to get hurt. They nod politely and stop immediately. No grimacing, no backtalk.

While helping to carry meals from the kitchen to the pool area, I suddenly acquire a shadow. I'm being followed by a very young man who asks if he can help, what my name is, where I come from, how long I will stay and what my age is. No matter what I say I can't discourage him; he's always right behind me.

"I prefer real women to very young girls and will follow you to the end of the world."

"I have already been there," I tell him walking along, "so we need not go this route again."

Eight years ago I had been to Punta Arenas in Chile and Tierra del Fuego and found out that the people there think of themselves as living at *al fin del mundo.*

He asks again to help but will not go past the stairs leading to the pool deck waiting there for my return to follow me back to the kitchen.

"Why don't you join your friends?"

"No, they'll throw me into the pool."

"Oh, so that's the problem!" He's a little guy.

Suddenly the electricity goes out. That's all we need right now. Since it will be dark pretty soon I think it best to collect the paper plates and cups after the people are done, before they all end up in the pool. Moving from table to table the happy crowd insists I have a piece of cake they had brought for the boss' birthday. A cream pie ends up in his face dripping down onto his shirt. How lovely!

Having no electricity has one advantage, this big group leaves early saying that they had a good time and, taking our advice to heart, make reservations for another fun event to take place the end of November. They thank Angela and all of us.

While all this is going on, the *Gringos* are coming back to no electricity and no water for them since the pump runs on electricity. Angela apologizes to them about this inconvenience and sends Marta along to the house with candles. One of the *Gringos* stays behind saying they want to reconfirm their return flights tonight. We have no phone for outgoing calls so Angela has to take him into town. Yes, it's a full day.

At eight in the evening all the outside lights come on again and, feeling hot and sticky I take another swim. When I leave the pool about one hour later and want to get into the house, the door is locked. The car is also gone which means Angela is definitely not here and probably took Ida along. I call for Marta, no answer. I look into the kitchen house, nobody. I look into the other house, where Marta and the others sleep, nobody. I call for Marta, Pedro, nothing.

"Great," I think, "here I am in a wet swimming suit with only a little towel, the door is locked and nobody is here. It's pitch-dark and I'm getting a little chilly. Where is everybody?"

Finally, after what seems an eternity, I see a figure walking towards me which, upon coming closer, I recognize as Pedro in his *Rambo* role.

"Dónde están todos?" I ask him.

"Buscando la guardia," he answers - Looking for a night guard.

I find out that the usual two guys haven't shown up tonight and Angela went with the two girls to find somebody. Pedro has the key and opens the door for me, saying he was at the front entrance when I called. *Rambo* took a long time to walk up here.

I'm barely changed, when I hear a car coming. It's Angela with Marta and Ida. Marta and I have no trouble deciding that this day definitely calls for a *Cuba Libre*, como agua, as Marta says. Happy Halloween! We got all the tricks.

Friday, 11/1/02

The *Gringos* are leaving today. They come by to say good-bye and how much they enjoyed staying, despite having no water at times and no electricity last night for a while. Two of them mention that they would have brought their wives along had they known they would be in such a beautiful place.

"Well," you can always come back. Now you know where to find this place."

"I think we will."

The house they stayed in is being emptied in a hurry again of most items so they can't be stolen. There was a break-in in August. Thieves had cut through the strong wire mesh that serves as windows around the brick wall and literally cleaned out the house. Angela said everything was taken, refrigerator, stove, TV, and furniture.

The guard had fallen asleep. She had only one person then and now she usually has two.

We have to go to the market again having used most provisions yesterday. On this warm day it's less of a pleasure as the market has all the odors of the orient and occident together with meat hanging outside on huge hooks.

Today another familiar face shows up, Hugo, who used to work here years ago for Angela until she had to let him go because he could not always be trusted. I had my doubts before and during a visit here with our friend from Lima, Maria, who had the same thoughts and we decided that both of us were not wrong.

At that time some CD's disappeared and Hugo accused Pedro who said he hadn't taken them. Maria and I thought he was innocent and talked to Angela. I don't think she was convinced then but neither did she let Pedro go. Months later she found evidence of dishonesty and let Hugo go.

Now he comes with his handsome son who was a baby when I saw him last. After we exchange a few words they go looking for Angela who tells me later he comes by once in a while.

Today is also very hot and we all feel sapped of energy. Angela and I even take a little nap in the *ice box* which feels actually good right now. In the late afternoon we go to Guayaquil to see how Amelia is doing. These things are being decided quickly and one has to be prepared in a hurry. I am glad because I know it is cooler there and I can bring some other clothes out.

Amelia has a new maid but she doesn't like her much and she can't cook either. Ivan takes her out to lunch and dinner daily to make sure she eats well.

Saturday, 11/2/02

El Día de los Muertos - the Day of the Dead. Everybody goes out to the cemeteries today to visit graves of loved ones and bring flowers. I had noticed the past few days that close to the huge cemetery we pass daily, the usual few flower stands had turned into a flower market in preparation for this day. As all the stores are closed and we can't get fresh rolls for breakfast, Angela, Amelia and I leave early for *La Granja* to have breakfast there. I'm surprised how cool the morning is in Guayaquil. In fact, the whole day turns out to be cool and pleasant.

Passing the cemetery there is much activity today. Many people are out dressed in their finest clothes, carrying flowers. We stop at a shopping mall with an open drugstore where I can buy some paper for my notes and another pen.

Arriving at *La Granja* Angela manages a few unusual things. Absentmindedly, she drives down from the paved part of the road to the lane being worked on, a drop of at least twelve inches, giving us quite a bump. Oops! Late in the afternoon she bumps a motorcycle lightly and then a car in the very crowded streets but crawling along as we are, nothing happens.

Sunday, 11/3/02

We had a delicious breakfast again, among other things something in the shape of a large egg, green in color, which is made of the green bananas with onions and some spices, tasting really good. I love these things made of green bananas, little patties called *patacones*, and steak like *chuletas verde* as well as frijoles and other specialties.

Pedro is playing Frank Sinatra music and famous Latin singers. He always has to play *good* music for Angela on Sunday mornings. Later, when the pool guests arrive - mostly younger people - he plays what they like. It's still cool in the morning and quiet when I take my walk around the property. Once the sun comes out, the people arrive en masse to enjoy the pool. It's a busy day for Marta and Ida certainly gets her exercise carrying trays of food to the pool. Berta is here to collect the entrance fee and even the cook, who had disappeared for a week, shows up again but Angela tells her that she isn't needed anymore. She needs a person she can rely on. Looking at Marta I can tell that she isn't super happy because she'll have to keep on cooking all the meals, but she says nothing.

At three in the afternoon, one of the many volcanoes in Ecuador, Reventador near Quito, erupts with much force covering Quito, the capital, with gray ashes. Reventador is spewing out huge gray clouds all over the city and the north of Ecuador.

In the evening, Marta finds a note in her pocket saying "Te espero a las cinco" - I expect you at five. She doesn't know who gave it to her and we all tease her quite a bit.

I go for a swim again. The water seems quite cool but is nice for swimming. It feels as if I'm alone in the world, it's so peaceful. As the beautiful rose-colored evening sky turns darker and darker, a lonely bat speeds around in crazy zigzags above me. Or is it two? I watch her fly about thinking of the time I was here many years ago, when a flock of bats had chosen a dark ceiling corner of the bathroom, which had a broken window, for their home. Heads down, they clung tightly to the ceiling like cones on a tree, taking off in a flurry of fluttering wings, making squeaking noises like mice, the moment one of us walked into the bathroom. It was amazing how quickly they escaped through the small hole. After a while, when the bathroom was empty, they would return until their night hunts outside.

I had never seen bats close up like that and wanted a photo. I got my camera ready, opened the door carefully, click/flash and there I had them before they left squeaking. Even this didn't deter them from returning.

Monday, 11/4/02

The day is nice and cool. Juan, the maestro, is fixing a leak in the bathroom only to discover that the whole area under the sink is full of termites who love the moisture. Angela says she'll have all the wood torn out and build a counter of cement and tiles. This house has been here for a long time, perhaps thirty years or more.

After taking my walk around the property I return to the cabaña and my favorite hammock only to discover, that the family who was here yesterday had left a real mess behind. The mother and an adult male - don't know if he was the father of the children - had cuddled in a hammock without supervising the children.

Marta has gone to Guayaquil to handle some personal affairs and is expected back tomorrow. We actually intend to leave for Cuenca tomorrow, a beautiful colonial city in the Andes I love. Angela wants to take her mother along but she doesn't want to come. Even though she's without help again, she wants to be in her place and cook her meals. She gets bored if she is here too long because she misses all the people she can talk with in front of her house in the city. We take Amelia back to Guayaquil but don't stay long as Angela feels with Marta gone, we should return. Ivanovich comes along but later in the evening we all drive back to Guayaquil again. I'm used to changes in plans having been here many times and take my toothbrush and a few items and we are off.

Well, not quite because we go to Milagro where they want to meet with some people to discuss various matters. The streets come alive with people and vendors in the evening, some of them having set up a little cooking station on which pots are boiling with the evening meal. A small board on a stand serves as table for people to put their bowls and plates down to eat. Cars are passing by and horns blasting if the traffic isn't moving while people cross the streets any way they like, a polychromatic scene loud and confusing but utterly fascinating. I like the beautiful children with their dark hair, big curious eyes and skin of all shades. They are truly darling. Where ever I go, I try to take photos of the beautiful children of this world, many of whom live in such awful poverty and neglect by their countries and the rest of the world.

Ivanovich says we'll take a different road home that brings us through a little town called Yaguachi nearby which, he says, is famous for an important battle Ecuador fought against Spain in its fight for liberty. He doesn't remember the exact historical date but says festivities take place here every year in commemoration.

When we arrive in Guayaquil later in the evening, Angela and Ivanovich want to visit a few more people with whom they have to discuss various matters because evening is a good time to find people at home. Angela has a tractor in repair for more than three months already which isn't getting done. The parts aren't available or the maestro isn't there, were some of the excuses she received but now it's being assembled she was told. She needs this tractor badly to spread out the mountains of dirt along the long wall of the property to improve the road there.

As we drive around Guayaquil, I am truly surprised how beautiful the city has become.

"How beautiful it looks here," I exclaim as we drive along the river.

"It does look better at night than at day, believe me," says Ivanovich. "The city is becoming more beautiful, however," he adds. "Tourism is now the main industry and the reason for the beautification."

Finally we arrive at home just before ten in the evening and watch some news on TV about the eruption of the volcano Reventador, which has closed the airport in Quito leaving many people stranded there. Even TAME, the Ecuadorian Airline has closed flights out of Guayaquil. We wonder why there being no problem with ashes in Guayaquil, while in Quito and surrounding the scene is total devastation; everything looks gray.

Tuesday, 11/5/02

We wake up early in Guayaquil and watch the seven o'clock news showing again the enormous disruption of life caused by the eruption of Reventador. The volcano is about eighty kilometers northeast of Quito so the capital gets the brunt of it. Reventador is three thousand five hundred sixty-two meters high, about ten thousand five hundred feet. The base is thirteen kilometers around and the cone two kilometers. I found this information in EL UNIVERSO, the newspaper I buy almost daily. EL UNIVERSO covers this disaster in great detail mentioning the economic loss suffered by individuals and the country as a whole.

There are presently two other volcanoes erupting off and on, Pichincha just south of Quito and Tungurahua further south, but Reventador had a far more powerful eruption and took scientists completely by surprise. Its last eruption took place in January and April 1976. The scientists say they don't have the proper instruments nor are there enough of them. For that reason, the three thousand or so people living close to the volcano could not be warned. Many lost their homes and their livelihood as their crops are covered with lava containing big rocks and ashes everywhere.

There aren't enough face masks, food, shelter, potable water and other things. They report that people fill the hospitals in Quito with pulmonary problems. They show dead animals covered with ashes. Some people lost all their livestock but no human lives were lost so far. Hopefully this remains true. The government promises help but the people say usually not much is forthcoming. The funds and heavy equipment are missing to truly help.

On TV, they show people in Quito sweeping the ash-covered streets clean with brooms, some not even protecting their faces with masks. The airport is shown with all the huge planes from different countries standing their covered in thick ashes. People were taken by bus from Quito to Guayaquil to continue with their travels. Later on in the day, with the eruption slowing considerably and the ashes cleaned up, flights are again leaving out of Quito.

They show the enormous economic loss suffered by some businesses, especially the ones which export flowers, fresh fruit and vegetables to the United States and Europe. The floral market is destroyed because flowers being grown for next Valentine's Day will not be there with the fields covered by thick ashes for now. The agriculture in the region has suffered much. EL UNIVERSO says that one million metric tons of ashes have been expulsed by the eruption and that the weight of the accumulated ashes has made some roofs collapse. Seeing all these awful scenes on TV, I feel sorry for the people and the beautiful city of Quito having to go through this disaster even though they are no strangers to volcanic eruptions, but every time this happens, it is an unnecessary setback causing suffering and loss.

At breakfast I'm surprised to see fresh rolls there and ask Amelia who brought them. She tells me that she went to get them. I ask why she didn't tell me, but she says the bakery is at the corner and not far. I look at her in amazement. Here is this frail-looking ninety-two year old lady walking all by herself to get us some breakfast rolls. She says she is only afraid of falling and breaking some bones.

After breakfast we drive the same route of the night before since some people were not available. I see some of the area again along the river and yes, Ivanovich is right, it does look better at night. Here are the little old wooden homes built on stilts at the edge of the river against the background of skyscrapers of modern Guayaquil. And is it ever modern! The contrast is stark.

Marta returns early in the evening from her trip. She tells me that she had to go to Riobamba to sign final divorce papers after being separated from her husband for seven years after eight years of marriage. He wanted to get married again. She says she feels fine, but I offer her a drink anyway which she gladly accepts. We chat for a while and I find out that she has a house in Guayaquil and is looking after and supporting a teen-age niece living with her. Her mother is only two houses away and keeps an eye on the niece while she is away.

Today is voting day in the U.S. I did my voting before I left there, which was an enlightening and unexpected experience. I called to request an early ballot but was told the earliest they would be available would be Thursday, the third of October. That was late for me as I was leaving early Tuesday morning, the eighth. To my question if I could come in on Thursday and vote there, the person at the other end of the phone said this isn't possible and there is nothing she could do. I asked for the supervisor who told me the same thing. What would he suggest I do? He had no suggestion. Only after mentioning I was under the impression he wanted to deprive me of my right to vote did he inform me of three places in the greater city area if I wanted to drive there. Surely the first person knew that also and their could-not-care-less attitude surprised me because I had heard and read that the various governments, federal or local, wanted us to vote complaining all the time about voter apathy. Well, so much to that belief!

Wednesday, 11/6/02

After a late breakfast, we take various trips into Milagro on different errands, one of them being *la bomba*, another water pump, which has been in the shop for four weeks now. They tell Angela that a certain electrical connection is no good. Angela responds she has a spare one at home and will bring it to them. They test the pump after the new part is installed and it seems to work okay, although I hear a strange scraping noise that just doesn't sound right, but then what do I know about water pumps.

Back at *La Granja*, Pedro and the maestro work all afternoon on the installation without being able to get it to work.

Angela has to go back to Milagro on some other matters and I go along but stay in the car and watch the world around me. We stop at a busy intersection. Right next to me at the street corner is one of these cooking stands, consisting of what appears to be a stove on which there are some pots. Around it is a wooden board serving as table and a bench for people to sit down and eat their meals consisting of mostly rice with some meat sauce being poured over it. It smells rather good and the customers come and go enjoying the meal and the company. Sitting there I observe one very skinny man ordering his meal, eating half of it and then pushing the plate over to the side where the shoe-shine boy sits. He then takes some water from a container and drinks before swinging himself on his bike again. The shoe-shine boy, as soon as he finishes with his present customer, sits down to eat the remaining food. This little act of kindness will forever be on my mind, showing once again that the people who have the least are the most caring.

Everybody helps himself to a drink of water out of a big tub using the same little empty plastic margarine dish. When all the food is gone they wash the pots out, take the setup apart and load it on the tricycle bike with the cart area in front of the steering bar and pedal off. This type of transportation for everything is seen a lot here. I saw somebody giving his grandma a ride. Many times fathers transport their children or a spouse this way. Looking at the street corner now, one would never have believed anything was ever here. All that's left is another little garbage pile in the gutter which will be picked up later by the collection crew.

At a news stand I buy EL COMMERCIO to find out about the elections at home. There are no results saying at typesetting the voting in California was still going on and it didn't want to put out any predictions. I thought that was a step in the right direction. It was not till late afternoon when we learned from *CNN en Español* what the results were. Too bad! This means war for sure.

In the early evening we leave for a neighboring village where, according to Angela, lives a maestro who's the only one capable of getting *la bomba* installed and working. Upon arrival at his house we find out from his wife that he isn't home yet. Angela says we have to wait because this is the last evening of the week he'll be at this house, because as of tomorrow he'll be at his other house in Guayaquil.

"He has another house in Guayaquil?" I ask. "This one here is rather large."

"Yes," she answers laughing, "and his wife in Guayaquil has exactly the same house."

"He has another wife?" I am astounded.

"The wife in Guayaquil is the first one and this one here is his second wife."

Turns out this maestro has two families and divides his time by spending the week here and the week-end in Guayaquil with the other wife. I find out that both wives know about the arrangement and that it's not a rarity here. It reminds me of some cases in the States I read about over the years where long distance truckers have families at each side of the country.

"Mind you," Angela adds, "he isn't married to this one here. The one in Guayaquil is his real wife."

I am reminded of a Spanish proverb I learned in my Spanish class at a college in California which states: *Nada es nuevo en la cara de la tierra!* - There is nothing new on the face of the earth. I don't know who said it, but I'll remember it until my dying day as I find it so absolutely correct.

The maestro isn't returning and after having waited for about half an hour we go home and should return tomorrow morning by six as he leaves for Guayaquil early. I wonder if this will happen. Neither one of us rises and shines so early these days.

Thursday, 11/7/02

We both wake up around eight in the morning and around ten, right after our breakfast, the maestro from the neighboring village shows up. He's a good looking man, tall and handsome, middle fortieth I would guess, with dark hair and dark eyes. Angela thinks he looks Mexican. She says that he works only for people with money which doesn't surprise me having to keep two households going. After puttering around for about two hours with our maestro Juan and Pedro, the maestro who can do everything, tells Angela she needs to take *la bomba* to Guayaquil to have it repaired.

So we leave for Guayaquil with maestro Juan and *la bomba* in the car to take it to a shop this maestro has recommended. Angela is understandably annoyed saying she spends thousands of dollars on equipment repair waiting for it forever and then still not working.

"On top of it I'm paying the people here who are breaking it because they are running it dry. I told Pedro so many times to watch the water level but he has become so lazy."

We again pass by the factory which specializes in balanced shrimp food for the shrimp pools of Ecuador. Long before seeing it one knows it's coming by the strong odor that permeates the area, depending which way the wind is blowing or if it is working or not. As usual I hold my breath for as long as I can but it's never long enough feeling sorry for the people who live around here.

Once in Guayaquil we head straight for the shop. I stay in the car and watch two boys working on a car on the other side of the street. After working on *la bomba* they tell Angela that the shop, which had the pump for four weeks, broke some parts.

"You know I paid him two hundred dollars for that."

I shake my head in disbelief. "Well, if the pump works now, you know what to do in the future - bring the pump here."

The evening traffic in Guayaquil is something else. People, cars, buses go any which way amidst construction everywhere. There are so many beautiful, modern buildings now that it seems like another city to me. Angela says much has changed in the last four years. The new mayor has a beautification project going, redoing or building new skyscrapers and houses, redoing streets with bricks, etc. Right now the construction project is an enormous hindrance to the daily life in Guayaquil, especially its traffic.

Then there is the Malecón 2000 stretching along the Guayas River in downtown Guayaquil. Therefore, once at home I change my clothes, put only a few dollars in my pocket on Angela's advice and walk to the Malecón which I haven't done so far. I run into Berto downstairs warning me to be careful, many *ladrones* about, and by now it's dark. However, everybody is out enjoying the cool, envigorating evening breeze. I walk at a fast pace looking at the people around me. Once I arrive at the Malecón 2000, I'm truly impressed at this long and wide promenade, partially at two levels, with restaurants and shops above and below. Beautiful old, big trees, bushes, fountains, flower beds and many benches grace the promenade which is crowded with people. I'm certainly not afraid. There are families out, lovers walking hand in hand or sitting on benches kissing, women and men dressed in business attire going home from work and everybody talking and having a good time. The restaurants seem to be busy as well and, as I walk along, what do I see but the Golden Arches of McDonald's. I'm not at all a fan of this type of fast food anymore. The only time I like to see the Golden Arches is when I need a restroom, theirs being generally clean. The *Colonel* also smiled at me earlier on another street corner. Too bad this unhealthy, grease-dripping food has invaded almost every country I have ever visited.

I'm at the entrance of an underground shopping area which I notice only as I walk along and peer into some windows set into a raised area. Well, since I love shopping, I walk downstairs and find a huge underground area filled with shops, boutiques, restaurants and everything one can imagine. I try to see as much as I can before the stores close at eight in the evening. I come across some Ecuadorian arts and souvenir stores and see a T-shirt showing the continent of South America with a line straight through Ecuador into Brazil saying *La Mitad del Mundo,* - the middle of the world. The equator goes straight through Ecuador by Quito, the capital, and is responsible for the country being named Ecuador.

On my first trip to Ecuador Angela had taken me to Quito and the Equator where they have created a park and memorial to pinpoint this line. Some Indians in their beautiful and distinct clothes sold their wares there. I remember having a photo taken with some of the girls nice enough to stand there with me towering over them, although I am only five feet and three inches tall. The people in the high Andes are of shorter stature but with enormous endurance and sure of foot.

I see many nice things and regret I have only a few dollars with me but there will be more opportunities. I arrive at the house shortly before nine in the evening without encountering even one *ladrón.*

Friday, 11/8/02

The sun is out today and it's quite warm already. Up till now I haven't seen much sun here, quite different from my previous visits. Angela says she has never seen weather like that this time of the year. The sky is mostly gray which may be due to the eruption of Reventador and the other two volcanoes. In fact, the former has acted up again. I read in EL UNIVERSO today that Quito is once again covered in ashes. Furthermore, the article says that the people in Quito complain about the government officials all having departed for Guayaquil rather than staying there and evaluating the situation to provide more help.

Angela and Ivanovich have some errands to take care of in Milagro and so we stop after a while at a Restaurant and buy some *empañadas,* good tasting but rather greasy. I try another pastry which looks and tastes better. When I comment on this to the owner, a blond, blue-eyed middle-aged lady she says, "These are baked and the others fried." That explains it.

They have a map of Colombia on one wall which is their home country. I find out there are many refugees from Colombia here, who try to escape the political situation and crime there to make a new life in Ecuador. This isn't easy in a country which has much poverty of its own and, like everywhere, creates some friction between Ecuadorians and refugees. EL UNIVERSO discusses this situation often saying that it puts an enormous financial burden on the country.

Back at *La Granja,* maestro Juan and Pedro try to install *la bomba,* but they can't get it to work. Ivanovich says somehow the pressure is not right. So it goes, more people working on it, more money and still no results.

Saturday, 11/9/02

We are back at the same shop in Guayaquil again with maestro Juan and *la bomba.* We left right after breakfast as they close at two in the afternoon. They have the pump in an upright position and it works just fine, while at *La Granja* it is horizontal. Maestro Juan thinks he can install the pump that way as well so we leave the shop and make our way through the unbelievable Saturday traffic in downtown. Cars making right turns from any lane in front of vehicles with the drivers being most accommodating. Some streets have lanes clearly marked but that doesn't necessarily mean anything either because if there is room for another vehicle to squeeze in between two cars, they'll do so. Yet I see few accidents although many cars, except very new ones, have dents, broken lights or their side mirrors missing. Seems everybody does their own thing and if the traffic doesn't move, they blow their horns.

At the house we find out that the new maid for Amelia has left again after only three days on the job. Angela is glad because she thought nothing of this new person and wants to take her mother to *La Granja* with us for the week-end.

"Have you asked her if she wants to come?

"No, not yet," she replies.

"Remember, she prefers to come for only one overnight visit and not for more days."

Sure enough Amelia says she is staying in Guayaquil and that Ivan can take her out to eat. Ivanovich is so good with her and takes great care that she eats well and gets to her doctor appointments.

So Angela and I leave alone and will return Sunday night wanting to go to Cuenca on Monday. Tomorrow night she would confirm with Carla, her friend, if it was convenient.

During lunch at *La Granja* Angela has some surprising news for me. She had learned that one of the sisters in Hamburg, with whom her former help was living, had been killed. This particular sister was living in Germany for the last ten years, came back to Ecuador about twice annually to buy property and houses here.

"How was she killed and how could she afford to come so often and buy all this? What did she do?" I ask.

"She worked in a factory and when she returned to her car, she was shot dead with one bullet I've heard."

"Only one bullet; goodness that sounds like execution-style killing. Working in a factory does pay well, but still the cost of living is high also."

"She also had a car and she was married."

We discuss this matter further and in detail, wondering what could have happened to her and whether she was involved in some extra-curricular activities. I didn't know this sister personally but Angela says that she was the youngest and the prettiest of all the girls. She also has a daughter of about eleven years or so. She has done much for her family here always helping out with money. How truly sad!

Later I take EL UNIVERSO and settle back into my favorite hammock being very interested in news I like to keep abreast with what's happening in the world. I enjoy reading about this part of the world and the problems faced by this beautiful little country. Right now much attention is being given to the forthcoming elections here. There are photos today of the two candidates visiting different cities, Lucio Gutierrez in Milagro and Alvaro Noboa in Pascuales.

While reading I notice that the tall young man with a full head of curly hair approaches. He and his girlfriend had wandered in earlier, were swimming in the pool, ordered some food and now are walking leisurely about this beautiful property. Approaching he asks in English if I am from the States. Living in New York he speaks English very well, introduces himself as Carlos reaching out and shaking my hand. He says he came back to see how things were but found them no better than a few years ago when he had left.

"People here earn three, five or eight dollars a day. How can you live on that?"

"I know it's impossible."

Carlos tells me he is into computer technology and also works in building maintenance earning between thirty-five and fifty dollars an hour. He's happy with the money but wants to see if he can't get into some business here, like perfume for instance, but it's difficult to find the forty percent alcohol and who would supervise the business here. His parents are too old and can't do that anymore.

We talk for a long time about life here vs. the States. He's very intelligent and a nice, well-mannered young man. Carlos likes *La Granja*, saying he didn't know that it was here, yet he remembers this area. I tell him that Angela had a chicken farm here at one time rattling his memory.

"That's it!" he says snapping his fingers. "I knew this place before, but what she has created here now, is truly beautiful for the eye and the mind to come to and relax."

I couldn't agree with him more. Finally he says good-bye, wishes me a pleasant stay and then they leave. What a very nice young man!

I take up EL UNIVERSO again, reading various articles about the sudden death of the man who was the director of the newspaper since nineteen hundred and seventy-three. Carlos Julio Perez, born the thirtieth of June nineteen hundred and thirty-five, educated at the University of Syracuse, had passed away at one in the afternoon two days ago. He was apparently well-liked and respected in Ecuador and the husband of one of Angela's friends. I saved all the papers with news about him for Angela to read.

Sunday, 11/10/02

There's a killer working here I learn over breakfast this morning. Angela tells me that he actually killed a person when he was a young teenager and had been in rehabilitation.

"I didn't know that," she adds deeply in thought.

"How did you find out?"

"He told one of the girls yesterday. He was drinking at that time when another man bothered him, they started fighting and he pulled his knife and stabbed him."

"But do we know that it is the truth? Maybe she just said so for whatever reason. She wouldn't make something like that up, would she?"

"I don't think she would make it up."

We are both surprised about this news because he appears to be a good person and hard worker. He's very young has a wife and a baby son. We both like him. He also seems to possess more intelligence. It was just the other day that he told me, he and his wife had decided not to have any more children so they can give this one a good education and a better life.

We discuss this matter further. Neither one of us has any fear because of these revelations. We just hope that he'll stay straight and continue to be responsible. Angela will do what she can to help him. He has changed somehow and seems to have a better attitude after Angela put him to work with Pedro.

After breakfast we take a trip into Milagro with Stalin, who is dressed very nicely. We stop at a bicycle shop because Stalin needs a new bike and Angela knows the shop owner well. She talks with the owner saying that Stalin is one of her best employees and a good person. What could he do for him as far as price goes? Stalin looks all the shiny bikes of different color over, paraded in front of the store. He tells the owner that he would like one from a particular group. The owner replies that they cost one hundred and fifty dollars but that he would give it to him for one hundred twenty-five. Stalin looks pleased. He pays the twenty dollars down and has to pay five dollars a week. We leave him there. In my mind I know that he will pick the dark red one. He did and shows it to us proudly upon his return. He has a big smile on his face. I take a picture of him with his new bike which I'll send back to him with Angela. He looks so happy. I feel happy for him and quietly decide to give him a little money towards his new bike when I leave.

On returning to *La Granja* Hugo is there again with his son. Angela says she wants him to do a promotional flier for her business. As they discuss the wording and how best to do it, I throw in a few suggestions having plenty of experience from my past job.

"Why don't you do it?" Angela suddenly suggests.

"Oh, I don't know enough Spanish for that."

"Sure, you can do it." So I write my first flier in Spanish

"You did well," says Hugo upon reading it. "I don't have to change a word. Hope it comes out nice because there is no such thing as a proof here. This is Ecuador, you know, they don't work this way here."

Maybe not in Milagro but I'm convinced one gets a proof in Guayaquil or Quito.

Later I walk by the pineapple patch and see the two *abuelitos* working there. They are making some of the furrows deeper to allow a better water flow. Some of the plants have plenty of water and sprout big fruit while others look puny, almost dying. Angela has her own wells and no water shortage at all, it just doesn't flow uphill

The *grandfathers*, as I call them, are two old, skinny men; one has a hard time walking and rides a bike from place to place accompanied by the other. I hardly ever see only one. They usually work with machetes clearing the sides of the ditch in places where Pedro and his lawnmower can't get to, or do other similar work. They both look frail and cannot do much anymore, but Angela feels sorry for them and keeps them around for the easy tasks. They get meals as well. Whenever we meet, we exchange some friendly greetings.

In the evening we drive into Guayaquil again to see how Amelia is doing. We learn that the maid had shown up again, but Amelia had let her go. We brought some potato salad and chicken along which Amelia eats with gusto. She has a good appetite while maintaining her weight nicely.

Later at night Angela calls Carla in Cuenca to say we intend to come tomorrow if it is alright with her. She advises we leave early as this road is dangerous, otherwise come early Tuesday.

Monday, 11/11/02

Angela can't find her driver's license. We look everywhere in the apartment, in the car all in vain. It must be in *La Granja;* but when we arrive there we don't find it either. Suddenly Angela discovers it in a side pocket of her handbag. By now it's too late to go to Cuenca today but we pack our clothes to be ready for our departure early tomorrow morning. Ivanovich has promised to drive with us which makes us feel much better. The road to Cuenca is quite something I only know too well.

When Angela talks with Carla later, she learns its good we didn't come today because they have a terrible thunderstorm with lightening and much rain.

We all go back to Guayaquil because Ivanovich is not an early riser and Angela says we had better be there, rather than wait for him to come to *La Granja.* Heaven would only know when that might be.

Tuesday, 11/12/02

We are really on the road. I had my doubts till last minute. We were up at five-thirty in the morning and ready by seven around which time Ivanovich sleepily comes upstairs.

"How are you my dear Ursula?" he asks in his usual friendly manner. "Did you sleep well?"

After some coffee and a breakfast roll Ivan is ready and his shadow, Cousin Mario, also comes along. Cuenca, here we come!

I find out we'll be driving a new road, a shortcut, I'm glad to hear. The other road is in bad condition for quite a stretch and dangerous. Because of all the rain the road is badly washed out in some area and trying to escape one pothole, has brought us right into the next on some of our previous trips. In some spots, as we climb higher, there is perpetual fog and the landscape resembles scenes from another world constantly misty distorting shapes only partially visible. This one should take no more than three hours.

Initially I'm not aware it is the new road. We come through a misty part again higher up in the mountains where fog or low clouds cover everything in a haze, except the branches of bushes and trees lining the road. To me this is like fantasyland, mysterious, not knowing what lies beyond. I actually love this part of the trip but Angela does not. She is afraid we could be attacked. One has to travel extremely slowly in this twilight zone where the vision might be no more than five feet ahead. Also there are curves. It is dangerous driving no matter what, even without being attacked. They tell me that there have been incidences where cars have been stopped and robbed. Well, with all the travel we have done here that has never happened to us. Ivanovich drives carefully through this hazy mystery land, where the branches and leaves are dripping water, until we come out of this stretch just as suddenly as it began. I imagine that here the cool mountain air hits the hot air of the low country creating this watery haze. Once out of this mist on the otherwise excellent highway, our car isn't moving so fast anymore. Ivanovich says it's the altitude; the car doesn't get enough air. Since the car also has a leaky radiator, we stop by some houses and check the radiator.

Ivanovich unscrews the radiator cap ever so slowly, even though Angela and I advise against it. Suddenly a giant fountain of hot, dirty brown water shoots up into the air spraying all over the place. All of us had distanced ourselves far enough so nobody gets hurt, not even Ivan, with the water spraying in the downhill direction. Cousin Mario puts cold water into the radiator - another no-no - but nothing terrible happens. Ivanovich finds something had come loose and ties it together with a piece of string! Seeing this brings back memories of our first trip to Quito, the chauffeur then had also tied something in the motor area together with some string, which worked out just fine.

Once again we are on our way - slowly. The car refuses to go fast as the climb becomes steeper and steeper. We climb and climb. Ivanovich shifts into second gear but the car refuses to move any faster until it stops completely.

"That's it, we'll never make it." Cuenca is only sixty miles away. Only sixty miles but they are the worst of the trip as we have to climb over a pass. After we stopped and filled the water into the radiator, Ivanovich says: "Now we'll fly up this hill, Ursula." Well, we were far from flying, crawling was more like it and now we stand still altogether out in nowhere.

However, after a few minutes and having checked under the hood, Ivanovich starts the car again and we crawl on. That procedure continues various times, stop - go, stop - go, until the car won't start anymore at all. We hear the water bubbling in the radiator!

We all get out and I look up at the mountain where the road is winding higher and higher and it simply doesn't seem possible for us to ever get up there.

"We'll never make it up this hill," I say dejectedly thinking there goes our visit to Cuenca which is so close and yet so far at this moment.

Ivanovich opens the hood and we listen to the water bubbling in the radiator.

"Have faith, Ursula, have faith," he says.

"This will take more than faith. We need a miracle."

At this moment, a four-wheel drive comes around the corner towards us with three men inside. They are looking over at us passing slowly, then stop, back up and come over to our side of the road. The driver calls over to us "Tiene agua?" stepping down, followed by two more men with guns.

"Sí, we have water," Ivanovich responds. Then the driver and Ivan discuss the problem until he advises Ivan to turn on the motor to cool the engine. Having been standing for a while already, the motor actually starts. They talk some more, then they bury their heads under the hood to look at various parts of the engine. The other two men only occasionally participate in the conversation. I ask them if this enormous peak up on the road ahead is the highest point.

"No, no. Sube más, sube todo el tiempo." they answer.

My heart sinks. I can't see how we'll ever make it up this steep, rising road into the Andes. I see Ivanovich opening the cap again, without a spouting fountain this time, while Mario adds some more water. Finally the three men climb into their vehicle after saying a friendly *adiós* and wishing us all the best on our trip, advising Ivanovich to stop and wait whenever necessary and we'll get there.

We all get into the car, Ivan shifts into gear, and we are actually moving - ever so slowly - but we move.

"Can you imagine," Ivan says, "three men with guns? I thought we were being attacked."

"Oh no, I didn't think so at all; the driver has a good face. I go a lot by people's faces."

"That's right," adds Angela, "I, too, go a lot by people's faces."

"Besides," I throw in, "they were from the *seguridad.*"

"That doesn't necessarily mean anything," Ivan says. "This could be a disguise. Out here you never know."

"That's right," Mario adds, "you don't know for sure."

"Well, I don't expect bad things to happen all the time because I believe one's thoughts can attract bad things if one is forever fearful."

I had not always felt that way but was at one time very fearful and shy, especially in my younger years. I remember my first job interview, with my mother in tow. I was not quite sixteen then. Later on my colleagues told me that they were hesitant to hire me. But that, of course, was many moons ago. I have come a long way since - in years and miles - and through times where I simply couldn't afford the luxury of fear.

At our next stop, Ivanovich opens up something on the motor to improve the air flow. The timing is set for sea level while the highest point, the pass, is at about twelve thousand feet.

"Why didn't I think of that before?"

We stop a few more times, letting the motor cool, adding some water and moving on at a snail's pace. Water is readily available. Everywhere smaller and larger waterfalls cascade down the mountains, many of them close to the road. Mario has taken over the duty of keeping our container filled with water.

"Well," says Ivanovich "at least I can also see the beautiful landscape going so slowly."

And beautiful it is indeed; spectacular mountains with beautiful valleys and many small but very clear lakes. In some places the clouds hang so low they seem to float in the valleys. Speckled high up in the mountains we see the small homes of the Indians surrounded by fields. Some mountain sides are terraced, very green cultivated terraces, falling down the mountain like waves. The earth here is very fertile and the vegetables grown are of enormous size. Every so often we encounter some Indians and see their homes here and there along the road. Coming around another curve, we have llamas in front of our car, some white ones and a very dark brown one.

"Stop, Ivanovich! Can you please stop so I can take a photo?" I ask urgently.

"Of course, take your time."

This is not the first time I see llamas in the wild. Eight years ago, on a trip to Argentina and Chile, I was fortunate enough to visit Puerto Natales in Chile, from where I took a twelve-hour car tour through Parque Paine that almost didn't happen. Upon arriving in Puerto Natales and inquiring about a tour to Parque Paine, I couldn't understand why none of the *Agencias de Viaje* was anxious to arrange a tour.

"No hay," I was told everywhere.

"I can't be the only tourist here. Don't you work together?"

They didn't work together then, I found out later, but right now I couldn't believe that I had come all this way in vain. As I walked along the cold streets of Puerto Natales at eight-thirty in the evening, I thought it can't be true. The businesses were mostly closed by now. What was I to do? I only had one day here to see this Parque Paine and so I talked to God to please help me with a tour after coming all this way and, like a miracle, I got one.

Turning into another street I saw a sign *Agencia de Viajes* and, coming closer, there was light on inside and a woman sitting at a desk. The door was open. In complete desperation I walked in saying in my best Spanish, "Necesita una tour al Parque Paine mañana y no hay!" gesticulating with my arms and hands for emphasis.

The woman looked up at me in surprise and quietly said, "Sí, hay." I stared at her, mouth open, momentarily speechless.

"Hay?"

"Sí, hay."

"Cuántas personas?"

"Hay dos y tú eres la tercera." - There are two and you are the third.

Her husband came and picked me up at seven in the morning. A brother and sister from Scotland were already in the car and greeted me friendly. For twelve hours we traveled through the park with the most spectacular vistas one can imagine. Scraggy Mountain peaks, the bluest or greenest of lakes with the clearest water, a calving glacier, condors circling overhead, and herds of llamas on the road in front of us and on both sides with little fear of people. Walking here and there to explore, a strong wind made me lean into it sometimes not to be driven off. We admired in awe. I remember thinking how strange it was that the bottom of the world and the top - I had been to Alaska many years before that - were so extraordinarily beautiful in their wild ruggedness and grandeur that made one feel at the same time uplifted and aware how insignificant we truly are.

All these memories come back to me now on this trip to Cuenca. Ecuador is a very small country, but one of the most beautiful I've ever seen, with spectacular scenery. I love to come here and admire the country and the spirit of the people.

As we crawl along - yes, we are still moving - we are now accompanied by a fast running creek. There are also signs everywhere saying trout fishing is good here. We have come over the pass when Ivanovich says to me, "You see, Ursula, we made it. I told you to have faith."

"Yes, you were right. But I don't know how we made it. These three men from *Seguridad* were our miracle."

The three-hour trip takes five hours but we don't care when we finally roll into Cuenca.

"One has to have an adventure," says Angela. "What would a trip be without an adventure? We wouldn't have anything to talk about." We agree and laugh relieved.

Suddenly we realize that we are very hungry and buy some chocolate bars which we practically inhale, they are gone so fast. I hardly ever do that but one has to break the routine sometimes. Angela calls Carla and tells her we have arrived and will go to the Mercado first to eat lunch. This Mercado has a variety of goods but what we are especially after is the meat area where they have whole roasted pigs from which they cut off portions as people come in and want to eat. We walk along the isle, try meat here and there offered by the Indian women in the various stalls, until we decide this one is the best. We each get a plate full of roast pork, mote, big white kernels of corn covered with ají, a spicy red chili sauce, some salad and potato. There are some stools and benches or one stands up to eat right there, the heads of the roasted pigs behind and around us. This is the Ecuadorian equivalent of our fast food places, except healthier. The roast pork is excellent and with the hot sauce I actually like the mote as well.

Finally we arrive at Carla's house. Ivanovich is tired after the long drive with all the excitement along the way. Mario and Angela also want to rest. I leave with Carla and Alfredo, her help, to do some shopping for the evening. While we drive she fills me in on what happened since I last saw her over three years ago. Carla speaks English to me. She doesn't want for Alfredo to hear all these family details. She has a daughter married in Canada and has just returned from a visit with her. I met the daughter during my last visit here and liked her very much.

While Carla is waiting for some baked goods in one place, Alfredo and I sit in the car and an interesting conversation develops. Alfredo is a young Indian boy from the coast near the resort area of Salinas, short of stature looking no more than fifteen years or so. I like him. However, when I do ask his age, he tells me he is nineteen, adding "Y me siento muy viejo."

"Very old, at nineteen, that's not possible."

"Sí, I feel very old."

"How come; you are very young, almost a baby!" I smile and he smiles also.

"I feel old because I always worked much and very hard, with the machete and in construction. In February, I'm going to be twenty and this is very old for me."

"Why can't you go to school now and learn more so you don't have to work so hard with the machete anymore?"

"I have a steady girl-friend and I have to earn money and can't go to school."

"My son went to work and to college at the same time."

"Sí, he worked and studied at the same time?" Alfredo is obviously impressed.

"Sí, so why not you?"

"I have an obligation to my girl-friend."

"Bueno, would your girl-friend not like for you to improve your life so you can also make a better life for her eventually?"

"No, because one should be done with school by the time one is twenty."

"In the States people study to their mid-twenties and thirties."

"That's very old. If I would go back to school, I would be much too old with all the others being so much younger than I."

Our conversation is abruptly ended when Carla returns, saying she has heard there is a religious ceremony under way. Would I be interested in seeing it? We walk to the church close by in front of which some kind of tower, the shape of a Christmas tree, has been set up. It's decorated all around. Carla tells me, the entire shape would be full of lights and beautiful to see. A large crowd is assembling. Finally a procession, led by the priest, enters the church and we follow. Carla wants to be up front while Alfredo and I stay in the back. Standing by the last pew a man sitting there moves over and motions for me to sit down. I thank him and sit down. At the end of the brief special service we leave and wait outside with the crowd for the things to come.

There are fireworks, very beautiful ones, set off right next to the people. A few misfire, pieces coming down all around us. Then they have some tall figures on stilts with spark throwers who walk right into the crowd. Everybody flees, including us.

Meanwhile, some balloon-like little crafts, filled with gas and fully lit, are being sent into the air, called *globos* by Carla. As these *globos*, mini hot air balloons ascend into the air in the dark they look very pretty, climbing higher and higher becoming smaller all the time.

Suddenly, things are happening at the tower. Spark throwing lights, beginning at the very bottom, climb up higher and higher all around the tower until they reach the top where they explode into thousands of sparkling stars. It looks very pretty, Carla was right. The crowd is obviously enjoying it. Little stands, selling food and knick-knacks, have popped up here and there and indulging parents, like everywhere in the world, buy candies and little toys for their children.

The house is dark upon our return around eight in the evening. "They are all asleep," I say to Carla which is exactly what they were doing. We wake them up, Alfredo sets the table and we eat some dinner and then sit and talk and talk forever it seems. Carla, like Ivanovich and his cousin Mario, is well educated and knows about worldly affairs. She is a long-time friend of Angela's. I remember her from my last visit here where I had given her the name *apurate lady,* hurry-up lady, because she would forever tell us *apurate! apurate!* because there was so much she wanted to show us. We were always on the run, but with a host like that one does get around. This time she is quieter, although, thinking of my excursion with her right now, still on the go.

She tells us that she is actively working for the present presidential elections to be held on the twenty-fourth of November, not even two weeks from now. Carla is campaigning for Noboa from the establishment, the ruling class, versus Lucio Gutierrez who comes from the people, being of indigenous ancestry. He is a lawyer and well educated. I know already she's working for a lost cause. The people are leaning overwhelmingly toward Lucio, whose picture is everywhere and whose name and campaign slogans are being blasted daily out of car loudspeakers in Guayaquil, *Lucio por presidente,* however, I say nothing to Carla who is aware of all that also but feels encouraged because Noboa has gained some.

Finally, well after midnight, I have enough and go to bed. Angela left us some time ago. The house, like many here, has no central heating and I'm really cold by now and can't wait to get into bed, but crawling under the covers, feels like lying down on a glacier. The bed feels like ice. My feet resemble icicles and everything around me is icy; I have to put some of my clothes back on again but it seems to help little. Lying there shivering the entire day passes through my mind again until finally sleep takes over. What a day it has been!

Wednesday, 11/13/02

We rise early and hurry into our clothes after the quickest of bath. After a delicious breakfast of trout we are on our way through Cuenca into some villages some distance from here. We drive through a most beautiful valley, a stream in the middle and steep green mountains seemingly going straight into the sky.

Indian homes line the side of the tall mountains, surrounded by fields again.

We visit the villages of Chordelec and Guayadeo, where the arts and crafts are at home. The prices are better here than in Cuenca. Not to forget the beauty of these places and the picturesque drive to them. We see much silver and gold jewelry, but also pottery and all possible items out of wool, various metals and wood are available as well. Most the stores are around the plaza.

I had bought a silver necklace here with an interesting pendant last time, showing an *Andino* as the people from the Andes are called, blowing on his reed flute, wearing a poncho and the typical round hat worn by the men. I wear this necklace quite a bit and receive many comments on it. It's unique. Everybody would like to have my conversation piece. I always joke around saying this is *my man on a chain* which made one of our bosses at my office reply that this is where all men should be. He ought to know!

I find the store again but not a second pendant. It was the only one three years ago and checking in other stores doesn't produce anything resembling my *Andino* either.

While we are busy shopping Carla and Alfredo, with help from Ivanovich and Cousin Mario are busy hanging up Noboa posters. Finally everybody is getting very hungry and we have some lunch at a wonderful seafood restaurant here serving trout among other things but I have mixed ceviche which turns out to be the best ceviche I've ever had.

Once back in Cuenca, we drop Carla and Alfredo off at the house while we do a little more sightseeing. Ivanovich and Cousin Mario haven't been here in many years and I'm always ready to go. Cuenca is such a beautiful city, built in colonial times, with large plazas and a beautiful basilica, famous for its round blue domes. This city is very clean and at an altitude of about 7,500 feet cool at day time and cold at night. We drive around then park the car and walk up and down streets with many arts and craft shops. There are wonderful galleries with everything one can imagine. Finally we end up at the market again where Angela always buys a sack full of special yellow potatoes we all love. She has taken a big basket along for this purpose which is being filled quickly.

Returning to Carla's house, we have a little snack and then leave for a party with some artist friends of hers. We're not very excited to go having had little sleep last night; however, our attitude quickly changes once we arrive at the house. Carla told us that the house belonged once to wealthy people, but is now used as an artists' school. We are greeted by some friendly young people as we walk through a brightly painted hallway into a little bar. Some wine is poured and one of the artists, Gabriel, offers to give us a tour.

We enter a large courtyard and see all the signs of construction in process. The walls and doors are gaily painted and everything looks - well, like an artists' school. There are various rooms for the artists to work in and display their creations. We admire everything. I fall instantly in love with an oil painting depicting a street in Cuenca, with a church and smaller houses in the background and end up buying it wondering where to hang it.

Having lived in Scottsdale for many years, I tell Gabriel of the Thursday night Art Walk taking place from seven to nine in the evening, drawing large crowds and suggest that perhaps they can do something like that in the future. He listens attentively saying that this is a great idea. Already they have live music in the bar each Wednesday night and, indeed, a guitarist is showing up a little later who plays and sings for us. More and more people are coming in so that we are surrounded by a lively and international crowd, including people from Chile and Argentina. The wine is flowing, we are all having a very good time and nobody wants to leave. When we finally go to bed, it's two in the morning and this time I don't even undress and fall asleep fast.

Thursday, 11/14/02

We awake at seven in the morning to marching music which Carla plays at the highest volume possible. The house seems to shake. Haven't we just gone to bed? Before nine in the morning we are on our way again. Carla needs to go to the election headquarters and Angela wants to get back to *La Granja*.

The weather is beautiful, the sun is shining, the car runs perfectly - its downhill now - and we are in a good mood, admiring the beautiful view once again, this time bathed in sunlight. We even stop so I can take some photos of a beautiful valley below us. Then we pass through the twilight zone again without any problems and before long it gets much warmer and we know we are almost down. What a difference from our trip up; we are talking and laughing, enjoying the view on this sunny day

In a small village along the way we see a meat stand by the road with halves of pigs hanging from big hooks. Ivanovich stops and we take a closer look. Angela gets a few cooked pieces of meat for all of us to try. It tastes excellent and she buys some to save a trip into town later. Some more people show up to buy meat and a few stray dogs hang around, looking longingly at the meat hoping they, too, will receive a piece or a bone.

We are back at *La Granja* exactly three hours later, unload most of the vegetables and potatoes and then drive into Guayaquil in the late afternoon to see how Amelia is doing and to spend the night there.

Amelia is glad to see us back again. On the spur of the moment Angela and I decide to go and eat at Tony Roma's. The restaurant opened a few days ago in one of the big shopping malls, *Mall del Sol*, where one of Ivan's sons started working. We promised him that we would come to eat one night. There are a few people in front of us, but the waiting time is short and we are being seated quickly. We see Angela's grandson, I take my camera, call out to him and when he looks around and sees his grandmother, a smile of recognition shows on his face and is caught on film immediately.

The restaurant has a nice ambiance and is very crowded. Our meal is good, not spectacular but good. The price is rather high considering that people's salaries - even though in dollars these days - are lower than in the States. Angela says it's too expensive and she'll not come back again because one can get a good meal for less. She thinks many people will come here only once now that it's new.

Friday, 11/15/02

I wake up thinking that I'll be leaving in two weeks from today - not such a pleasant thought. I like it here as the country is beautiful and I have a good time with my friends.

At breakfast Angela says we'll be returning tonight to Guayaquil as we have an invitation for the evening. This makes me think it would be a good time to stay here for the day and take a closer look at the Malecón 2000. Angela agrees but, like everybody else, warns me to be careful.

From Parque Centenario I walk down the present obstacle course called *Calle Nueve de Octubre*, a very busy street. Guayaquil is being beautified and this is one of the main shopping streets being paved. Right now the street is torn up here, paved there, ditches dug, wire fences and shaky wooden planks one has to cross to get from the street to the sidewalk with piles of dirt and bricks everywhere. The traffic is horrendous, frustrated drivers are blowing their horns, the policeman is holding a handkerchief to his nose and mouth to protect himself from the dust, and many pedestrians wiggling their way across, around and though that maze. It's an adventure! Skipping, walking and balancing along, I hope I can see the finished product some day, because it should be absolutely beautiful. Police and security guards are everywhere and really no need to worry.

After about ten minutes I arrive at the Malecón 2000 by the Guayas River. First I walk along Simón Bolivar, the main street running parallel to the Malecón 2000, looking into shops here and there when I suddenly hear a voice saying, "Hola Ursula! Cómo estás?"

Turning I look into the face of the young man wanting to follow me to the end of the earth a few weeks ago. "Hola! Estoy bien y tú?" He says nothing about following me anymore and is in a hurry.

I walk along the Malecón 2000 from end to end, beginning at the foot of el cerro Santa Ana and ending with the Indian Market, enjoying this beautiful promenade lined on the one side by the river and on the other by a broad street with modern buildings and skyscrapers. Many tall, old trees provide shade, a beautiful garden aglow in the brightest of colors of many flower patches artistically arranged and perfectly kept; a feast for the eye as well as one's sense of beauty.

Finally I feel a little hungry and go to the Resaca Restaurant right on the Malecón. The view from the upper deck of this restaurant is wonderful. A nice breeze provides natural air-conditioning and makes this spot very comfortable. Seafood lover that I am, I order a bowl of ceviche which is good.

Sitting there, I have a wonderful vantage point and watch the people passing below. I notice a couple sitting on a bench below me, a young pregnant girl talking emphatically to a young boy. Both look no older than fifteen. I feel sorry for the girl so young and beautiful and pregnant. The boy mostly listens, not looking happy at all. Teenage pregnancy is also a problem here I heard on T.V.

Upon my return, Amelia and Berto, sitting by Segundo and his stand, greet me with relief that nothing happened to me and I fill them in on my wonderful day without *ladrones*. Besides, the police are out in force. I don't stay long with them but go upstairs to change clothes for our evening out. Angela returns late and by seven thirty we go downstairs to hail a taxi.

"Isn't it too late by now," I ask. "I thought you had said we are expected at six."

"Up to two hours late is okay."

"Okay. What do I know?"

We stand and wave for a taxi and the oldest, banged-up, almost falling apart taxi stops. Angela looks at the thing and asks the driver, who had jumped out at once, if the taxi has a good strong motor because we have to go up a steep road. The driver doesn't know the area but his car has a good new motor, oh yes. We both climb in not without apprehension. We drive through the city taking a wrong turn once and, after asking for directions, we come to the street I remember from previous visits here, where another friend of Angela's lives. It's rather steep with houses to one side and the road falling off to the other which makes for a wonderful view over Guayaquil bathed in so many lights. The old taxi rattles along the narrow road which suddenly comes to an end as we leave the houses behind and find ourselves entering a forest. The road now consists of two, somewhat paved tracks in the grass, forest to both sides.

"Adónde?" asks the driver.

"Al bosque," - into the forest - I answer laughingly, because I can't believe it either that we are on the right track and hope no car will come towards us.

"Un poquito más," says Angela. We are almost there.

We still climb higher, surrounded mostly by forest, but now there is a house coming up and as we approach dogs are barking. Angela says to stop. She gets out and calls for her cousin. The lights are on in the house but nobody seems to hear her. Eventually she finds the door bell and rings it. It doesn't take long and the American friend of her cousin, at whose house we are, comes out to greet us. The cousin follows close behind. She looks good but has definitely gained a few pounds since my last visit. After the greeting we all go into the house followed by the barking dogs now accompanied by more dogs kept in the backyard until finally they settle down and we can talk.

We are standing in *La Sala,* a huge L-shaped living/dining room, every wall of which appears to be covered with book shelves and more book shelves filled to the rim. The dining table is completely covered with books, so are the chairs and more piles of books everywhere. Being a book lover myself, I comment on the enormous amount of books and am being told that he loves to read. That's obvious.

We are sitting down in a comfortable corner in front of a big TV with a glass of wine exchanging a few words while the TV stays on because everybody is waiting for *El Clon,* the TV show that has all of South America in its grip. Even after this show the TV remains on.

Our host is a very tall man who has lived in this part of the world most of his life. Right now his health is not the best and he walks with difficulty. While thinking what a good-looking man he must have been in his younger years, the door opens and in comes a young man, who is introduced to us as his son. I immediately feel I have the younger version right in front of me. He returned not long ago from his studies in Europe and speaks various languages, including German, fluently.

The son sits down beside me. Finally I have someone to talk with and an interesting conversation with a very nice, well educated young man. He was born in Ecuador and to him this is home. Because of his father he has dual citizenship and wants to come to the States one of these days - at least to visit. He grew up here but was later sent to Europe to study. This seems to be the custom here among many of the well-to-do. On one of my first trips here, I met a cousin of Angela's with four children, who had all attended German schools and been sent to Germany to study and speak German like the natives. So does this young man. I'm impressed.

I learn that he studied some years in Germany and in England, taught in Spain and had returned to Ecuador only a little over a year ago. He is running the ranch and not in town all the time. In his spare time he reads a lot and follows his interest in painting. It is easy to talk with him and we fall from one subject into the next. I tell him about my son and granddaughter and ask him if he has a girlfriend. He says he did in Europe but it broke up because European women are so independent suggesting perhaps women want to take revenge on the men now.

I can't help laughing out loud saying, "Oh, do you feel revenge is called for? I had never thought of it in these terms. Women have just become more independent now because they were forced to through divorce or death and young girls are raised and educated that they can stand on their own two feet in the working world. They feel much more equal now, less inclined to be subservient or whatever you here in your macho world are looking for and think of as revenge?"

"I don't think it was men only but society as a whole changed," he replies.

"What changes society? It's usually a little ripple caused by certain developments, which eventually turn into an unstoppable swell. Sometimes it's difficult to say which came first, however, the many broken families have contributed greatly to the present situation, where women feel they had better be self-reliant than depend on a husband or future husband, who may or may not be around forever."

He understands that but still feels European women are too independent and when I comment that he might find American women the same way, he nods his head saying he would like to come and see for himself. Right now is not the time. He has to take care of the business. I suggest that women here might fit better into his way of thinking. At this time the doorbell rings and a daughter of the cousin arrives with her boyfriend. They stopped by to take us home. It's quite late by now but being involved in an interesting conversation we didn't notice how the time passed.

Saturday, 11/16/02

Angela and I leave early for *La Granja* because she expects a group today. They swim, play soccer and relax in the hammocks.

Berta is here again to help. It's a warm day and we have quite a few people coming from the community to enjoy the pool. Even Stalin comes by to help a little. He is so proud of his new bike which he purchased a few days ago. Stalin smiles much more these days and seems more open. I'm so glad about the change I see in him which proves again that kindness brings kindness in return.

The news that day talk about starving children in Argentina, even though the country is a big meat producer but poverty has increased since the financial turmoil not long ago. Another concern is that Ecuador seems to be getting more and more involved with Colombia.

Marta, Berta and I are having our *Cuba Libre* when Angela returns announcing we are going to Guayaquil to spend the night there. Fine with me!

Sunday, 11/17/02

Today is the day the body of the dead sister is arriving here from Germany, accompanied by her daughter and the man she lived with in Hamburg, married or not. Berta tells us that the daughter is supposed to stay here with her father but that she refuses to do so and will return to Germany. This is understandable. She lived her life there. The dead sister was only thirty-three and very beautiful I'm told. I wonder what happened to her. Did she get mixed up with the wrong crowd or what actually occurred? Did we get the true story? So far nobody knows who killed her or why and I wonder if they will ever find out. Angela says she came back every year two or three times spending lots of money. She couldn't have done all that with money earned from a factory job that much is certain. Her other sisters in Germany and Belgium seem to live a normal life. Sometimes the price for riches is simply too high.

It's a very hot day. The sun is out which makes a big difference. People are coming in constantly, all wanting to cool off, play basket ball or soccer and then jump in the pool again or just plain relax. The kitchen is busy as well.

We brought Amelia along for a change and, of course, her dog Zucchini. She loves her dog and the dog loves her. Being spoiled and liking meat only, he sits patiently by the table waiting for Amelia to throw him a piece of meat from her plate which annoys Angela. She does not believe in this habit which reminds me of a cat we once owned and also started feeding from the table. Consequently, she would meow constantly if she didn't get anything, a big annoyance to us, although we loved the cat dearly. Of course, it was our fault and we learned our lesson. The next cat we had would sit longingly, but quietly like Zucchini, while we ate knowing she would not be forgotten.

Zucchini often cannot finish his food because it's simply too much for him having had the tidbits from the table before. The cats don't fare so well and if Zucchini doesn't watch his dish, they help themselves to his food. With Zucchini being partially blind, the cats have an easy time snatching some of his food before he chases them away with a growl. Otherwise he sleeps a lot, follows Amelia wherever she goes or just sits in front of her staring at her.

By the way, the fence is still not finished, the gate hasn't been installed and *la bomba* is not working either. Maestro Juan has been absent for a few days because his father passed away, Angela told me. He lived in Ambato, northeast of here close to the volcano Tungurahua, and the Maestro has many obligations right now. Maestro Juan is always very pleasant and a good worker as far as I can see. He is an intelligent person and reliable. There is not much he can't fix as far as I have seen. *La bomba* is the exception.

As the evening approaches we return to Guayaquil. I'm glad because I know Amelia prefers it this way. Amelia has a new help, Angelina. We were all wondering how she would work out after the other disappointments we had. Angelina is quite rotund but appears to be a caring person from the way she takes care of Amelia. This is the most important thing for Angela and Ivanovich, that Amelia is looked after well. Angelina had asked for Sunday off, but should be returning tomorrow. Amelia is so far pleased with her pleasant ways, even though she can't cook well according to her. This doesn't concern Angela or Ivanovich much because he takes Amelia out to eat as often as possible. Angelina is mostly to be company for her and she is nice to Amelia which is more than one can say about the other women before her.

Monday, 11/18/02

I'll spend the day in Guayaquil. Ivan's wife had said she would go to *el cerro Santa Ana* with me just to let her know when. However, ɹrns out she can't today after all with such short notice. I'm still ɹoking for a pair of sandals. I take a taxi to the *Polycentro Mall* which Ivan's wife had recommended. I don't remember having been there and think this is a good opportunity for me to look around what there is and what the prices are.

The mall is not too large but modern with quite a selection of stores. I take my time looking and find that one can buy everything but that some imported items are rather expensive. After spending some time there trying on various sandals, I go to the *Mall del Sol* which is so much larger. I had seen a pair of sandals there I liked the night we went to eat at Tony Roma's, but when we came out, the store was closed. By now it's about three in the afternoon and I feel hungry and go to check out the food court down below. They have a great variety of ethnic foods just like the malls in the States. The barbequed chicken with baked potato, vegetable and a big salad and coke, all for four dollars and fifty cents is at least as good as Tony Roma's for a lot more money and without a big salad.

Returning home I stop at the photo shop at Parque Centenario to pick up the pictures from Cuenca I left there in the morning. I want to leave the pictures for Angela, Carla and the artists in Cuenca here, rather than mailing them later from the States. I'm very happy with the photos; the colors are absolutely perfect in every way. On top of it, I receive two little photo albums holding forty pictures each and all this for nine dollars for developing two rolls of film with twenty-four pictures each.

Angela has brought Ida along from *La Granja*. Sometimes she brings her along for company or because she wants her to do some work at the apartment in Guayaquil. Ida is rather intelligent and has a good knowledge of many things. She can also be quite funny, like tonight, when she is blocking my view of the TV and I ask her to move a little.

"You are not made of glass." I say jokingly.

Ida laughs and answers; "Here we say e*l carne de un burro no es transparente* - the meat of a donkey is not transparent. I will never forget that.

Tuesday, 11/19/02

I spend another day in Guayaquil. Ivan's wife and I agreed to go to *el cerro Santa Ana* in the evening around seven leaving the whole day for myself. I walk to the Malecón 2000, to the Indian Market at the other end which is quite an exercise because the Malecón stretches along the Rio Guayas. Fishing boats float on the river which I love watching hauling in their nets or throwing them out over the water. Sight-seeing boats add to the activity on the river.

At the Indian Market at a stall with a big selection in T-shirts a young girl from Otavalo pulls out shirt after shirt until I see one I really like: Three ants are walking across the shirt, each carrying a leaf. It says *Amazonia* underneath. I had seen the identical scene in reality and this brought back instant memories of my trip on the Amazon in Peru years ago. The little boat would stop for daily excursions into the Rain Forest. One day a sheer endless line of ants, each carrying part of a leaf, crossed our path; our path? No, we crossed theirs I came to realize! At first glance it seemed like walking leaves until, intrigued, I looked again and saw the ants underneath. I had read about leaf-cutting ants but this was the first time I saw them in nature. It was fascinating to watch how these small ants carried such big pieces of leaves.

"Oh, I have seen exactly this!" I exclaimed aloud.

"You have! Where?"

"In the Rain Forest of the Amazon in Peru"

Now they want to know where I come from, how long I'm going to stay and how tall my son is because the shirt is to be for him. I make the mistake of pulling my wallet out to show them a picture of my son and his family, because instantly they pull out some shirts for Hailey-Schatzi, my granddaughter. By the time all is said and done, I also have two shirts for her.

Shopping and sight-seeing, I paid little attention to the time until my stomach begins to growl and I go back to the Resaca Restaurant to have some more ceviche, this time of clams, which I also like. When I return home, Amelia always wanting to feed the world invites me for some *muchines* again. I had some the night before with coffee. They taste good and are made from the green banana, filled with cheese and then deep-fried, not exactly my regular fare. I didn't want to eat but could not get away and end up having two *muchines* and a cup of coffee. Somehow it turns out to be too much. I feel a little sick to my stomach and have some pain right under my rib cage on the right side. This is most annoying to me because I'm generally healthy and don't like to be limited by pain or illnesses.

Ivan's wife sent word for us to leave for *el cerro Santa Ana* and Angela, Amelia, Ivanovich and Berto all warn me that it is *peligroso* and I shouldn't take my handbag and just put a few dollars in my pants' pockets and take my camera. I follow their advice but, sorry to say, regret it quickly. Ivan's wife is nicely dressed with handbag and all and here am I, typically tourist looking, speak *Gringa*.

We take the bus down to the Malecón and then get out at the foot of *el cerro Santa Ana*, which is one of two hills in Guayaquil, covered with brightly painted houses resembling building blocks glued to the side of the hill from the distance. It looks a little like Sausalito across Golden Gate Bridge, except Sausalito isn't as colorful.

The main staircase up is rather wide and consists of steps and more steps and a landing and more steps, one climbs all the time and I learn there are four hundred and forty-four steps. In front of every brightly painted house there is a planter box containing beautiful plants, flowers or small bushes. Benches line the main route so one can take a rest. Everything is very clean and nice. These hills were once home to the less desirable elements of society and, I'm sure, some of them are still there but to a lesser degree. In the name of beautification, these houses and streets have been restored and are now a wonderful place for an excursion. I'm sure the people who live here now take new pride and joy in being a positive part of the city. I love el cerro Santa Ana and simply can't see the danger of which everybody speaks. Neither does Ivan's wife, I think, because she doesn't look afraid either.

We meander up the hill, turning around every so often to look back down onto the city at our feet, glowing with evening lights. We are invited by some vendors and the police to walk along some of the side streets, look into this and that restaurant even though we say we have eaten. Just to look, we are being told and we are very welcome. There are also stores, most of them closed by now, but one here or there is still open. So are ice cream and soft drink stalls. Many people are walking up, enjoying the cool evening breeze with us, or sitting in restaurants having dinner. I'm surprised how beautiful this hill is, even up close, and how clean. Where is the danger, where are the *ladrones*? I don't see one. Ivan's wife and I climb up to the top, holding an old light tower surrounded by a fortress like wall with cannons pointing in all directions. This is, of course, a perfect point to cover the Guayas River below. A chapel graces the other side of the hill which we also visit. It is pretty up here and the view, in all directions, is marvelous. There lies the city with its thousands of lights like so many diamonds sprinkled around. The ribbons of light of the two bridges we are crossing on our way to *La Granja* are to one side and along the banks of the Río Guayas, close to the center of town, the strings of lights of the Malecón 2000. Truly a beautiful view of this city of about three million people! I am so glad I came and I know right now and here that this will not be my only visit up this hill.

We start down again and stop at one small restaurant we had passed on the way up, with a nice view, for a drink and a little talk. There are a few other guests enjoying the cool evening and a friendly waiter of African ancestry comes over to serve us. When we want his service again he comes quickly to see what we desire but then never brings us the drink. Finally, I catch his eye and motion to him. He hits his forehead with his hand and when he comes back, apologizes. I laugh and say, "Estás muy ocupado, no?" We all laugh at this joke with only three other guests present.

Wednesday, 11/20/02

I only learn today what happened at *La Granja* yesterday. Angela had not come back when I left with Ivan's wife last night.

Angela hired another security guard last night - I don't know where she finds these people so quickly and how trustworthy they are. He and *Rambo* made the rounds for quite a while until *Rambo* went to bed. It was then that the hired guard asked Pedro to give him both pistols since he was now the only guard. Unfortunately, Pedro obliged and handed his pistol over to the hired guard, who then disappeared with both pistols and the bullet-proof vest. Marta discovered this a few hours later. She has the habit of walking around at two or three in the morning to check on the guards if they are awake, ever since she was able to take a pistol away from a sleeping guard. She always carries a pistol herself. She woke up Pedro to tell him that she couldn't find the guard. They discovered then what had happened.

This particular one had been recommended by José, one of the people working for Angela. I believe the guard is either a cousin or a friend of José. When Angela learned of this development yesterday morning, she and Ivanovich tried to find this person, but there was no trace of him anywhere.

Angela relates this story to me, asking, "Can you imagine? And you know what else happened! Stalin took fifty dollars out of Ida's pants and didn't come back to work in the afternoon." Stalin is the only one who goes home to eat lunch because he eats so much, he says, although he is skinny as a rail. All the others eat lunch at *La Granja*.

This does surprise me. Stalin has his new bike to pay for, but somehow I have not thought of him in terms of *thief* and asked Angela, "How does Ida know it was Stalin and not somebody else?"

"Because she saw him going into the house and he was the only one there."

"Stalin came into our house?"

"No, Ida had her pants in the other house where the people sleep."

"Why would she have her pants in the other house if she always sleeps here in our house? That's not very smart. She knows nobody comes into our house. We keep it locked when we are not in."

"I don't know either why she did this."

"Did she see him take the money, actually take it?"

"No," replies Angela, "but there was nobody there but Marta and Pedro. José was away and maestro Juan is still in Ambato for his father's funeral."

I feel terribly sad and disappointed to hear this news. Stalin seemed happy, more approachable and he was much friendlier. On the other hand, of course, there is the new bike to pay for. Opportunity makes people do all sorts of things. What a shame! Not returning to work in the afternoon makes for an even stronger case against him. Of course, we had heard about the police inquiring about him at another place. Perhaps he has to go into hiding for another reason. Anyway, I'm sad.

The matter stays on my mind as I'm considering every possibility. What if Pedro had taken it; he once tried to implicate Stalin for something which I had seen the two *abuelitos* do. Only when I told him so, did Pedro admit, "Ah, sí, es la verdad." But then again, I don't think that Pedro would do such a thing. No, I really don't think so. That leaves only Marta. Absolutely not!

Then another thought pops into my mind, what if Ida pretends the money is missing hoping that Angela will cover her loss?" This is a possibility even though an unlikely one. I wonder if we'll ever learn the truth. I make a mental note that all this happened on a full moon.

"Hola, Ursula, cómo estás?" Rosa, an old friend of Angela's I met years ago, comes towards me, giving me a big hug. She had gone to *La Granja* yesterday with Angela and Ivanovich and will join us again today. She is a nice lady, very lively, talks a lot and worked for many years for a German company here in Guayaquil who, she says, treated her very well. She is retired now and has, like so many people here, lost a lot of money in the Filanbanco scandal. To me it's unbelievable how the top people of corporations can get away with this. After all, nobody can hide hundreds of millions of dollars these days. If nothing is being done about recovering this money tells me governments are as corrupt as the perpetrators. That goes for any country in the world.

Ivanovich is joining us. He wants to see about a tractor to be repaired, an ongoing saga for more than six months. Unfortunately they paid in advance, something I can't understand. "One doesn't pay until one gets back the repaired goods in working order."

"Yes, but if they tell you, they will do it right away if paid in full, you do so hoping to have the job done quickly," he answers.

"You'll get things done quicker if you don't pay because they'll work quicker to get the money but not this way."

"I have told them the same, but they don't ever listen," Rosa adds.

Of course, the tractor is still not ready. The person, on whose property it's parked, would like to be rid of it also. I personally think they have meanwhile used some of the parts on other machines.

By the time we are done with all these errands, Rosa is hungry and we go to eat in a little restaurant set up in something like a large entrance or a garage open to the street. The space is filled with tables and chairs and very crowded. The soup is excellent, the rest not so great. Because my stomach is still not back to normal, although much better than yesterday, I give my lunch to the old lady sitting on the pavement by the entrance begging. She thanks me and starts eating immediately.

By now, the afternoon is going fast and we find it's too late to go to Milagro today.

At around five thirty in the afternoon, with my handbag this time and camera, I leave again for this *muy peligroso* place, el cerro Santa Ana. I want to be there while it's still daylight to take some photos. I walk the obstacle course of *Nueve de Octubre* down to the Malecón 2000 then make a left turn to get to the foot of el cerro Santa Ana. I always enjoy the walk along the beautiful Malecón. It's crowded as usual with families and office people on their way home. Once at the foot of el cerro Santa Ana, I start climbing the wide staircase. Again, no *ladrones* but many nice people, friendly police and still open stores this time. I climb slowly up the stairs, stopping every so often to enjoy the view of the city below me. I notice something today which had escaped me before, namely that there are photographs of the houses the way they looked before they were restored and painted in frames attached to each house. What a difference! I was told that the Municipal Government is paying for this restoration also; what an excellent investment, I think. I take my photos, look into the stores which sell mostly souvenirs and handicrafts and finally reach the top.

"Hola niña," I'm being greeted by a friendly voice which belongs to the waiter from the night before who forgot to bring our order. He's sitting on a bench with a woman and going by his hand movements and all, he is telling her about our encounter.

"Hola niña," he repeats smiling broadly, "cómo estás?"

"Hola! Bien, gracias," I answer smiling waving to him, before I walk on. It made me feel good to be greeted by somebody in such a friendly manner in a totally strange place. I could see that he was pleased also and heard the woman say to him, "she remembers you!"

When the city lights come on I start back down again. A bat is flying an erratic pattern right beside me and lovers are huddling on benches. People are out, the restaurants filled and I just love the whole atmosphere.

Once down at the Malecón, right by the museum, I hear music and follow the sound. There is a big outdoor stage where many performances take place. Upon arriving, I am told that this is a practice session for the opera to be performed on Thursday. I absolutely want to go there on Thursday.

Later Angela and I watch the evening news on TV and learn that a horrible thing has happened - the entire ammunition storage building in Riobamba blew up. There aren't many details so far, apparently a hand grenade went off either by accident or intent and the ammunition exploded like star wars, destroying not only the facility but many houses close to it, shattering windows in others. So far there are six people dead and many wounded. The pictures are awful; people crying and mothers looking for children or vice versa. Everyone is trying to account for all family members. I feel sorry for Ecuador; first the eruption of the volcano Reventador and now this explosion - one disaster after another. It's too much to handle for this small country.

Thursday, 11/21/02

This morning starts out with another explosion, this time in Guayaquil, but it's a minor one. The TV news is mostly about Riobamba, some about Guayaquil. EL UNIVERSO, the newspaper, says so far six people are dead and over three hundred wounded. The photos are of people crying, looking for their missing loved ones. They show pictures of window glass hanging in precarious positions from window frames and the reporter warns people not to walk along these streets as this glass could come down any moment.

Rosa comes over again to accompany us to *La Granja* and Ivanovich joins in also. He and Angela have various errands in Milagro. Once there, I go straight to my favorite hammock updating my notes. It's wonderful here. I can also see over much of the area. Right now I'm watching Pedro, Marta and Ida trying to knock almost ripe mangos off the tree by our house. They are having lots of fun trying to get the fruit with long, branch-cutting sticks.

When they are done, they come over and offer me some mangos. They are pretty good already. I take this opportunity to talk with Ida about the stolen money. She tells me she had the fifty dollars in her pants' pockets. The pants were rolled up and lying on a bench in the house some of the employees sleep in and where everybody goes in and out.

"Why were your personal belongings over there when you sleep here in the house with Angela and me, where the doors are locked?"

She answers she keeps her clothes there generally and only spends the night in our house. The only one she saw entering was Stalin. I doubt, however, that she was looking at this building all the time as I still have a hard time believing Stalin was the culprit.

"I don't believe Stalin took the money," I say to Ida. "Did you confront him with this?"

"No, I didn't discover the loss until evening that day and Stalin never returned to work."

"Stalin not showing up to work could be coincidental," I suggest.

"Sí, he has problems with his wife and her parents with whom they live," adds Marta.

"Bueno, that could be the reason for his not showing up but you didn't discover the loss until evening which leaves all day open for somebody to enter."

Suddenly, out of nowhere, a thought jumps into my mind, Hugo! Hugo is not working much, always in need of money, and Angela had told me he was here that day. She had invited him in to lunch. Considering Hugo's past history, I couldn't shake the thought that it was him. I asked Ida and Marta about Hugo, and both confirmed he was here for a while and had lunch with Angela. Later in the evening I mention my suspicion to Angela as I didn't want to say anything to the two women. She looked at me in surprise.

"You are right, it might have been him! I had forgotten about him being here that day. The theft happened the one day Hugo was here. But now it's too late to confront him. How can we ever prove anything?"

We can't prove anything. However, in my mind I am pretty convinced it was him. I wished Stalin would show up again with a reasonable explanation for his absence.

At lunch time, politics come up. Rosa is very much into politics; Angela is very interested as is Ivanovich, but this time he says he doesn't care who becomes president of Ecuador because they are all alike. We were talking about the ongoing election of a new president.

"They promise but never deliver afterwards. There is always some excuse or the other, why they can't keep their word."

With the second round of elections only a few days away, there is much propaganda on TV and in the newspapers. It is Noboa, the establishment, against Gutierrez and the underprivileged. Contrary to the average citizen in the States, who has been silenced by fear of not being 'politically correct,' politics is definitely a topic in Ecuador, like in most countries of the world. Rosa thinks Noboa is gaining and will win. Carla in Cuenca had the same idea. I think they are both wrong. From all that I have seen, Gutierrez will win. The underprivileged want more of a voice and the country is certainly having a hard time economically with the eruption of Reventador and the ammunition depot explosion in Riobamba among other things. The pictures on TV are not pretty and the general populace suffers much.

When we drive back to Guayaquil, Ivanovich is going as fast as he can. We leave at six-thirty and I want so much to go to the concert taking place today at seven-thirty in the evening outside the Museum of Anthropology and Contemporary Art at the Malecón 2000. According to EL UNIVERSO, *La Misa Criolla* is presented by Ariel Ramirez of Argentina, who also composed a famous piece of this music, called *Alfonsina y el Mar*, dedicated to the poet, Alfonsina Storni. He himself is a pianist and came here from Argentina with his band of nine to present this famous piece.

Ariel Ramirez, says EL UNIVERSO, was born in Santa Fé, Argentina, is seventy-nine years old, has been playing the piano since age four and created more than four hundred musical works. The concert is free to the public in a setting that could not have been more spectacular. Ivan's wife had told me that many cultural presentations are taking place here, free to the public, and that she attends many. We were to go together tonight, but with time being of the essence, Ivanovich drops me off there just in the nick of time. I run up the stairs, pass by the policeman who, with a smile on his face, wants to check my purse. I know he doesn't take this serious himself and say: "Just hurry up; I'm late."

I enter at the back of the stage and have to walk around to where the audience is sitting. It seems to me, all of Guayaquil is present; there is no empty seat left. Then I see a bench with unoccupied space and sit down, facing the stage. I feel so lucky to have such a good seat at such late time. Right behind me is el cerro Santa Ana aglow in light, with a full moon above. The air is pleasant. A cool breeze makes the evening outside more than comfortable. Since the concert takes place on the most elevated platform of the Malecón 2000, looking down on the other side, there are all the shining lights outlining the lower Malecón. I have been to outside performances before, but never have I seen a more spectacular setting than here in Guayaquil.

The concert begins on time with Ramirez and his musicians coming on stage dressed in the typical ponchos of Argentina. One presentation follows the others, many sung by the tenor Javier Rodriguez, accompanied by various Ecuadorian choirs. Rodriguez has a powerful voice. All the presenters are excellent. They are dressed in church gowns or ponchos, depending on the song presented. It's a feast for the ears and eyes and even though I'm not familiar with these pieces, I'm overwhelmed by this wonderful performance. From comments behind and around me, I realize that the populace is well familiar with this music and very appreciative. I am so grateful that I was given the opportunity to have this experience here in Guayaquil, the city which is getting more beautiful all the time. This evening will always be engraved in my heart and mind as one of the most wonderful nights of my life.

All throughout the performance people still keep coming in and standing all around, two and three deep. When the concert is over, and after standing applause by the audience and an encore, I leave thinking it's impossible to find Ivan's wife, because there are many sides one can leave from. Ivanovich had said he would come and pick me up at the end but I don't see him, even though I wait a little. There are simply too many people and I start walking home along the Malecón 2000 and *Nueve de Octubre*. On this beautiful night many people are walking that I forgo the taxi and walk home all the way.

I arrive back at the house without any problems, no *ladrones*, nobody attacks me, at about the same time Ivanovich returns. He had gone to look for me and is much relieved to see me save and sound at home. I'm sorry to hear that his wife had not gone. She was waiting for us to come back from *La Granja*. I wished she would have come, even a little later and I'm so excited about the experience that it takes me a long time to go to sleep.

Friday, 11/22/02

After a restless night with some dreams - I dream more here than at home - I hear that Amelia doesn't feel so good and doesn't look her best either. Consequently we don't arrive at *La Granja* until the afternoon. After our meal, I go straight to the hammock to read EL UNIVERSO. I'm interested in the news and am using the time in South America to learn a little more about this part of the world, their problems, their thoughts, and how they see world events. Our news in the States are so limited in every direction and often very biased.

Riobamba is still very much in the news. They now have seven people dead and five hundred thirty-five wounded. Many are still missing. Graphic pictures portray the human suffering. Women are looking for their children and people in general are looking for relatives. This is harder now, as many wounded have been taken to Quito hospitals. Riobamba hospitals are more than capacity filled.

The explosion seems to have been an accident and not an attack, the newspaper says. That is possible, because the paper says the ammunition depot was not very well secured or protected in any way. Neither is the country prepared for the tragedy and has no emergency plans at all. Hopefully this will change now because EL UNIVERSO writes that people were running every which direction. How sad this all is.

Here at *La Granja* all goes its usual way. Stalin still isn't back and Angela thinks he is hiding out from the police for the theft of a gun or pistol he has been accused of taking before he came to work for her. She says the police suspect him. This is the other thesis to this ongoing drama. I really don't know.

It's warm today and I don't move around a lot but read the paper and watch my favorite red birds, the hoyeros, who seem to trust me more and more by coming closer all the time, provided no other guests are around. They are picking crumbs off the floor of the cabaña. After all, I have company here many times and some days I could not even get into any hammock because they were occupied.

My first pictures from here came out great. I'm especially proud of the one of *el abuelito de los iguanas* - the grandfather of the iguanas - sitting on top of the wall, head raised in full alert, not trusting me one bit.

We return late to Guayaquil because Angela, as usual, still has to do some errands along the way. Rosa is talking all the time and seems to be anxious to get back home. She says "Yo hablo, hablo todo el tiempo." I laugh out loud, because this is definitely true; her mouth and vocal cords must be worn out from talking so much. I'm glad when we are home and alone. At one point we were considering going out still, but then Angela said, "Or should we do that tomorrow?"

"Yes, let's do that tomorrow." We stay home, look in on Amelia who is still not looking that well and watch some TV before going to sleep. Angela takes great care of her mother and spares no expense to care for her. She wouldn't dream of sending her into an old age home because here the families take care of their own parents.

Saturday, 11/23/02

Rosa seems to have become a permanent companion and turns up early this morning again. We drive her to a bank in a shopping mall where I have to accompany her because Rosa is afraid she may not find the bank. Walking along she apparently doesn't trust me either asking, "You know where we have to go?" I assure her that I'll find this bank branch.

Back at the car, we go straight to Milagro and intend to spend the night there because tomorrow is Election Day in Ecuador and Angela is registered to vote in Milagro. I'll be so glad when this election is over and I won't have to listen to the loud propaganda blurted out of so many loudspeakers all over the place.

La Granja is already crowded with people swimming and relaxing. It's hot today. All the hammocks are occupied so I settle down comfortably inside under the ceiling fan, which is of big help right now. I read EL UNIVERSO which contains more information and photos of the Riobamba explosion. A lengthy article on the presentation of *La Misa Criolla* says that 5,600 people attended last night's performance. The article confirms my own opinion of an excellent performance all around. It talks about maestro Ramirez, his son, who stepped into his father's shoes and is also a pianist, as well as the tenor with his powerful voice. The article mentions that they are Argentineans, but continues to say the maestro stresses that this is not important. They are Latin Americans and he feels he is a *citizen of the world*. A man after my own taste!

The more I travel, the more I realize that people everywhere have a lot more in common than what separates them. Too bad, the governments of various nations don't know this simple truth and still refuse to grant liberty to a people and a land to call their own. Just as most people work best when left to themselves, no nation wants to be oppressed by outside forces whatever excuse is being used by manipulating governments and propaganda. I have time to think about many things as I sit here and contemplate the world around me. But then, how many people take the time to think for themselves. Some of the news we are bombarded with don't even make sense. One knows when one hears it that it's a lie. It's so much easier to repeat what the newscasters say and not waste time thinking. After all, one may miss a football game or a favorite *nothing* show on TV.

Pedro is leaving for Guayaquil to vote tomorrow. As security guards we have José, Marta and Ida. Absolutely nothing can happen to us! Ida also takes a rifle and the three walk towards the far end of the huge property. They think they heard a noise. Angela and I stay by the house. We hear a shot. Angela says, she told José to fire once but then we hear another, different sounding shot. When the three return, Ida says she also felt like firing a shot.

Coming back to José, he is a slight man with some front teeth missing, who presently works mostly on rebuilding the front wall and gate. He's always very friendly, but a little inquisitive, wanting to know this and that about my personal life. In the course of one conversation, he was telling me what a wonderful husband he is and how well he treats his wife. Then, one day I find out that his wife had thrown him out, he didn't know where to sleep until Angela, feeling sorry, provided a bed for him in the other house. This came out when we were all sitting outside and caused much laughter, putting a sheepish grin on José's face.

Sunday, 11/24/02 - Election Day in Ecuador

Marta leaves early in the morning for Guayaquil to vote, Ida leaves after breakfast by which time Berta arrives. It is quiet in *La Granja* nobody comes in the morning, all are busy voting. We turn on the TV and learn that voting in Riobamba has been postponed due to the disaster. I wonder what that means and if we'll have a result today or not. They do not say when Riobamba will vote. Be interesting to see how they'll handle this. I'm sure the whole country is anxious to know the outcome of today's election.

Berta and I take a walk around the property to see if all is as it should be. I ask her about the dead half-sister, who was brought back last Sunday for the funeral. She tells me that the husband and her daughter have returned to Germany again. The daughter absolutely didn't want to stay here and will be living with her two aunts in Germany. There is also another version now of her death: she was killed for her car, which was stolen she now tells me. Still, all the money she spent she could not have earned by working. Something is fishy but she doesn't say anymore and I don't want to press any further either. All these unsolved mysteries!

It's the season for mango to ripen. Many ripe ones are falling on the ground. Berta and I pick up as many as we can carry. Daily we find more and more ripe fruit under the trees. They are delicious. I also learn the proper way to cut and peel them. One cut down each side, peel the skin back by hand from each end to expel the flesh, then cutting the skin off from what is left around the kernel. Now why didn't I think of that!

Angela is ready to do her civil duty and drives off. She returns quickly and I ask her, "No lines, ha?"

"They all know me and they let me pass."

The place fills up with people in the afternoon when done with their voting which is mandatory in Ecuador. For certain official business one has to show the slip that one voted. Marta comes back in the early afternoon; Pedro doesn't show up anymore and neither does Ida. I pack all my things because I don't think I'll be back here these last few remaining days and take one last look around this beautiful, peaceful place wondering when I will see it next. It is a true oasis, a quiet place especially this morning. There was no noise at all, no music, just the singing of the birds.

Back in Guayaquil, we turn on the TV to see how the election is going. Gutierrez is definitely ahead, although Noboa did gain some, but basically the people are expecting Gutierrez to be the next president the newscaster says.

"I'm surprised they are bringing all this without Riobamba having voted at all," I say to Ivanovich.

"Riobamba doesn't count. It's very small and won't make a difference one way or the other."

"Okay," I think, "so it doesn't count. Probably all votes would be for Gutierrez anyway, the population being largely indigenous."

Later on a happy crowd is celebrating in the streets below, shouting at the top of their lungs, "Lucio Presidente, Lucio Presidente!"

This election outcome to me is the result of centuries of the establishment of Ecuador having forgotten a very large portion of its people. It has happened in Peru and Venezuela as in many other countries. It's a protest vote! The only question remaining now, is Gutierrez up to the challenge he will definitely face? He wants to attack corruption first. I do hope he is successful as this is definitely a big stumbling block for progress, but hard to fight with incomes of many being at the low end of the scale. People, who don't earn enough to support their families, will do anything to gain some extra income. Yes, corruption is a big problem.

I'm thinking of the destruction caused by Reventador and the explosion in Riobamba and wonder if the people affected most by this, will ever see any aid other than a little soup for the day and some blankets for the night. I talked with Berta about this earlier, while reading the paper and looking at pictures of people sitting in the rubble of totally or partially destroyed houses.

"They'll get nothing," says Berta.

Lucio Gutierrez has his job cut out for him. I hope he is successful and does the right thing for the welfare of all the people of this small, beautiful country, which I love so much.

Ursula B. Borck

Monday, 11/25/02

We are actually on the road again. Angela had talked about going to Manta, a resort and U.S Air Force city by the Pacific Ocean. I was there once before about nine or ten years ago with Angela, her husband and a granddaughter. We were in Quito, the capital of Ecuador, for a few days and drove a northern road across the most beautiful country towards the Pacific Ocean. I craned my neck left and right to see everything. All the roads from and to the Andes are spectacular and words can't truly describe the beauty of the land. One has to see this country with one's own eyes to understand what I'm trying to explain. Even Angela said she had never been on that particular road. Perhaps this book will make some people want to go to see with their own eyes.

So now Angela, her nephew Mario and I are on our way to visit Manta again. I'm looking forward to this visit but afraid we'll never get there because Mario drives so slow until Angela tells him to speed it up a bit because right now he's moving at the speed of a turtle. I can't help but laugh and try to hide my face but glad she does say something because he drives faster now. We travel closer to the Pacific Ocean without the spectacular vistas of the higher altitudes but there are still interesting and beautiful spots. Along the road we encounter many houses built of split bamboo covered with grass or palm fronds sitting high on stilts for protection from flooding during the rainy season. Everywhere we see brightly colored laundry fluttering in the wind. Children, dogs, pigs and chickens hang out along the road lined with many fruit stands, baked goods, soft drinks, furniture made of cane, etc.

In La Cadena, they specialize in cushions, very nicely done and stuffed with the blossoms of the Ceiba tree growing here. Angela buys three cushions for seven dollars. There are many little towns along the road which slow us down with huge speed ramps in the middle of the road to make sure no one races through here.

Speaking of Ceiba trees they have unusually shaped trunks. The younger tree trunks are thinner on the ground, becoming thicker in the middle and then again thinner towards the top, from where a crown of strong short branches spreads. The older trees have enormous trunks spreading towards the ground into many folds which then become the roots. Most unusual! The bark is extremely

100

smooth and some trees have flowers, but none had leaves so far this being the spring season. The blossoms of these trees make excellent stuffing for cushions, etc.

We pass one tree with many black globs on it. It looks at first glance like birds' nests hanging there. As we come closer, I realize that the tree is full of black vultures. We are past so quickly, that I can't have my camera ready. However, we encounter another *vulture motel* and I do get my photo.

Manta has grown considerably since I saw it last. It has modern high rises right next to the older homes and villas and quite a few hotels. There is also a large Air Force base here and not only for Ecuador, but the U.S. as well I'm being told. The harbor is even more picturesque than I remember it with yachts and many fishing boats, some returning just now and selling their catch, surrounded by seagulls and pelicans fighting to catch whatever they can. Not far from there people are repairing a boat with children standing around watching which makes for a colorful scene typical for this part of the world which I enjoy watching. We sit down in a restaurant to eat lunch across from the bay which offers a wonderful view. My ceviche is delicious and served with some dried banana strips. A man comes buy selling carvings made from the tagua nut and carries some extremely beautiful ones I can't resist. These carvings are rather unique to Ecuador and make wonderful gifts. The tagua nut grows in clusters within a big round fruit casing and can be eaten just like the coconut when ripe with milk to drink as well. As it hardens in about four months, it can be carved into figures, buttons and is even used for industrial purposes. It is called the ivory of Ecuador which it resembles in color.

We do a little more sightseeing and then in the late afternoon start our trip home, stopping at various stands, where Angela finds a few things to take home. In the morning, we had bought some *pan de yucca* cakes fresh from the oven. Were they ever good! I like to try the local food whenever possible and enjoy most of it with very few exceptions.

While Angela is shopping, I start talking with the parents of the cutest little girl. They are obviously proud of their darling little daughter and allow me to take a picture of her with her father. I always try to take photos of children because they are so beautiful, wherever I go. I wished I could buy something from them but they sell all big and heavy items made of clay, stone carvings or metal not suitable for me to take on the plane.

At home, Amelia has caught a cold and is neither feeling nor looking well. I feel sorry for her because she seems to have one problem after the other right now.

Tuesday, 11/26/02

A ngela leaves in the morning for *La Granja*. Ida has not shown up so far and Angela has left word with Marta to tell Ida to come to the house in Guayaquil but nobody has seen her, although she should have been back last night or this morning. Angela has a new cook for *La Granja*. The agency brought a nice looking woman of African descent over this morning while we were having breakfast, who doesn't mind being out in the country and so Angela takes her along. Hope she works out because Marta is quite tired of doing the cooking for everybody, besides she has other duties to fulfill.

I stay in Guayaquil walking to different areas I had not been to before, eventually ending up at the Malecón again to have some white fish *ceviche* in a different restaurant today. It's very good.

In the underground shopping mall, I sit down with a coke in one of the restaurants to watch the activities on the Rio Guayas and to cool off a little. The sun is out which makes a big difference. Eventually I walk to the Indian market at the end of the Malecón to buy a few more tagua nut figures and shirts.

When I arrive back home towards evening, I'm glad to see Amelia sitting up eating chicken soup. She looks a little better today and offers me some chicken soup also which I accept because it sounds good to me just now. Unfortunately, I also find out that Angela had come back early with Ida and couldn't get into her apartment because she gave me the keys. Later at night she says not to worry about it.

There is some more excitement that night. Poor Amelia feels worse again and Ivanovich calls the doctor, who comes and checks her vital signs. He gives her some shots against the flu and the pain that she says she has right under her rib cage. Angela had taken her blood pressure before and checked her blood sugar. We are all standing or sitting around her bed while the doctor explains what he did. The shots seem to make Amelia tired; her eyes are closing and we all leave her room hoping she'll be better by tomorrow.

Wednesday, 11/27/02

First of all I wake up at five in the morning and discover that I have diarrhea. "Oh great," I think, "I hope I haven't caught something." Angela wants to know what I have eaten the night before. After taking all my different vitamins and some Advil, I feel much better by late morning, but take it easy and stay at home.

I buy EL UNIVERSO to find out what goes on in the country and the world. On the front page there is a photo of the present President of Ecuador, Gustavo Noboa and the President-elect, Lucio Gutierrez, saying they met to ensure the transition will be smooth. For an outsider like me, it's not easy to keep all these Noboas apart. One is president and another was running for president although they carry the same name, they are not related I am being told.

Another article talks about the immigrants from Ecuador in the United States saying that percentage wise they are the most economically successful per the Center for Studies of Immigration, a private group in Washington. Another headline catching my eyes announces that Inspections in Iraq start today.

The plan today is to go to Salinas, a resort on the very tip of a peninsula protruding into the Pacific Ocean like a pointing finger, less than two hours drive away. I had been there on my very first vacation in nineteen hundred and eighty five. I never made it back and am wondering if we'll make it now.

Suddenly we have a crisis. I go across the hall to check on Amelia only to find her in utter pain. It hurts really badly under her rib cage she can hardly move in bed and complains about a big pain in her right leg. I try to console her saying that Angela and Ivanovich will be back soon. Amelia moans and groans more, her face looks actually gray. I ask Angelina, her help, if there is a phone number where we can reach Angela or Ivanovich. No, there isn't, and Angelina hasn't been here very long either to be of much help this moment. I go downstairs to find Ivan's wife but she isn't home. I go upstairs again to find Ida, who is to clean the apartment, but Ida is nowhere around. Then I track down Mario to see if he has the phone number of *La Granja*, but he doesn't either. He is dressed so nicely today probably in anticipation of our trip to Salinas. I comment on this and he smiles telling me that he is leaving right now to take his daughter to the doctor who also has the flu.

I'm becoming desperate because I don't like the looks of Amelia at all and head back upstairs when I run into Berto who says that Ida is chatting with the maid in Ivan's apartment. Now I'm really annoyed because when I called Ivan's wife, Ida didn't respond either. Berto suggests I talk with Ivan's sons, who have their telephone sales place below. Explaining the situation to them, one son comes upstairs with me and unlocks the door. Sure enough, there is Ida. I am fuming and ask her "Didn't you hear me call earlier? Amelia is very ill and in great pain."

"No," she answers but follows me immediately, seeing how angry I am and knowing how I feel about Amelia. I told her once when she spoke in a disrespectful tone to Amelia that she shouldn't forget to whom she is talking, namely the mother of her employer and a very nice old lady, who deserves to be treated with respect.

Ida knew the telephone number at *La Granja* but when she calls nobody answers. Heaven knows where they all are. Meanwhile Amelia is moaning and groaning even louder. Ida thinks we should call the nurse from downstairs where she has an orange drink stand these days. When she returns with the nurse, I'm not sure she should give her the shots as I didn't hear the instructions the doctor had left for her. After all, she is an old lady and one has to be careful. So the nurse leaves again.

Angelina tells us now that Amelia had been in pain all night but not as severe as right now. That does it for me. "Call the doctor, Ida," I tell her. She calls the doctor but is being told that he isn't in right now. "Tell the girl to have him call here right away when he returns; we have an emergency." Ida does all that and I just hope that he'll call back quickly.

Meanwhile, Ida finds the cream Amelia uses for her legs and starts massaging her leg with it also bending her foot back and forth. She finds a knot in her vein and muscle and keeps massaging the cream into Amelia's leg which makes Amelia wince now and then but she seems to appreciate the effort and her legs are getting better. I'm holding her hand and talk to her every so often. Half an hour had passed since the call and still no call from the doctor. Knowing how busy doctors are and that one cannot necessarily expect a call right back, I say to Ida, "Call the doctor again. Maybe he has returned and if not, emphasize that Amelia is in severe pain."

Ida goes to the kitchen phone and returns quickly with a big smile on her face saying the doctor was indeed there and told her it was okay to give her both these shots.

"Okay, go and get the medicine from the pharmacy downstairs and the nurse because I cannot give shots.

Ida runs off and returns shortly with the medicine and the nurse following her, who does what the doctor had ordered while I sit there and can do no more than to hold Amelia's hand again as I had done before, stroking it softly. She is moaning all the time. I thank the nurse for her help. She's a very nice lady. I had spoken with her before. She returns to her stand and I sit with Amelia. Slowly, the shots seem to make her feel better, she is no longer moaning and when Angelina fixes her a cup of coffee, she actually has it and she even drinks a bowl of chicken broth Angelina brought, all the time concerned that I eat something right now also.

"Amelia, you have to eat now and not worry about me. I'll eat later." I have to almost argue with her but realize that this is a good sign because Amelia is always concerned with the welfare of other people. This all had been going on since about eleven in the morning. Now at about two in the afternoon, Amelia is more comfortable and I follow her wish to go and eat something myself. The soup and salad are very good, the fish not so. In fact, I wouldn't have known what I eat if Ida hadn't told me that it is fish. It was fried to death and dripping in fat. I could hardly eat it but didn't want to say anything, wondering how often Angelina cooks for Amelia and if that has something to do with the pain under her rib cage. When Ida asks me if I want some pineapple for desert I eat this with gusto which makes me feel better. After all, something is not right with me either, but with all the worry about Amelia, I totally forgot about myself.

I look in on Amelia again who seems to be sleeping, her eyes are closed and she is breathing evenly. I quietly step out again and return to our side of the hallway.

When Angela and Ivanovich return at three in the afternoon, they are alarmed to hear what had all happened to Amelia. Ivanovich is outraged, because the doctor had told him that Amelia should have her shots in the morning. He had instructed Ida accordingly, but Ida forgets easily and is a little lazy as well.

Now that everything was under control and Amelia feeling much better, Angela says, "Let's go to Salinas."

"Now," I ask. "It's too late."

"No, no it takes less than two hours from here," she answers.

I don't think it's such a good idea but by three forty-five we are on the way with Mario driving. We are about forty-five minutes out of Guayaquil, when Mario suddenly stops the car. We have a flat tire. We get all the tools out and put the spare tire on and in less than half an hour we are on our way again. We discuss the pros and cons of going on with our trip versus returning to Guayaquil and decide we can make it if we can buy a tire along the way. We arrive in the next little town called *Progreso* and try to buy a tire but no such luck. They don't have this particular size and it's most unlikely that we'll find it. Now we'll definitely return because it's not good driving with the smaller tire and what if we have another problem? Salinas is just not meant to be on this trip. Next time then!

We turn around and want to start back when Angela sees a stand with fresh *muchines* and buys some.

"Do you want some?" she asks me.

"No, I have had enough grease for one day." They both laugh. I told them of my fried fish experience with Angelina.

We stop one more time to buy some fresh vegetables and then arrive safely around seven-thirty, in Guayaquil. Ivanovich is with Amelia when we look in on her and we find out that she is much better. I take some vitamins myself and an Advil before going to bed that night.

We watch the news and talk a little about *La Granja*. Angela tells me that Maestro Juan is back, has installed the wrought iron gate again and it looks great. The wall is completed and pretty soon the fence will be put on and the front side of the property will look nice again. The new cook is very nice and it looks as if she'll work out. Stalin has still not returned to work and nobody knows where he is. *La bomba* isn't working either so far, but that hopefully will change soon.

"I'm glad you remind me of this," Angela says. "I'll have to go to the shop and get it."

"I hope not tomorrow because if you do, you'll never be back on time."

"Oh no, not tomorrow but next week I'll go."

She asks me again to stay longer over Christmas and New Year's. Unfortunately, this is not possible for me. I've made arrangements to be away for this time only. Also, I'd have to change my air ticket, etc.

"There will be another time. Who knows, perhaps I'll be back next year."

"That would be nice, Ursula, why don't you come back next year and stay longer."

"Thank you so much. I won't promise anything right now, but if I can, I'll return because as you know, I really like Ecuador."

How nice to have a friend like that!

Thursday, 11/28/02

It's Thanksgiving in the States and my last day in Guayaquil. Angela and Ivan leave after breakfast saying they'll return earlier than usual which I'll believe when I see it.

"Well, this is Ecuador," Angela responds.

I pack my bags which are entirely too full again. I brought gifts for everybody and now I bought gifts for back home. No end to it. When done I leave in the early afternoon to have some lunch outside. I don't trust Angelina's cooking anymore and I want to walk one more time along the Malecón 2000 and up to *el cerro Santa Ana*.

It's hot out and time I am leaving the country. I was lucky as far as the weather is concerned this year, luckier than I had expected. Now, however, summer is here. I walk down *Nueve de Octubre* one more time, climbing over all the rubble of the broken up street, new bricks, wire and sand, all the while stepping very carefully. The street work is progressing nicely. I have read in EL UNIVERSO that it will be completed in December and I think how nice it will be once it's all done and what a shame I can't be here and enjoy its completion. I have walked this street many times because my friends always remind me to walk where there are many people.

It's really hot today. Perhaps I should have stayed home. Once at the Malecón 2000, I walk through the beautiful gardens, a true pleasure for the eye. The size of some of the leaves and the blossoms of flowers are truly amazing, considering how puny they look as potted plants at home. The huge old trees offer much desired shade today. I take a few more photos of all the color and beauty around me.

Even though I'm not walking fast, I feel wet all over from the heat and humidity. Finally I arrive at *el cerro Santa Ana* and start slowly climbing the many steps - in the sun now. I can literally see drops of perspiration falling down from my hair as I walk up, head bent down, thinking I must be crazy.

I arrive at the restaurant where Ivan's wife and I had stopped one night and am greeted again with a smile and "Hola niña" by the waiter. "Hola," I respond asking him what kind of lunch they serve. It turns out it's not what I have in mind and so I say good-bye and climb on further up the hill arriving at the little restaurant *El Vigio* I had seen earlier. All one can see is the sign and a very narrow balcony with chairs and tables made of branches. "Muy rustico," I think, arriving at the restaurant which attracted me from the moment I saw it.

Totally bathed in perspiration and water dripping from my hair I look up and straight into the face of the owner who says he can provide lunch. He shows me the menu and recommends *corviche* made from the green banana and filled with some fish, not containing *mucho graza* he answers to my question how greasy it is. Since I also like the beans I ask if he has some and he says yes, putting the ready meal into the microwave. He comes out with a Pepsi and starts talking with me by introducing himself.

"My name is Victor Hugo."

"Victor Hugo?"

"Sí, Victor Hugo Andrade de Chimborazo" he replies.

Well, what do you know! I am having lunch with Victor Hugo today!

He has the typical indigenous features and is obviously proud of his name and as nice as can be. He wants to know where I come

108

from and the usual conversation develops. Then he pulls out a photo of his four months old son, his pride and joy. He owns the restaurant but not the building, is doing well and hopes to be able to open another restaurant in Cuenca, his favorite city, in about two years. We have the liveliest of conversations when he finds out how much of Ecuador I know, that I like the country and its people and that Cuenca is pretty close to my favorite city also.

"It won't be hard to travel back and forth because with the new road now one is in Cuenca in three hours."

He also compliments me on my Spanish. However good or bad my Spanish is I'm glad I speak what I speak because I would be missing out so much otherwise. He gives me a plan of *el cerro Santa Ana* which shows where everything is and he tells me that the restaurant we plan to visit tonight has good food.

As we talk, his wife comes up and brings him some soup for lunch. I joke with him about not liking his own cooking, ha? We all laugh and he says he just wants a change sometimes. His very attractive wife brings many photos, mostly of their very cute baby son, which I get to see also.

Sitting still all this time, I don't feel quite so hot anymore and start walking again - but not up the hill any further. Oh no, it's too hot. I don't have the energy for that anymore and slowly start my descent. Three people are coming up towards me, one woman trailing slightly behind, all walking very slowly also. With a smile on my face I say to her, "I see, I'm not the only crazy person around here today." She laughs out loud, knowing exactly what I mean and then proceeds to fill the couple in front of her in and they also begin laughing.

Angela and Ivanovich come back late but we all go out to *El Galeón*, the restaurant Ivan's wife and I had been in on our trip up the hill. I liked it immediately, its ambiance, many cozy rooms on various levels all decked out in wood, glass and fancy chandeliers and decided right there and then this is where I wanted to have the farewell dinner. Amelia, seemingly having made a total recovery, comes along also and actually climbs up the hill. I look at her and can't believe that this woman, who looked as if she would not live past the day yesterday, is climbing about fifty steps to get to the *El Galeón de Artur's* restaurant. Angela and Ivan's wife support her, she rests on a bench here and there but she makes it up the steps climbing even more steps inside the restaurant. The owner has a certain, very nice table in mind for us on the second level. Amelia is great and when I comment on this turn-around to Angela she replies, "It's always like that; one day she says she is dying and the next day she is as well as can be."

The owner himself waited on us and made sure Amelia was comfortable. From the table we have a view over the city and the Malecón 2000 all aglow in the evening lights. The dinner is very nice and Amelia eats everything on her plate and looks very good. The owner then brings two high-quality booklets on Ecuador for me to take with me.

More people come, a guitarist performs for us all, playing and singing so that we have a most enjoyable evening, just as I thought it should be. At first Ivanovich was a bit hesitant to go to this restaurant. He had the dining room in one of the big American hotels in mind but I told him this is not what I came to Ecuador for. I want the real Ecuador. When we leave he says: "Now I know why you liked this place. I haven't been here before, but I also enjoyed it very much and will keep it in mind for the future."

Hours later we leave and drop Amelia off at home. Ivanovich takes her upstairs and when he returns he says to us, "Do you know what my grandmother just said to me? She told me she is hungry because she hasn't eaten in hours." We all laughed.

When Ivanovich replied that she had said she was full, she answered, "Yes, but that was hours ago. Now I'm hungry again."

Angela also wants to stay but Ivanovich, his wife and I leave again on a sight-seeing tour of Guayaquil by night. Ending up at the Malecón 2000, we have a few final drinks at the Resaca Restaurant which is very crowded on this cool evening. We talk and talk without realizing how the hours are passing. It's one in the morning when I go to bed and the thought of having to rise and shine at five doesn't appeal to me at all.

Friday, 11/29/02

I don't think I slept much at all; at least it seems that way. I don't rise at five in the morning either but at five twenty. Rush, rush is the word, but all works out. Even Ivanovich, surprisingly, is up early and he and Angela take me to Simon Bolivar Airport where we arrive at seven in the morning. My flight is to leave at nine-thirty for Miami; I have plenty of time. A large crowd is at the airport already. We talk a little while and then say our good-byes because Angela has a busy day ahead of her again with the same large group returning today who had shown up without calling first. I don't feel like leaving and thank them both for the good time I've had with them, knowing I'll see Angela in a few months in the States. The check in line is not long and by eight forty-five I've passed all the checkpoints without being searched. That's a change and I hope that my good luck will continue.

I'm barely seated in the plane when a stewardess comes around offering us the various papers of the day. I take the EXPRESO and see on page one two photos of Noboa with Fidel Castro and Chavez of Venezuela who are visiting the country presently. The newspaper is thin and it doesn't take me long to go through it.

We are in the air now and I look down on the sprawling city of Guayaquil one more time before it's out of sight. Sitting there, I've plenty of time to reflect on the past so many weeks and the happenings during that time, many of which bring a smile to my face. I'll miss my friends and all the people around me for the past weeks very much and am sorry it's over so quickly. Where has the time gone? I'm never very anxious to return home because once home, responsibilities start again. I remember returning from South America after almost five weeks and a lady sitting next to me on the plane looking totally aghast, when to her question "You must be so glad getting back after such a long time," I answered "No." It's interesting to see the reaction of people when one gives the unexpected answer.

Besides, I have a good time everywhere and really feel at home on the planet earth, rather than in only one particular country. Most people can't understand that, but that's okay, because I can't understand people either who lack the desire or are afraid to travel and see the world, filled with so much beauty and wonder, so many interesting cultures and people, all contributing to enlarge one's horizon in more ways than one. This brings a saying back to me I read years ago: 'A mind once enlarged will never go back to its original size.' I know that what I've seen with my own eyes and experienced, nobody can ever take away from me anymore.

I also enjoy my fellow travelers and feel a common bond between us, namely curiosity about what is out there as well as appreciation and acceptance of what we may find that is different - without fear.

EIGHT MONTHS LATER

IN ECUADOR

Wednesday 8/13/03

"When are you coming down to Ecuador again?" Angela asked right after our greeting in July at my son's house in the San Francisco Bay Area, when she and her husband came to visit. I had just returned from a great trip to the East Coast of Canada where I visited the beautiful Maritime Provinces with a girlfriend of mine who lives in Montreal. Angela didn't have to wait for my answer as I'm always ready to go. Now, once again, I'm back in Guayaquil in my *home away from home* eight months after I left last year.

We planned on leaving in two weeks, but actually left three weeks later because Angela, balancing on high-heeled sandals, unfortunately stepped into a hole, stumbled, hurt her knee and could hardly walk. She also broke the little finger on the left hand.

I was ready to leave, and I mean ready, because of the heat in Arizona in the summer. I almost camped out at the airport because the American Airlines flight left before six in the morning. I hardly slept and woke up before the alarm went off.

The distance from the arrival gate to the departure gate in Dallas/Fort Worth was considerable but I walked because I would be sitting all day long. Once aboard the plane, I ended up with a wonderful seat in a row with extra space and a little TV screen all to myself, wondering what one has to do to get this seating again in the future.

In Miami I had more exercise getting from one gate to the other and surprised to find the 'full' flight to be half empty. The departure time arrived but nothing happened. The doors of the plane were closed but the plane didn't move. We stood there for about one hour and a half during which time the captain came up about four times telling us that we would leave as soon as the Customs Officers were done with going through the 'bowels' of the plane where all the luggage is and whatever other cargo they had taken on. Nobody ever showed up in the cabin. Finally we moved into the flight departure pattern and lifted off. I was thinking of my friends in Guayaquil waiting for my arrival. Much to my relief they were also delayed and didn't wait long at all.

After talking half the night away I still can't sleep when we finally go to bed. Next morning Angela shows me the enormous bruise on her swollen knee saying it was much better already. Her little finger was in a metal cap so she couldn't hurt it again. Amelia greeted me in her most gracious way saying how happy she was to see me again in 'my home.' I had brought her a robe which she thought was much too beautiful to wear. She is 93, still walking on her own just as she had when I left last year. Amelia looks good and joins us for breakfast which, to my delight, starts out with a huge piece of papaya, one of my favorite fruits. This is another nice thing in Ecuador, the very fresh fruit for breakfast because fruit is plentiful and grows to enormous size. We sit at the breakfast table for quite a while exchanging all the latest news. Amelia wants to know about her great-granddaughter and family who live close to me, as well as my son and family.

Later on we take a little walk to *Nueve de Octubre*, the street where last year I had to skip, jump and balance over boards crossing ditches, not to speak of the dirt and dust one had to deal with. Now I look in amazement at the beautiful street paved with stones of various colors and different patterns with wide sidewalks laid out in tiles. A true transformation! Of course, now we have to balance over boards laid over ditches in front of Angela's house as the entire Parque Centenario area is being improved as well. Segundo, the Indian vendor, is still there with his stand and greets me with a wide smile and a hug welcoming me back.

"I'll be buying newspapers from you again, probably starting tomorrow." We talk a little and he tells me that he'll have to move. Once the street beautification is completed, the new mayor doesn't like vendors like him with a stand on the sidewalk in this part of the city. He doesn't know where he is going to be and isn't happy.

"Where will I be buying my paper then? You are so convenient for me outside the house."

"Sí, I have my clientele and good business. They all know me and buy from me on their way to work or home. I have six weeks to be out of here."

"Six weeks only! That's not much until the end of September; then where will you be?"

"I don't know. They'll give me a spot somewhere, I think."

"That's totally crazy. They have street vendors in the States also."

"Sí!"

"Sí, pues, don't move until they actually make you."

The sidewalk is broken up all around the house now and one has to step very carefully among all the rubble not to break one's leg. Access to some businesses is definitely an obstacle course and at one's own risk. Of course, so is driving. Angela and I talk about the construction going on and she adds that it's hard to find a parking spot these days as they cannot park in front anymore but by the side of the house only. A security guard is standing there also and I feel sorry for him and Segundo having to be out in this mess and noise all day long.

After our shopping at *Mi Comisariato* on *Nueve de Octubre* we take a taxi home because Angela can't walk anymore which doesn't surprise me having seen her swollen knee shining in all colors of the rainbow. In the evening we sit and talk and I am just happy to be back here.

Thursday, 8/14/03

I can't wait to visit the Malecón 2000 again. As I walk down *Nueve de Octubre*, I think how enjoyable it is compared to last year. The milk and coffee colored Rio Guayas is flowing high transporting many water plants down river with its strong current. The air is pleasant, a little humid, but not too warm and the sky is a little overcast just nice to walk. After the last few weeks in Arizona everything is pleasant.

I arrive at the Indian Mercado at the end of the Malecón at the stall where the little Indian girls had sold me the various T-shirts last year. The girls recognize me instantly and I am being greeted with big hugs. They admire the photo of the older sister I took last year before the younger sister grabs it and puts it into her purse. She'll go home to Otavalo, north of Quito, to visit her parents. Otavalo is famous for its market all year round

I hurry home to eat lunch. After lunch we look at the news on TV and to our surprise find out that New York is in the dark. There's a power outage and everything is standing still. Hordes of people are walking home and nobody knows exactly what happened. Terrorism is ruled out but a problem in the power grid affecting the whole northeast, including Toronto and Ottawa in Canada, seems to be responsible. We look and can't believe what we see, suddenly thinking how easy it may be to eliminate our security system, speak home front defense. I hope somebody thought of that and has made arrangements for emergency set-ups because apparently nothing is totally guaranteed. Of course, it would be so much easier if diplomacy were used rather than bombs on other parts of the world. Then I have another thought, what if it were created intentionally as it is so much easier to control people with fear. I'm having many doubts by now about what we are being told or what is done to us.

There is extensive reporting on this power failure showing thousands of New Yorkers in the streets walking and children being taken out of a train standing still. I'm glad I'm not one of these stranded people in the streets of New York. Later in the evening they report that power has been largely restored, lights are on again and one sees buses running.

Friday 8/15/03

Today I buy El UNIVERSO again from Segundo asking "What's new in the world?"

"Nada; always the same thing," he answers.

The front page of the newspaper sports a big photo of New York showing a stream of people walking. Apparently one is not sure yet of the cause of the outage. There are complaints that the power grid in the States is only of third-world quality and that in the 'super power!'

"Well, it brought a problem to light. Now do something about it!"

There are articles in the paper about the previous President of Ecuador, Gustavo Noboa, being called to justice for many wrongdoings during his administration regarding foreign loan settlements he arranged by himself rather than the group of people responsible for it. Also, like other predecessors, he seems to have ended up with a large bank account in Panama. Seems to me, Panama is the Switzerland of this part of the world. Apparently there are also some questions regarding business his son was involved in. It's always the same story, corruption everywhere and not so different from the States anymore where, according to our news reporting, more and more heads of corporations end up in prison. With the exception of one who is still on the loose: Kenny boy!

We run some errands with Ivanovich who then takes us to the new Malecón opened meanwhile at the Río Salado and called Malecón Rio Salado. It's opposite from the other Malecón 2000 located at the Río Guayas and much smaller although with a pretty view on the Río Salado from here. Standing on the overpass crossing *Nueve de Octubre*, which runs from the Malecón 2000 to the Malecón Rio Salado, provides a nice view of part of the city. We eat lunch in one of the many restaurants. There are benches and playgrounds for the children, but I don't see any open stores so far. Yet, it's a safe and clean area in the city where people can walk and relax.

In the evening we visit Angela's cousin again. No taxi this time because, as Angela tells me, they don't want to go up the steep and narrow mountain road which is hard on their motors. Instead, Invanovich drives us accompanied as usual by his cousin Mario. They drop us off and will be back later to pick us up again.

It's nice to see Angela's cousin and her friend again. They live in such a beautiful big house up on a hill looking down on Guayaquil. Nothing seems to have changed, the dogs are barking and the living room is loaded down with books. After a short while the son joins us also. We had a very interesting conversation nine months ago about many different things. He was born in Ecuador but mostly educated abroad as most children of well-to-do Ecuadorians are and spent many years in Europe. Apart from English and Spanish, he also speaks German perfectly and without an accent. He thought then women were too independent. Asking him now how he's doing in this department, he says he's dating but nothing serious.

"You know in my age range women are either married or divorced with two or three children." Besides, this is still a very class and status oriented society and you can't just marry anybody."

"Well yes, I can see where it is more difficult and you don't want to marry just anybody with a flock of children, but if there is one child only, that wouldn't be so bad, would it now? Besides, I know somebody here whose wife was actually 'below' his status in the eyes of society. She is very nice and attractive and grew into her role. They have four beautiful and intelligent children, all grown up by now and judging from the crowd attending the wedding of one son some years ago nobody is holding anything against them."

He nodded his head in agreement looking at me but said nothing.

"So status alone should not deter you provided, of course, this person will not be an embarrassment to you."

He agreed but I think he simply hasn't fallen in love again.

"Are you still taking art classes?"

"Yes, I've just started up again. In fact I have two drawings which are copies of other drawings I have to do for class."

"You do! Can I see them, please?"

"Yes, of course, if you like."

I follow him back into a room with books and clothes all over the place and a nicely made up bed in the corner.

"Is this your room?"

"Yes. Why do you ask?"

"It looks just like my son's used to when he was younger."

"I just came back from the ranch," he answers smiling, "and I had to go to art class so there was no time to pick up."

Then I see the two copies of the face of a man and a woman, both very well done.

"This is great! You have talent!"

"You think so?"

"Definitely; have you tried to draw from nature yet?"

"No, right now I am supposed to copy and here is the next one I want to do."

"Try and do your own sketch some day. It doesn't have to be a face, maybe the landscape at your ranch or the house, a tree - anything. This is very nice. Would you mind if I showed this to Angela?"

"If you want to, go ahead."

I show the sketches to Angela and his father who seems to be surprised saying he had no idea that his son was so good.

Saturday, 8/16/03

We are finally on our way to *La Granja* as we usually refer to Angela's tourist center in Milagro, the pineapple capital of the world. I'm really looking forward to seeing *La Granja* again and the people there for whom I brought some gifts as usual. We also have a real estate agent in the car with us and a potential buyer for the property. I was really shocked when I found out upon arrival in Guayaquil, that *La Granja* is closed to the public. The local electric company and Angela were in disagreement as to the monthly charges for some time. After years of good relations, the electric company suddenly said she didn't pay enough whereas Angela feels she pays more than plenty. Water usage is included and so is garbage pick-up, however, she has her own water and garbage pick-up doesn't happen. Consequently, Pedro has to burn everything on the property. The end result is that while she was here in the States, they stopped providing electricity which basically closed her down. To me this was a personal insult because I fully agree with Angela that the enormous amount they want is entirely inappropriate. "Now I really want to sell," Angela says to me. "It's too much work for me and nobody else seems too interested in it."

I know this is true but it makes me feel sad because I know she loves this place - I love the place by now - and only last year when I was here called it paradise. Now she is willing to part with it all and live a more relaxed life without worry as soon as the right buyer would turn up. To find the right buyer will not be easy because money is scarce around here.

The first thing I see is the beautiful wrought iron gate at the main entrance installed the day before I left and the completed fence. It all looks so nice now. The road is finished - no more gravel, bumps, equipment and driving problems. A beautiful four-lane highway makes car travel easy and smooth and much faster, increasing the property value.

While Ivanovich blows the horn and Pedro comes to open the gate for us, I can hardly wait to get out and look around. The greeting with Marta and Pedro is a happy one. The two together manage the place and are now the only people here most the time. Angela asks Marta to show the real estate agent and the prospective buyer around and make sure she has all the keys with her. I follow a little later on my own to acquaint myself once more with *La Granja*.

What a sad homecoming it turns out to be. Everything looks dilapidated. The grass is not cut and quite high in the back, the beautiful big pool is empty of water but covered with dirt at the deep end, there are leaves everywhere and the whole place looks unkempt. As I go back to the last house where the *Gringos* stayed last year - Angela told me that the *Gringos* had come back early in the year and this time brought their wives along just as they had said they would - I find the terrace full of leaves and the duck pond empty. Everything is a far cry from the way I remember it. Depressing! As I walk along the back wall of the property, an iguana suddenly darts away. I wouldn't have seen it if it hadn't moved. The beautiful red birds I like so much are fluttering around and the morning doves take off as soon as I approach. Where I saw happy people before and heard music, empty silence reigns now interrupted only by some birds singing now and then. I'm hoping that this buyer will come through because I see problems everywhere and to see the place out of operation is not a positive either. Marta tells me right away that she misses the people and the activity around them and that it's lonely now.

The prospective buyer, a young man, likes *La Granja* very much and wants to buy it, or so he says. We'll see. Angela told me earlier that the grandfather of the young man had fallen in love with *La Granja* years ago and asked if she would sell. She had told him then that she was not ready but she would let him know when that time came.

Now here we have the grandson of the old man who tells me on the way home that he is in the tourism business and with the new road all the way to Milagro, he'll have the tourists from Guayaquil in a minibus there in no time at all. He says that he has mostly international tourists and guides tours all over Ecuador. Now we have to see what will happen. He is part of a consortium and tells Angela that they will have the money together and be ready to sign the papers by the end of August. Hmm!

Sunday, 8/17/03

We are again on our way to Milagro because Angela needs to see quite a few people and take care of errands after her long absence in the States. Stopping at the toll gate to pay the car stalls and doesn't start again. Angela is furious, the girl in the toll booth isn't happy either and other cars line up behind us, still the car will not start. Ivanovich had said the battery was low but it always started again. Well, it doesn't now. The girl inside the toll booth asks the police, who are always present, to push us. They do push while Angela steers the car to the side when it suddenly starts again. Great! She thanks them and we move on with a few jumps like beginning drivers. Ivanovich doesn't fare too well either in her remarks. I'm back in Ecuador, it's too funny. One always has to have a sense of humor and go with the flow.

In Milagro, the first trip is to a shop where we buy a new battery which is being installed. I watch a big green lorry sitting on a chair outside singing at the top of his lungs. I was unaware these birds could make such beautiful sounds. The bird is also talking. Some kids try to touch it, but are being pecked at quickly and they pull their hands away very fast.

Then we drive from place to place, find some people at home, others not. The streets are crowded with people and stands. Some kind of a fair is taking place and when we find a spot to park the car we get out and buy a few items. Then we are off to the vegetable market where we buy papaya the size of a water melon for seventy-five cents and a slightly smaller one for fifty cents. Pineapple, the larger size are fifty cents while the smaller size are three for a dollar.

In the evening we visit the very big and very new mall San Marino in Guayaquil which was not open last year.

"You see," says Angela, "now we have three malls relatively close to each other and competing for customers. I don't know why they do that because they may not have enough business and can't exist. It's always the same thing."

"Yes," I agree, "it's just like in Phoenix where they also have newer and bigger malls literally killing some of the older ones for lack of business. I've seen this a few times over the years I've lived there."

"Oh yes? You have the same problem there?"

"Of course; there used to be more outdoor malls whereas now everything is indoors just like here the reason being the same, the heat."

It's nice to be inside a cool, air-conditioned mall leisurely meandering in comfort. San Marino, three stories high, is beautiful, incorporating historic landmarks of the city of Guayaquil. Pointing out certain outside construction representing this and that building, Ivan's wife explains to me the different styles.

We have Amelia, Angela's ninety-three year old mother with us. Ida, Angela's employee, is holding Amelia on one side and I hold her other arm while we move slowly in the very busy mall this Sunday. We eventually manage to get her on an escalator requiring a push from behind from Angela with Ida and me pulling. This old lady is amazing!

We make it to the food court and find a table. I have some delicious *ceviche de pescado* which I eat often here because it's good, fresh and a meal by itself. Everybody gets what they want while we watch the masses milling around. The noise level is also considerable. I notice the beautiful children again, the girls in their pretty Sunday dresses, something I had noticed already in the afternoon in Milagro. Whether poor or rich, people dress their children so cute, especially the little girls look darling in their fancy dresses.

Monday 8/18/03

The phone wakes us up early this morning. A former employee of Angela's is calling to see if he could work for her again. She tells him that she doesn't need anybody right now and turning to me, she says: "You see they all want to come back."

"Yes, because they have a good life here with you. They don't have to work hard and eat well."

Once again at the Malecón 2000 I walk to the Indian Market where I find all the sisters from Otavalo present. I take another photo of them together and buy one of the sleeveless little dresses so light and comfortable to wear around the house or pool in our hot climate. They ask many questions about my son and granddaughter and how I like it here again, etc.

I buy EL UNIVERSO from Segundo and find out that there is trouble here with the Indians of Ecuador who are unhappy with the new president, Lucio Gutierrez, one of their own. He is in power less than a year but they feel already that he isn't doing enough for them. I remember on previous visits to Ecuador, that roads were blocked north of Quito in protest of the government and now they are planning to do the same. They can protest, Lucio tells them, but they can't block the highways.

Angela has been busy supervising Marco, Amelia's new employee, who is mostly there to look after her. He is a typical 15-year old kid of African descent, very tall and very thin, but also very picky when it comes to eating and has rather a fresh mouth to Amelia, but she likes him. He wasn't here last year when I left; in fact, he wasn't there when Angela left for the States and she is not too fond of him because he is so lazy she says. Marco accompanies me to the store a few times when I have heavy things to buy and carry like water or soft drink bottles, etc. He would love to study further but had to leave high school because the parents are divorced and his father doesn't pay anymore. I feel sorry for him because here is a young boy who wants to study and cannot for lack of funds just like Ida. I wonder how many young people like them there might be.

Ever since we've come back, Angela has been after Marco to fumigate Amelia's apartment because we found a few too many Cucarachas. Spraying has to be done on a regular basis, also in Phoenix, like in all hot climates. Now she is right behind him making sure he gets into all the corners and crevices, pulls out the furniture and generally does a good job.

In fact, she tells me this morning that her mother had almost died during the night because Marco decided to fumigate her bedroom in the evening while she was sleeping there - all this after we had told him to wear a face mask while performing this task. Amelia had choked and coughed trying to breathe while Marco and Ida tried to help her without waking us. Angela is furious threatening to let Marco go saying he's so smart but he doesn't think.

"Can you imagine, my mother could have died!"

Amelia spends most of the day resting on Angela's bed because she needs to wait until her room is aired out properly.

Tuesday, 8/19/03

We are on our way to Milagro today with a lady lawyer in the car to handle some matters for Angela. She is rather charming, talks a lot and promises Angela to peruse all the papers and have it settled in ten days from now. Hmm!

In Milagro it's 'dole-out day' as Ivanovich calls it. We see long lines of people waiting and he tells me they are the unemployed and poor who are receiving their government support today. It's a sad line, mostly mothers and children and old people, snaking around the corner into the next street. These are the people world-wide who don't count in the eyes of their governments. A nation may be prosperous as such, but that means nothing to the disenfranchised existing on a pittance. Ecuador is not a wealthy country and I think these poor people will never be in a position to better their lives. It's very sad.

There is also more news in EL UNIVERSO about the Indians protesting against the government and when we watch TV at night, there are breaking news that seven bombs have been found in Quito, the capital. Some exploded but didn't kill anybody nor was anyone hurt.

I had asked Segundo being indigenous himself, why the Indian people are so angry and he answered because Lucio doesn't keep his promise to them. To my response that Lucio hasn't been in power very long, inherited so many problems, including the previous president, that he probably needs more time, Segundo nodded his head silently.

I hope the Indians here do not go the way of the Shining Path in Peru or the ongoing conflict in Colombia. They showed a leaflet on TV in connection with the bombs in Quito today saying that the Colombian opposition is in solidarity with the Indians of Ecuador. The news commentator mentioned that this protest seems to be in response to Lucio's recent visit to Alvaro Uribe, President of Colombia.

I also read something good in EL UNIVERSO, namely the *Feria of the Book* is opening today in Guayaquil and is the first of its kind ever here. It will be held at the Malecón 2000 and is open till eleven in the evening.

Wednesday, 8/20/03

Rosa, Angela's long-time friend who is well-informed and always has a lot to say, has breakfast with us and we fill each other in regarding news, the situation in the country and whatever pops into our minds.

On my walk to the Malecón in the direction of the outdoor theatre at the foot of *el cerro Santa Ana* I notice that the upkeep of the Malecón has not changed. Everything is clean and tidy and the cleaning crews as well as the security guards are ever present. Towards the Museum of Anthropology right next to the theatre, I see another structure going up and upon inquiring learn that it is to be an IMAX theatre. I will not be here anymore when it opens, but in the course of my stay I certainly see it grow.

I walk towards the very end onto a narrow boat-shaped boardwalk looking out over the Río Guayas. Towards my left is the foot of *el cerro Santa Ana* going right down to the river. I instantly recognize the house being renovated shown in EL UNIVERSO a few days ago. It is beautiful and is part of the rejuvenation and beautification of Guayaquil's *el cerro Santa Ana*, where old homes have been turned into beautiful houses with views over the city or river. The whole area is now a top tourist attraction with a beautiful view after having climbed all four hundred forty-four steps.

Then, looking further to my left and down the river, I notice some children swimming in the brown waters of the Río Guayas. Their house is directly at the water and the tide is in so they are jumping in from their deck. The thought of them swimming in these brown waters doesn't appeal to me until I remember my own experience a few years ago while on a four-day Amazon boat trip from Iquitos, Peru, to the border of Brazil. Somewhere along the river the boat was anchored and we were told we could swim. We were only two courageous souls who dared and actually ventured into the brown waves of the Amazon hoping for some refreshment and relief from the heat and humidity. Once in the fast flowing brown waves I had quite a time to stay at the same level with the boat and had to swim against the tide all the time not to be drifting off. It took some effort as I was in the water a good twenty minutes before I returned to the boat. The other person had given up earlier. Returning to the deck I realized that I had been swimming where they were also fishing for piranha with raw meat! Lucky for us, this apparently isn't the favorite playground of these ferocious little fish because they only caught one measly little piranha.

I look at the children again frolicking in the water, tossing a ball between them and having a genuinely good time. The brown water doesn't look so bad anymore.

In the afternoon, Ivanovich, Angela and Rosa accompany me to a chiropractor. My left lower back causes me some problems ever since I walked from one gate to the other in Dallas/Fort Worth with my heavy bag. It's getting worse and sometimes I can't even sit down but have to jump right up again. Ivanovich says he has this good chiropractor, a blind man, who had helped him years ago. Now here we are in the waiting room and when my turn comes around, I'm full of expectation. He takes down some information and then leads me back into a small room with a dark plastic covered table saying I should take my blouse off and lie down with my face on a square piece of paper towel. Then he feels my entire spine, pressing here and there, finally rubbing some lotion on my back and pointing an infrared light on me. After about ten minutes he comes back, turns off the light and takes out some little gadget which I recognize as an electric hand-held massager. With this he massages my lower left side for about five minutes, snaps my neck to one side then to the other and pushes down on some spots on my back which hurt and repeating this on each side saying that the session is over.

"Es todo?" I asked.

"Sí, es suficiente.".

I dress and go into his office where, to my surprise, he hands me a lengthy prescription for three shots, eight pills of this and eight pills of that and three of Vioxx.

"All this is for me?"

"Sí," he answers.

I'm surprised; Chiropractors in the States usually don't prescribe pills and shots because they believe that one can be healed if the body is properly aligned. We both return to the waiting room and the others where he tells Ivan that my back is not very good and for that reason he didn't give me one of his strong hand massages that Ivanovich had told me about. That doesn't make sense to me in view of the fact that he had bent my back to the point I thought he was breaking it which could have done more harm than a strong massage. He tells me I'm to come back Saturday.

"Pues, vamos a ver," I answer. I pay him my fifteen dollars and we leave. Outside I express my surprise at the prescription from a chiropractor, but Rosa tells me oh yes I have to take them; this is how it's being done here to take care of the inflammation. However, I'm not into taking medicines and luckily haven't needed many in my life.

"Now I know why you have so many *pharmacias* here," I tell them. "The doctors in the States prescribe lots of medications but this here seems to be just as bad. After all it doesn't make my spine better."

"But it helps with the inflammation," says Angela.

It occurs to me that this is correct and why hadn't I thought of this myself and taken some of the Advil I have with me? I'll do this at once when we get back.

"I'm not going back to him," I tell them.

"You are not?" asks Ivan.

"No, but you can tell him that he helped me already, if he asks you."

Rosa wants some *chancho* - roast pork - and has Ivanovich go and buy some rolls with *chancho* for us. I decline because I'm still full from the meal we had earlier. Later at home I try a little piece of pork and find it doesn't compare at all to the pork we always eat at the Mercado in Cuenca that the Indian women cut off of a whole roast pig.

Thursday, 8/21/03

The TV is on early. We watch the news about the Indian protest march against the government today and then they announce one of the horrible bombings in Iraq killing the senior representative of the United Nations, Sergio Vieira de Mello of Brazil, a very well liked and respected diplomat. This is a great loss. Then there is another bombing of a bus in Jerusalem. It's too bad that always the ones who have not created these international political problems are paying with their lives for others' folly.

After breakfast we leave for Milagro where Angela has to buy provisions for Marta and Pedro at *La Granja*. On the way out we always pass by a big building with a neon sign reading *Extasis*. I point to this 'House of ill Repute' and turn to Rosa, who shoots back before I can say anything "Sí, the melon factory." We all roar with laughter. This is certainly one way of looking at it.

In Milagro we go to the Mercado I know well from last year. To my surprise it has absolutely no odor at all this year. Big improvement!

Back in Guayaquil, I suddenly get the urge for apples and go to *Mi Comisariato*, a major grocery/department store chain, closed yesterday due to the death of the founder/owner. I read a very nice article about him in EL UNIVERSO today saying he was born on August 30, 1916 in East Prussia, Germany, came to Ecuador in nineteen hundred and thirty-six, started a store some years later which turned into a successful chain. He was also a great community leader and philanthropist.

In the evening I take a walk to the Malecón 2000 and, to my surprise, find the gate at *Nueve de Octubre* closed. After walking along the fence I eventually arrive at an open gate and enter. A policeman stationed at the entrance tells me that the other side was closed off due to a bomb scare which is presently being investigated.

"Qué horrible?"

"Sí es," the policeman answers.

When I return later to the gate blocked off earlier, it's open again. Nothing had been found. Apparently some people like to disrupt normal life. After all, this is where many people come in the evening to enjoy this beautiful area and the cool evening breeze along the river. Children are running and playing trying out all the equipment on the playground under the watchful eyes of their parents. Ice cream and soft drink vendors are raking in the dollars.

Friday 8/22/03

Angela has hired a new cook for *La Granja*. She has the two *abuelitos*, the grandfathers as I call these two skinny old men, cutting the grass and generally cleaning up. One of the grandfathers has a bad leg and rides his bike everywhere accompanied by the other. They are usually together, eat here and all this cooking for everybody is too much work for Marta, who has other duties as well.

Elena, the new cook, is a young, beautiful, very light-colored girl of African descent. She is eighteen years old and I must say I like her immediately. Actually everybody has a favorable opinion of Elena. She has a friendly smile although she's shy being so new here. In her tight little shorts and the fitting sleeveless top she's quite a temptation for the opposite sex. I can see Marco's eyes already wandering in her direction and all over her. Should be interesting to see how this will all go.

The first job Elena gets is ironing Angela's clothes which Ida had washed about six days ago and then left sitting on the couch. TV watching is more fun than ironing clothes. Later she is cleaning the house because Ida can't clean the house well either.

Nevertheless, Angela is mad at Ida for something else she didn't do and leaves her and Elena at home to thoroughly clean the house while we are gone. Upon our return it really looks spic and span.

In the late afternoon I walk to the Malecón and have to open my handbag when I enter. Indigenous people march against the government everywhere so the security is high. I see many police around - even with security shields; however, nothing happens anywhere in the country. It's also the day Colombia's president Alvaro Uribe visits Ecuador. He's in the country for about twelve hours to encourage the Ecuadorian President Lucio Gutierrez to join hands in the fight against terrorism and narco traffic not appreciated here by certain factions. Later in the day we run into another problem - no gasoline. The government has put a higher tax on the gasoline and the gasoline stations refuse to pay it. Consequently many gasoline stations are refusing to accept new loads. Invanovich has to travel around for quite some time to fill the tank of the car.

This brings back many bad memories for me of the so called gas shortage chicanery we had to live through more than 30 years ago in the United States. Living in the San Francisco Bay Area then, we knew we were being had because the oil storage tanks were so full that they couldn't accept more oil which forced about fifteen huge oil tankers to anchor out in the bay because there was nowhere to unload and the berths were also full. It's amazing what governments allow to happen to their citizens for a big profit of a few! I remember one time standing in one of these long gas lines for over an hour - in vain - because the car in front of me got the last gas. I drove more often on fumes of gas than the actual product, but luckily was never stranded.

Ecuador, although rich in oil reserves, has a poor quality of refined gasoline so that one has to buy *Extra* for one dollar and sixty-eight cents which equals our regular or super for two dollars and nine cents. So what is going on here and who profits from all this? There is quite a bit of talk on TV and in the newspaper about the poor quality of the gasoline and how it is ruining cars. EL UNIVERSO talks almost daily about it saying that because of this problem, each car owner can expect to pay about eight hundred dollars extra annually for car repairs, a very steep price considering incomes in Ecuador do not equal those in the United States.

Saturday, 8/23/03

Marco, Amelia's help, left for a few days to go home to Esmeraldas in the north of Ecuador at the Pacific. Ivan took him to the bus station last night and Angela leaves Ida to take care of Amelia while we go to Milagro to take Elena to *La Granja*. She will be cooking there for everybody and also be company for Marta. In fact, I think the latter is the real reason that Angela hired her. Pedro leaves today for a few days in Guayaquil with his family. His wife and four children live in the city and they don't see each other too often. His wife is working also and comes to visit him about every other week and the children are all in school. Marta will be leaving for a few days as soon as Pedro gets back. Hmm!

While sitting in the car waiting for Angela and Ivanovich to return, I asked Elena if she will like to be on *La Granja* very different from the busy city life.

"Sí, I want to be away from home."

"Oh! You don't get on with your parents?"

"No. My mother's husband is not my father and he always bothers me."

"I see. This is a big problem everywhere." Elena nods her head and her soft brown eyes look sad. I feel sorry for her.

"Do you have a boyfriend?" I ask

"Sí."

"What does he say to your having taken this job?"

"He will have to wait."

Once in *La Granja* I take a walk around as usual and then spend time in my favorite hammock. A young couple walks up. They tell Angela all they want is some solitude. As I approach the ramada, a distinct, pungent smell permeates the air and is coming from the ripe fruit which have fallen off the Guayaba trees. I pick some nice big ones up and start eating. Guayaba is a very tasty fruit and also makes excellent juice. Altogether, the freshly squeezed juices I drink here cannot be compared with what we buy in the store at home. Standing there and eating the Guayaba, Ivanovich walks up with Elena. He had shown her around and she bends down immediately to help me pick up the ripe fruit to take back for juice. We leave Elena in Marta's care and drive to Milagro where we have a delicious lunch in a nice veranda style restaurant. Ivanovich and I enjoy the wonderful fresh *ceviche* of shrimp and white fish.

Tonight is the night we go to the Hilton Colon Hotel. They have a wonderful Bar/Lounge area with a band to listen to. It's rather crowded but we find a table towards the side looking down into the hallway of the hotel. There are many foreigners here going by the different languages we hear. Two wedding parties of happy people also pass by, both brides are very beautiful. It's a pleasant place to spend an evening listening to the music and watching the world go by.

Sunday, 8/24/03

Today at breakfast Angela tells me that her two main employees get on very well at *La Granja*. This thought had popped into my mind when I saw them again the first time being all alone in this big place. Still, I'm a little surprised and ask Angela "How do you know?"

"Ida told me. You know, Pedro has slept with every girl there ever was," she adds.

"He has, ha; even though he has a beautiful wife in Guayaquil?"

"Oh yes. She comes to visit about twice a month."

"What about Elena now?"

"I told her to take a stick to bed with her so she can defend herself. I'll not leave her out there alone with him. When Marta leaves I'll bring her back here."

"This will probably be best in view of the fact that Elena is trying to get away from an abusive stepfather, poor girl!" I really feel sorry for Elena and all the other girls in the world who live in such circumstances. And there are many of them. Yesterday, while sitting in the car, Elena had told me that they were four girls at home and one boy from three different fathers and that she doesn't get on well with the stepfather, clutching her little backpack which probably contains most her worldly possessions.

After breakfast I visit the *Feria del Libro y del Palabra*, the first one of its kind in Guayaquil. It takes place at the Museum of Anthropology at the Malecón 2000. I spend more time there than I thought I would because it's interesting. There is quite a selection of books on display and for sale in the different categories - even one section of books in English. The newspapers are represented as well, especially EL UNIVERSO which had a book out on the history of Ecuador. I'm tempted to buy it if it weren't so heavy. The book has quality photographs on heavy paper and so I sit down right there and start reading as much as I can. Then I listen to one author's presentation and discussion of his book. A huge crowd is present obviously enjoying this cultural event and many purchases are made. Of course, Harry Potter is also there much to the delight of the younger generation.

Monday, 8/25/03

After breakfast I walk down *Nueve de Octubre* as I do almost daily for exercise. Today I enter a home and house wares store and find they have an impressive selection of cook ware, china and table ware, garden and patio furniture as well as some office pieces, in particular computer tables. Really, one sees everything here just like at home in the States.

Later, reading EL UNIVERSO, I see a photo of Jefferson Perez on the front page, the Ecuadorian who won the Gold Medal in Paris just now walking 20 km, presently the pride of the nation. Earlier in the morning when I purchased the paper, I asked Segundo: "What's in the news today? Is there anything good happening in the world?"

"Sí," he answered pointing to the photo of Perez swinging the flag of Ecuador.

"This? Yes, it's good news but only sports. I'm talking about politics."

"No nothing good there."

Another theme of increased reporting is that the previous president, Noboa, has been allowed asylum in the Dominican Republic. The newspaper and TV news say that he has done much harm to Ecuador, embezzled millions of dollars which is in an account in Panama. Now he has been freed to leave the country. So the story repeats itself. Many of the past presidents have ended up this way after robbing the country blind first. It is said they can't prosecute him as world opinion would be against Ecuador which they can't afford. This is beyond me. How can world opinion be against prosecuting criminal behavior? Are they all criminals? Until corruption and theft in these countries is not resolved, there cannot be any real progress.

In the afternoon we go grocery shopping to another big chain called *Super Maxi* which Angela prefers. These super markets are of enormous size, larger than many we have in the States. The selection of food items is excellent. The prices are very close to what they are here in the States with some staples being lower. Produce and fruit grown in Ecuador are less expensive there being plenty of it.

In the evening Ivanovich and his cousin come up and we talk for a long time about many things of the past as well as an article which appeared in EL UNIVERSO yesterday regarding the situation in the Galápagos Islands which belong to Ecuador and are considered World Heritage. The article airs the complaints of some tourists not being able to fly on certain dates because there are not enough seats on the plane and, once there, there is a shortage of hotel rooms, tours and restaurants. Ivanovich had mentioned a few days ago that he was thinking of perhaps one day going to the Galápagos and getting into the tourist business there. Therefore, when he comes up I give him this article to read saying, "You might have a good idea going into the tourist business in the Islands."

I had my own rather similar experience with getting to the Galápagos in 1992 and, according to this article, nothing has changed. Once again in Guayaquil with Angela, who had actually planned to go to Lima with me, but when I read the newspapers talking of bombs going off in various places in Lima due to the Shining Path Party, I said to Angela this is not a good time for us to go there. We might be walking along Miraflores enjoying the beautiful shops and area, and are being bombed to bits and pieces.

So, on the spur of the moment, I decided to fly to the Galápagos. I walked from Travel Agency to Travel Agency and couldn't get one seat on a plane, which seemed very strange to me. The planes were all booked, I was told. Finally my American Express Gold card came to mind which promised extra services. That's it, I thought and marched to the American Express office, handing them my card and telling them what happened and that I was promised certain extra services with this card which I needed right now. I ended up with a very nice young man who listened to me attentively and said he would try his best, but that the planes were quite full. He asked for my phone number and not quite two hours later he called to tell me I was booked on a TAME plane leaving next day for a four-day excursion which was all the time I had left. I have - over the years - had many good experiences with American Express.

Boarding the plane next morning I found it to be a far cry from full. There were two other tour groups from Germany and some local people. Lots of empty seats! There is an ecological limit as to how many people are allowed to visit the Galápagos annually, but I also arrived at the conclusion that they didn't really want individuals, preferring large tour groups only.

I had received a voucher for a hotel room and was told it might be difficult finding one, recommending a certain place to me. Arriving in Baltra and going through immigration, I had to pay a hefty tourist tax, forty dollars at one desk and taking another little step, ten dollars at the next.

"Each step here costs a lot of money," I commented, making everybody roar with laughter. (Now it costs one hundred dollars I read in the paper).

I found a room in a small hotel owned by a man who had lived and worked for more than thirty years in the States. When his American wife passed away, he came back to Ecuador and went first to the Galápagos for peace and quiet. He never left. He married again and together with his new wife built this small hotel. They had two sons together, but he outlived this wife also. Now at seventy-nine, he took life easier. He certainly didn't look his age at all, slender and wiry he moved easily. In fact, he mostly ran apparently not able to walk at a normal pace. His English was still great so that I didn't have to put my *radar* out to understand him.

"Jimmy?" I asked. "This was not an Ecuadorian name in your days?"

"No," he answered. "My name is actually Hannibal. Can you imagine me going through life in the States with a name like Hannibal?"

"No," I answered and we both started laughing at that thought.

Jimmy was to secure two one-day trips for me on boats visiting different islands while I walked around Santa Cruz visiting the giant turtles called Galápago, after which the islands are named, and the Darwin station, etc. not to speak of all the iguanas sunning themselves everywhere. When I started walking shading my eyes to look into the distance for the marine iguanas, I almost fell over the ones right in front of my feet. They are not afraid of people and don't run away. Returning later, I found out he was unable to secure any tour which made me very unhappy thinking this can't be. Jimmy said he would try some more and I left again walking a different street when I saw a sign advertising tours in German. That was the answer. I approached and addressed the man sitting there in German saying I needed help to find two tours and could he do something for me.

The man looked up, stretched his hand out and introduced himself as Henry Schaefer. He said it wouldn't be easy confirming what I already suspected; they don't care much for individual tourists preferring groups that fill a boat. He made many calls almost begging, "Una sola persona," until eventually he came up with two tickets for me for two separate tours to other islands, saying, "Tell Jimmy, that he'll get the credit for your tours. He's my friend and I don't want him to be left out."

"Can I pay you something then?" I asked.

"Oh no," came the reply, "I have a daughter here who has a restaurant. Come and have dinner at her place tonight. That'll be payment enough."

Returning to my hotel, Jimmy still hadn't been able to secure tours for me and when I showed him the vouchers from Henry he was annoyed because the same people had told him there was nothing. Even telling him the credit would go to him didn't help. He stormed off angrily in the direction of the tour office across the street from the hotel. When he returned he told me that he had given them a piece of his mind. I believed him.

I met with Henry in a little outside bar on the side of the street for a drink. His daughter had no liquor license and so I invited Henry for a drink for all he had done for me. He told me his life story. Henry Schaefer was born in Berlin but had lived in Ecuador for more than thirty years and was married to an Ecuadorian lady who lives in Guayaquil, where she worked. Either she would come to visit here or Henry would go to Guayaquil frequently. They have one daughter who, outside of her restaurant, also was a tour guide and I would probably have her tomorrow. He had lived here for more than three years by now and just loved it. Having been in the corporate rat race for many years, one day he simply had enough and called it quits. He told me he came here to recuperate.

"Out of one month became two and three and more. The longer I lived here, the less I wanted to leave. Then I found out there was a real need for more tourist services and especially someone who also spoke German because we have an enormous amount of German tourists coming. So I started my agency. When my daughter was finished with school, she came out to visit but liked it immediately and accepted a job as tour guide. She speaks four languages perfectly and this is what is needed here with people coming from all over the world. She just now opened her restaurant and I hope it will go well for her. So here we are and love it because it's so beautiful and peaceful. My wife doesn't like it as there is no entertainment so to speak of here. I feel otherwise. The whole world comes here and I meet so many different and interesting people. Of course, she also has to take care of her elderly mother who is living with her."

I met the daughter a little later when we headed to her restaurant. Everything is so close in this small place and one just walks from one to the other. The dinner was good home cooking and her restaurant a pleasant place. She was our tour guide on both boat trips which I took with one of the German groups on the plane with me. Karina speaks both English and German very well dispensing much detailed information. Some of the islands reminded me of Arizona, desert and cactus, except here surrounded by wonderful beaches and the clear warm water of the Pacific with sea lions, albatross birds and giant tortoises, not to forget the iguanas, seals and variety of sea birds. An ecological paradise which is the reason Ecuador keeps a tight lid on the number of tourists visiting the Galápagos annually.

Upon my return each evening, Jimmy would be sitting in front of his hotel at the edge of the ocean at a small table with two chairs facing each other. "Hola," I would greet him and he would motion to me to sit down in the other chair. Then we would chat, me telling him how my day went and he would tell me another paragraph out of his life. Jimmy had left Ecuador as a very young man of twenty-one without telling his family. He went to the States; married had a son and a very good life. The son, by the way, lives in the Phoenix area he informed me and asked me to call him upon my return.

"But you know how hectic the States are. I finally had a longing for a more quiet life. Guayaquil, however, has also become so big and busy that I went to see what the Galápagos were like. I came, I loved it and here I am and will stay. I have two more sons. The boy you just saw is the youngest at fifteen and the older one is eighteen. From the hotel and my Social Security check from the States - I am an American citizen, you know - I live very comfortably here and in peace. Look around you; we are at the ocean, the beautiful sunset and no rushing about. I couldn't have it any better."

I had to agree with Jimmy. It was indeed beautiful. The spectacular sunset tonight, the silence - only interrupted by the lapping of the waves against the rocks - and the silhouettes of marine iguanas lying on the wall or rocks against the sky was very calming. Jimmy had it made and how lucky for me that I was allowed to be here in this paradise, if only for a few days and that Jimmy shared a part of his life with me. I enjoyed our conversations immensely and was looking forward to them. Thinking of my job in Phoenix, I was tempted moving here, but Henry had told me that non-Ecuadorians couldn't work here in the tourist business.

Jimmy's and Henry's stories were similar in that each came here looking for peace after a hectic life. They had found it and now Ivanovich says he would love to live there sometime in the future and get away from it all. He would probably be good in the hotel business, because he had managed hotels in the States many years ago. I can't help thinking how many fascinating people I meet on all my travels and how they have enlarged my life by including me into theirs and sharing with me - even if only for a brief moment!

When I returned to Guayaquil and told Angela about Henry, she at once replied: "Oh yes, I know him. His wife works here in Guayaquil and they have a daughter. She is a good friend of mine and we used to get together a lot." Angela knows everybody here, I noticed that before. In fact Henry had also mused that he knew Angela from years ago.

Tuesday, 8/26/03

Marco, Amelia's help, came back from Esmeraldas yesterday. Now he is looking after Amelia again who, unfortunately, doesn't feel well and complains about a headache more than ever. Angela and Ivan have taken her to doctors and chiropractors but somehow this headache doesn't ever leave her totally. Angela and I talk about it while in the car on the way to Milagro and she says she'll take her mother to a doctor again after our return to Guayaquil.

At *La Granja* Marta is dressed in a sweat shirt because she is cold while I'm hot in my short-sleeved blouse. Elena is there also, both look happy and everything looks clean in the first part of *La Granja*. Pedro is still away in Guayaquil with his family and due to return on Thursday. A police truck is parked there, very visible from the street, to deter undesirables.

Back in Guayaquil, we take Amelia to the doctor and find out she should have a few tests done like an MRI of her head and neck, blood and urine tests, etc. We plan this for tomorrow morning.

EL UNIVERSO today shows a picture on the front page of a boy looking through a telescope at Mars right now being closest to earth. There is general excitement in the country with many official and scientific buildings making telescopes available for the general public to take a peek and people are taking advantage of this.

There's a very disturbing article about the herbicide used by Colombia to destroy coca production. It shows a plane spraying this poison from the air saying it also lands on other crops in Ecuador's border area which causes grave concern about the effect on the health of the people living in this area. Investigations are taking place.

A phone call in the evening from Angela's husband in the States keeps us informed and I learn that I am being missed by Angela's granddaughter, Christina.

Wednesday, 8/27/03

Angela and I are up early today. Ida is not here, she went to see her daughter and mother last night and so we have no breakfast until later because we are taking Amelia to the clinic. Marco comes along also. We take a taxi because the traffic in the morning is awful and there is little parking. We arrive early and after signing in and a few questions, they take Amelia away and we sit and wait. I've come prepared with EL UNIVERSO to see what's happening.

There are quite a few people in the waiting room of the Nuclear and Diagnostic Medicine Department. Everything seems to go just as in the States. The reception is set up the same way with check-in and all is done in a very professional manner. The waiting area has many chairs so the patients and family members are comfortable. Everything is clean and people are extremely friendly. I pull out EL UNIVERSO, give the sports page to Marco and start reading. Again there is a photo of Mars on the front page saying that the observatory in Quito, the capital, will open its doors at 7:00 p.m. so that the people can come in to observe. Gustavo Noboa takes the entire second page and a big article regarding Tony Blair and the investigation of the strange death of David Kelly gets my attention.

One of the many active volcanoes, Tungurahua is acting up again expulsing ashes and big rocks up to 400 meters into the air. Volcanic activity never seems to stop in this small and very mountainous country with about seventeen active volcanoes.

After Amelia's tests are completed, we return home and have breakfast all being famished by now. Then I take my walk to the

Malecón 2000 and head to the lower end where the Indian Market is. I have a photo for the Indian girls from Otavalo I want to give them. They like it and we take another one, this time with me on it as well. Then I find a nice pair of blue pants for my granddaughter Hailey-Schatzi and buy them. When I asked her in May what her favorite color was, she had told me 'blue.' Now that the Otavalo girls see me oftener, they become more open and are not as shy as they were before. The middle sister is home in Otavalo for two weeks they tell me. I learn that the oldest is called Consuelo but the youngest one has a name I have a hard time pronouncing and remembering. To my surprise she suddenly speaks to me in English which she pronounces very well. They now take English from first grade on all throughout school, but I certainly don't encounter it a lot and find very few people who actually speak it so this must be new.

Thursday, 8/28/03

We are on our way to Salinas the Copa Cabana or Waikiki of Ecuador. It's about two hours driving from Guayaquil and sits at the tip of a little strip of land jutting out into the Pacific. I haven't been there since my first visit to Ecuador in 1985 and been told that it has changed much. Ivanovich is driving and his cousin Mario and Ida are also along. The three of us share the back seat and both of them being rather heavy, I can't say that this is the most comfortable ride I've ever had.

The sky is overcast which is good because we won't be quite so hot in the car. In Salinas it's cool and windy until the sun comes out and we walk along the beach. I'm really surprised how this city has grown from when I saw it first eighteen years ago, when only a few skyscrapers dotted the beach while now it looks like other famous beaches in the world. Many people are sunbathing and some even swimming. A broad promenade makes a stroll very pleasant. I test the water and find it would be great for swimming but I didn't bring my swimsuit along. Salinas curves a little with the yacht club at the outer edge. Hotels and apartment buildings, many restaurants and bars, travel agencies offering all sorts of tours, including whale watching dot the promenade. The latter would really interest me but unfortunately it's too late today. Invanovich says he would also like to go on a tour and inquires about it returning with a pamphlet. The agency tells him they need a minimum of six people to go out with the boat. He leaves our phone number with them and they promise to call us.

We came here to buy jumbo shrimps, called *langostinos,* and to have *ceviche.* We don't go to a fancy restaurant to eat *ceviche* but to the fish market where Angela knows exactly the right place. The *ceviche de camerones* is excellent and served with fried bananas. While we eat, fish sellers surround us with boxes full of crawling *langostinos,* shrimps of all sizes, as well as some very big fish. Angela haggles with the vendors and after walking away, gets the price she wants. The purchases are put into the coolers we brought for this reason. Everything is fresh from the sea and we can look forward to a few good seafood meals at home.

Afterwards we drive around Salinas, looking at another beach and the beautiful houses here. Right now few people are present because it's winter in Ecuador. In the summer, December through March, called la *temporada,* multitudes of people come here. Salinas, being close to Guayaquil, makes it very easy for people from that city to come out for even just a week-end on Friday night while the families will stay for various weeks. It's beautiful here and it would be nice to have a small apartment in one of these modern high rises overlooking the promenade, the beach and the Pacific. Ivanovich shows me a spot at the beach further out where he and his brother used to play and swim to an old half sunk cutter which is still there. Cherished childhood memories - they are always with us. Angela used to have an apartment here where we stayed the first time I came out but sold it for lack of time to enjoy it. Life changes for us all.

Friday 8/29/03

We wake up around eight in the morning because of a phone call from Rosa. After being off the phone, Angela tells me she is not feeling good and thinks she has the flu. In fact when I am done with my shower and dressed, she is still in bed and sleeping again. Rosa walks in at this time and is surprised to see Angela ill. She and I have breakfast together and then try to have Angela take some vitamins or something that might help her but she refuses. Finally around eleven in the morning Rosa manages to talk her into taking Lemon Flu. Rosa and I have a lengthy conversation about everything. Her favorite expression for most politicians and people in government is *sapos.* Sapo is the word for frog, thus the meaning in this case is *jumping at an opportunity and taking advantage of it* for their own good and not for the benefit of all. I have to say, Rosa hits the nail on the head. We have rather an animated conversation about the political situation in Ecuador and politics in general. She tells me that she was a millionaire when they had the *sucre*, their former currency, and now with the dollar currency the money has shrunk considerably.

After my walk and while sitting at lunch with Rosa, Angela suddenly joins us saying she feels better. We are so glad to see her at the table with us eating a little because if she doesn't get up, she's really sick.

"You see, I told you this Lemon Flu is a wonderful medicine," Rosa says to her. "Now you have to take another pill and then later in the evening again." Angela does as she says and then goes back to bed.

Since there is nothing I can do right now, I think this is the perfect day to go to the new Mall, *San Marino*, with Ivan's wife if she has time today. She and I had agreed to spend some time there shopping and looking around. For the next four hours we walk around the three stories and through its many wonderful stores and boutiques with goods from all over the world. There are beautiful shoes and leather goods from Italy, Colombia and Brazil, china and crystal as well as jewelry. TGI Fridays is here also as a separate restaurant whereas the other fast food providers are in a large food court. This time we each have a delicious piece of cake before we leave. Speaking about these cakes I see in Ecuador, they are of a quality one finds only in specialty bakeries here in the States. Finally we arrive home late at night and find Angela watching TV telling us she feels so much better now and we all sit up and talk for a long time still.

Saturday, 8/30/03

Angela is up early and seems to be her usual self. I take my walk after breakfast and buy a newspaper from Segundo. The volcano Tungurahua is still active and dispersing ashes. This has been going on for about thirty-four months now. The *campesinos* living around the area are complaining about not receiving much help from the government. EL UNIVERSO further reports that a bomb exploded in Iraq killing the Shiite leader and in England Tony Blair finds himself without a minister of communication. So it goes, day after day.

There is also a nice little report in the section called *El Gran Guayaquil in* EL UNIVERSO which features five young students who want to change the country by changing attitudes. They are concerned with tolerance, equality, corruption, solidarity and coherence and feel that a change in the way people think and act, especially in the government, should be brought about. I feel they are speaking to and for the world. One big point is tolerance and doing away with racism in that one accepts the fact there are different countries, cultures and people who need to be respected and accepted as they are. This youthful idealism of the one girl and four young men, all of whom are sixteen years old and very nice looking, is something wonderful to see bringing back memories in probably all of us. But then what happens that most of us lose this idealism? It's usually *me first* felt by most of the world right now.

In the afternoon we pick up another water pump that has been repaired to take to *La Granja* in Milagro. The real estate agent hasn't called and it seems like the sale will not go through and Angela wants to get *La Granja* up to par and open to the public again. I'm very happy to hear this conclusion because I'm concerned about the empty pool being damaged. We have no electricity but Ivanovich suggests there are generators. Pedro will install *la bomba* and we leave for home again.

Arriving in Guayaquil around 7:30 pm, Ivan's youngest son comes running towards us saying that Angela's mother had a fall. Alarmed we rush upstairs and find Amelia on the bed in great pain moaning and groaning and her face almost white with agony. She had slipped in some water spilled by Zucchini, her black poodle, and that the only ones home were Elena and Marco who had a very hard time getting her back onto her bed.

"I've told them to put the dog dish further away because I was afraid something like this may happen," says Angela.

"Yes, that's bad," I agree realizing the whole problem in a second so to speak when I see Elena passing the bed pan up to Amelia's bed. Ivanovich and Angela examine her as well as possible and think nothing can be broken as the pain is very high up on the inner thigh.

"She probably sprained this big muscle," suggests Angela. She gets her an icepack and rubs her leg with some special cream she has and is busy with her until past midnight. We all feel terribly sorry for her and wonder if she'll ever walk again at her age.

Sunday, 8/31/03

Amelia is still not better so Angela and Ivanovich take her to the clinic and have her checked out and perhaps spend a few days there. The ambulance comes quickly but to get Amelia down is a major effort. The elevator can't be used because it's not large enough to have the stretcher in there. She has to be carried down the four flights of stairs. Every time they move her a little, she cries out in pain. I feel so sorry for her that she has to go through all this. Ivanovich goes with the ambulance while Angela stays here to supervise a very thorough change and clean-up of Amelia's bed and room.

"This is my chance right now to get everything turned around and cleaned while my mother is in the hospital. You know how she is; I can never move or change anything when she is here. Now Marco has to really clean and spray to make sure there are no bugs either."

With these words she goes to work with him while Elena accompanied Amelia to the hospital. They literally take the place apart and move every piece of furniture to get to all the spots that normally don't get cleaned. Then she telephones a repairman to fix the bed which, like a hospital bed, can be moved into different positions electrically except it hasn't worked lately. Angela is very thorough in doing all this.

Ivanovich comes back and says the X-rays show only a minor hair fracture in the lower right hip and that the doctor thought it was mostly a sprain that causes the pain. Having once sprained an ankle myself, I know only too well how it hurts. Hip replacement was discussed but this seems a little far-fetched. Nothing definite is decided and Amelia is to stay in the hospital for about three days to observe and check to see what should be done. Later both of them go to the hospital to check on her and then they want to go to Milagro to see if *la bomba* is working.

When they return later that evening, they say that Amelia is sleeping now and more comfortable. Thank goodness for that. We still discuss all the implications of Amelia's fall for Amelia and Angela and the entire household and foresee difficult times.

Monday, 9/1/03

Angela is in a bad mood this morning concerning the employees.

"They are so lazy; that Marco, he does nothing and I have to tell him everything. I'm going to let him go."

"As far as that goes, you'll have to let Ida go also. I've never seen her take the initiative to do anything on her own." I feel a bit sorry for Marco. He's only sixteen.

"All he wants to do is eat."

"He's a teenager. When my son was his age he also ate a lot. Look at Marco he's as skinny as a rail."

"He also doesn't eat everything. He doesn't like this and he doesn't like that as you know."

"Yes, that surprises me also. Either he was very spoilt or he grew up very poor because all he likes is eggs and rice and chicken, eggs and beans. Oh yes, he likes some fish."

"That's right," Angela confirms.

"Is he looking after Zucchini now?"

"No not much! I have mostly been hand feeding the dog. Have you noticed he's getting stronger?"

"I noticed that also. Where is Zucchini now? I haven't seen him all day."

"He's in my mother's bedroom!"

"Marco needs to take him for a walk, doesn't he?"

"He doesn't like to do that because he's afraid the dog gets away."

"Well, if he's on the leash he cannot get away."

"I don't know where the leash is right now."

"This is something he does need. I can understand where Marco wouldn't like to take the dog downstairs without that."

After breakfast we drive to the hospital to see how Amelia is doing. She looks better. Her face is presently not tortured by pain as it was earlier, although she tells us that she has pain all the time. They have her on an intravenous line through which they also administer the painkiller.

Ivanovich checks on the medicine he bought for her last night and thinks there is some missing. He has to fill the prescriptions himself that the doctor writes out for Amelia rather than the hospital giving her what she needs. In fact he has to buy all the supplies for her even soap, towel and toilet paper as it is needed.

"How can it be missing? They probably gave it to her," I say.

"No, they only put so much into this bag and this is the second bag she has, so there should be more." He questions Elena what they have done and how Amelia is being treated and how she behaved, etc. Elena sleeps on a couch in the same room. We had brought a pillow and blanket for her. There is nothing here only the bed, the couch and two plastic chairs. There is no TV. It's very drab and I feel sorry for both of them to have to spend the day in here. Furthermore, when I ask Elena if she has eaten, she says she hasn't.

"They gave you no food last night either?" I ask.

"Last night I got something but nothing today."

It's about eleven in the morning and so I go out to buy her some rolls and a coke for lack of much choice right now. Ivanovich is also upset and tells the nurse upon entering to provide Elena with some food. From being a cook poor Elena has turned into a nurse. I wonder how she likes her new situation.

At *La Granja*, Pedro installed *la bomba,* but the water pump isn't bringing up any water. Pedro and Ivanovich discuss the matter arriving at the conclusion that this is due to the extremely low water level. They didn't have much rain this spring. The rainy season resembled more a dry season. As *la bomba* runs on oil it should work. Ivanovich and Angela discuss the next step to be taken now, namely purchase a generator for electricity. Angela says she needs to get the place operating again. I couldn't agree with her more.

"You see, I can't leave for very long from here. Something always happens when I'm away. This is also a reason I want to sell because I'm so stuck right now."

When we return to *La Granja* from Milagro, Pedro tells me he cleaned the pool and for me to go and see. Marta adds that she slipped in the pool and hurt her chin which has some black marks. So that's what it is - Marta had to help to get the job done, pobrecita!

Back in Guayaquil we eat a quick dinner I prepare in the microwave hoping that Angela will realize how well it works for vegetables, fish and certain dishes. By the time Ivanovich comes upstairs we are long finished with our dinner to his surprise. Ida is watching also to see how it turns out and when it comes to salad, I've started preparing this most every day.

Later in the evening when Angela and Ivanovich go to visit Amelia again, I enjoy the cool evening breeze as I walk along the Malecón towards el *cerro Santa Ana*. I walk at a fast pace, even up the hill all four hundred and forty-four steps, working up a sweat. It's all worth it as I look at the city below glistening in the lights with the Malecón 2000 clearly outlined by a chain of lights. The old light tower on top is all lit up and so is the chapel. Some people climb up the stairs inside the tower, others enter the chapel to pray. I put some money into one of the telescopes pointing at a distant area of the city and find out I see things I didn't even know were there. The wind is blowing strong up here providing coolness. Having taken in the view from all angles I begin my descent after having cooled off, while many people are still coming up just now. Even older people tackle all these stairs.

Walking back along the Malecón, I see the tide is coming in carrying all the water lilies ripped off around in a big circle. It reminds me of Reversing Falls in St. John, New Brunswick, where I had seen the water flowing down stream partially turned around at the edges of the river by the incoming tide in a similar circle only still more forceful. Watching this circle dance of the water lilies for a while makes me think of life in general going around and expanding in ever larger spirals. I finally arrive home again at nine in the evening, the same time Angela and Invanovich return from the hospital saying they want for Amelia to stay there a little longer.

Tuesday, 9/2/03

First thing this morning we all go to the hospital. Amelia looks good. She can even move her leg a little so some progress seems to be happening. We stay and talk with her for a while, make sure she has everything and is comfortable. I have started bringing the Newspaper to Elena who enjoys reading it. There's absolutely nothing for her to do otherwise for most of the day. She's got to be bored.

From there we go to two different places to check on generators, that is to say, Ivanovich does the talking and asking and looking while Angela and I only go along for the ride so to speak. Later on we go to Milagro to look after things there and even end up having dinner because it's late in the evening and Angela says she can't wait until we get back again. We eat in a little restaurant right by a repair shop Angela favors which I don't find too inviting or too clean. The food tastes alright, although one doesn't know who prepared it. We then drive straight to the hospital before going home. Amelia is asleep but quickly wakes up and we stay with her for a while during which time the doctor comes in to check on her. He makes her move her leg to see how she is doing. He discusses her situation with Angela and Ivan and tells them that he will have the leg X-rayed again tomorrow to see how the hair fracture is doing and then they will decide how to proceed. We bring some food for Elena and send her out to buy something across the street just so she gets out of the room for a little.

As I read EL UNIVERSO today, there is a picture of a man on hunger strike to protest the detention of people for more than a year without a hearing. He looks emaciated and the accompanying article also says that he is thinking of crucifying himself to draw attention to this injustice and bring a change about for everybody.

Wednesday, 9/3/03

There's no water this morning. Sometimes we have a problem with *la bomba* here also and then we have to wait to get the tank filled. We have some drinking water which will have to do for a quick little wash. This is why I'm always turning on the faucet with trepidation, will the water flow or won't it. Most the time it flows, thank goodness!

Secondly, looking in the mirror I have some strange little red blisters in various places on my face. I have no idea where they come from overnight. It doesn't look so wonderful and Angela is also surprised when she sees them and says I should do nothing but wait a little longer. I think eating in this strange place last night might be the reason.

Thirdly, Rosa just walks in the door. I find out she'll be going to Milagro after visiting Amelia. I'll stay in town today anyway because I've read in the paper that there will be an International Bolero Festival starting tonight at the outdoor theatre at the Museo Antropologico y de Arte Contemporaneo, MAAC for short, at the Malecón where I was fortunate enough to attend *La Misa Criolla* last year. The International Bolero Festival will take place over four evenings. I want to go tonight and take it from there.

When I open EL UNIVERSO today, there is an article with photo telling how the volcano Tungurahua is spreading heavy ashes over various provinces in the sierra and the coast. The police help in cleaning up and worst of all, people's respiratory systems are suffering. The clinics see many patients - it's a repeat of last year.

Then there is good news. Quito, the capital, is preparing for its 25-year celebration being added to the Cultural Heritage of the World. There is a photo of la Plaza Grande in front of the Government Palace in the old heart of Quito. In fact, Ecuador has various centers being considered Cultural Heritage of the World. Apart from Quito, there are the Galápagos and Cuenca in the Andes and Zaruma, the old mining town. There will be many festivities with people arriving from all over the world and Quito is preparing to shine, showing off its history and spectacular mountainous setting with the Andes as backdrop.

Later I talk with Ivan's wife and tell her about the International Bolero Festival. She also likes to attend cultural events. Angela doesn't want to go. Ivan's wife thinks we should send Marco ahead to get us tickets but I fear Marco will never find the place and ask Ida to go along only to find out she doesn't know either where to go. I explain to them and they are on their way while we leave a little later because I've no confidence in either one of them. Turns out I'm correct. They have no tickets when we arrive, but neither is there a line at the ticket booth where we purchase our tickets and walk to the unnumbered seats which is the reason to be here early.

The evening turns out to be wonderful - my first ever Bolero Festival, the third of its kind for Guayaquil. The performance starts at seven-thirty and does not end till almost ten without intermission. The performers are the finest and well-known in South America. Tonight we have El Trio Pambil, Omar Montalvo and Patricia Gonzalez with Guillermo Vives. This festival takes place to honor Patricia Gonzalez, perhaps the most famous Bolero singer of Guayaquil who, for 35 years developed her career in Ecuador, Colombia and Mexico. She has a powerful voice, a great performer with a remarkable sense of humor. The performers are here on special invitation by Patricia Gonzalez, one of them being Guillermo Vives of Colombia, who is very good. For more than two hours we listen to music. The audience has grown to the point where additional chairs have to be brought in and then there are still people standing. The applause doesn't end it seems and a breeze keeps the temperature very pleasant, almost cool now. I don't want the evening to end and consider myself fortunate to be here and part of this experience. I know already that I'll attend the other performances as well.

Thursday, 9/4/03

First thing in the morning we visit Amelia again who tells us that she is still in pain. Elena appears to be holding up very nicely. She is a quiet, pleasant girl. I hand her EL UNIVERSO again which she accepts gratefully. There is also a TV now because Angela brought one in from *La Granja*. After returning to the house, I stop at the pharmacy below and show them the strange blisters I have in my face, more today than yesterday. They recommend a cream called Quadriderm saying that many people have this problem here. This seems strange to me because I've never had this on my previous visits. They tell me it's because of all the dust and dirt in the air. There's of course more these days with the streets all dug up but I still suspect the strange little restaurant in Milagro to be the cause of my affliction. I wash my face and put the cream on as instructed and hope for the best. Then I take my daily walk and ask Segundo to save me a paper for later in case he's running low. He does so and we always talk a little before I go upstairs and make myself comfortable in my favorite chair. There's one article today regarding the Galápagos and the upcoming 25-year anniversary of them being acknowledged as Natural World Treasure of all people accompanied by a beautiful photo of el Pináculo, the Pinnacle, on Isla Santiago which to me resembles a shark's fin standing straight out of the clear blue water. A sailboat appears to be dwarfed by the sheer height of the rock. Now I'm dreaming about the Galápagos again wondering how Jimmy and Henry are doing.

Another article in EL UNIVERSO tells that yesterday - finally - medical supplies have been delivered to the people around Tungurahua as well as masks and protective eye glasses. This will be of some help, but I'm sure so much more would be needed. These forever erupting volcanoes present a huge financial burden for this small country, not to speak of the possible loss of life also occurring during major eruptions.

Then there is another problem the reporters write about more and more, namely the immigration of Peruvians who, so they say, take jobs away from Ecuador. Seems like a world-wide problem - people everywhere wanting to improve their lot in life or, for many in this part of the world, simply surviving. In this modern age of instant communication, people become aware if the grass appears to be greener on the other side of the fence, and in living color at that. It would be so important for the heads of governments to do their utmost to provide jobs for their citizens instead of accusing and fighting each other over nothing. The same would apply to the heads of corporations who, by merging or taking each other over to become ever larger conglomerates, eliminating jobs and future customers in the process - all in the name of the bottom line RIGHT NOW - without concern for other people or vision of the future.

The second evening of the International Festival del Bolero is also a big success with a most appreciative audience. There are some different presenters today, among them Beatriz Gil, a very talented, young woman. The crowd is not quite as large as the night before but applauds just as enthusiastically. People in the audience can see themselves on large screens between different presentations, if *cerro Santa Ana* - faced by the performers but in the audience's back - is not shown. A very strong wind blows cold tonight and I'm without a jacket. We walk home very rapidly.

Friday, 9/5/03

Rosa shows up early in the morning and we all have breakfast together after which she leaves with Angela for Milagro. I want to stay here to attend the Bolero Festival in the evening and have to get there early before all the good seats are gone.

In the news there is much talk these days about President Gutierrez's trip to China and the cost thereof and what he gained in return for the country. There is another problem, namely his marriage isn't going so well; Gutierrez didn't take his wife along to China only one of his daughters.

The city of Guayaquil is not the only place being beautified. The International Airport Simon Bolivar is also being turned into a larger, more efficient facility with more parking along *Avenida de las Americas* implementing all the latest security measures. In November the international side is to be opened and the entire project should be finished by the end of the year. Right now it's a nightmare to take passengers to the airport with practically no parking and barely space to let people out of the car. On my next visit here, I should enter a beautiful new and up-to-date airport.

I leave on time in the evening for the third performance which is really international tonight. There is Lucho Gonzalez of Peru, Mariachis, María José Tejada and Ignacio Izcaray of Venezuela and, of course, Patricia Gonzalez of Guayaquil. It's another enjoyable but very cool evening; even Patricia Gonzalez comments on the cold weather. But the music is wonderful and much applauded by a happy crowd.

I read an article in EL UNIVERSO today about the Bolero saying that some think the Bolero originated in Cuba while others say it started in México but the only thing certain is that the songs and the music appeal to people today as in the past. This last part of the statement couldn't be more correct.

Walking home afterwards, I pass by the IMAX theatre which is growing by the day. The dome is finished and even at this late hour of the evening work continues by strong lights. It should be very beautiful once finished. As far as architecture goes, the Latin world certainly doesn't have to hide behind anybody, in fact I think others could learn from them when it comes to form and eye appeal. That's just my opinion although I've heard others agreeing.

When I arrive home, Angela tells me that Amelia asked: "Where is Ursula?" The doctor thinks Amelia should go home as there is nothing the hospital really can do for her. It all has to simply heal and that takes some time.

Saturday, 9/6/03

A very early phone call wakes us up and a frantic Elena tells Angela to come quickly to the hospital because Amelia is out of control, had ripped the glucose line out and wanted to get out of bed, yelling at everybody around her. She says that they tried to tie Amelia's hands to the side of the bed, but Amelia ripped free of that also.

She gets up immediately saying, "I'll have to go to the clinic."

"I'll come with you," I answer getting up as well and taking a quick shower, thinking we'll be leaving soon but we have breakfast first and arrive at the clinic later in the morning.

Amelia has calmed down by now but seems to be delirious not knowing what she had done. She doesn't really seem to recognize us either and is babbling about things of the past and talking with her mother. She also sings some songs of her youth. Her skin feels sweaty and she doesn't look well.

"It's all the medication they have given her that's making her crazy," I say. "I don't know what you had to buy every day and why all these prescriptions for what? She didn't need anything else but perhaps a painkiller. I've just read a lengthy article in the newspaper at home addressing exactly this problem - overmedication of the elderly in particular. One woman took her mother off everything and brought her home where she became a normal person again after a few weeks once all this medication was out of her body. This is crazy."

"Yes there are all these prescriptions. Every morning the doctor leaves them here for Ivan to buy," confirms Angela.

"I've been wondering about this myself," says Ivan. "The painkiller I can see but there are all kinds of other things."

A young resident doctor enters at this moment. Angela and Ivanovich discuss Amelia with the doctor saying that they wanted her off all the other medications. The young doctor responds that this isn't up to her; they have to call the head doctor. When he enters he tells them after a while that then there is nothing he can do for Amelia because everything he had her take was for her best. He also said that she is diabetic because her sugar was low when she came in first. Angela took her reading just now and it was extremely high. She is alarmed. They had informed the doctor that Amelia was on diabetes medication. Fed up, Ivan calls her regular physician. When he arrives a little later, he looks at Amelia who is better by now and talks with her. Then he looks at the X-rays and says nothing is broken; all that she needed is rest to heal.

So we pack up everything we have here to take home with us in the car while Ivanovich calls the ambulance service to take Amelia home again. This agitated her because suddenly she doesn't want to go home although she had requested the day before to be taken home again. "Don't leave me here," she had said. Poor Amelia went through a lot that day and put the family through many concerns as well. Everybody wants to do the right thing by her.

Angela is so glad that the mechanism of the bed works. The repair was finalized yesterday. Now they wash and dress her and put her in a clean bed before the doctor comes by to check on her again after having read the records from the clinic. He says she still needs the glucose because her potassium is low. Amelia is calm now, looks much better and smiles when she sees me, stretching out her hand as she usually does while earlier she didn't recognize me at all. I'm glad she is better and hope she'll walk again. It's much harder for somebody her age to fully recover after a fall. We are all hoping for the best.

I keep sharing my newspaper with Elena and point out a photo in the El Gran Guayaquil section showing an area of the Rio Salado where wooden shacks on stilts stand in the water surrounded by a huge mass of debris and garbage floating around the houses. I can't believe I'm seeing what I'm seeing.

"This is where my mother has her house," Elena tells me.

"This is where you live?"

"This is where my mother's house is and where I lived before I came here" she adds pointing with her finger to a certain area. "Si, es horrible."

"It must smell terrible."

The accompanying article talks about how three fishermen got stuck in the debris with their boat and it took their combined efforts to free themselves again. The city has contracted with a company to have section after section cleaned up. Of course, the people living there share much of the blame by discarding their garbage like that. On the other hand, thinking of Angela's situation in Milagro, being charged for garbage pick-up that doesn't happen this is perhaps similar. They show a woman living there complaining about the constant foul odor enveloping the entire area and this in the warm, humid climate of Guayaquil! It will certainly take a major effort and cooperation from all sides to clean up and keep it clean.

In the evening, Ivan's wife, her mother and daughter and I are off to the final night of the International Bolero Festival dedicated to Patricia Gonzalez, the lady from Guayaquil, admired and liked for her contribution to the arts.

We go by taxi because the mother is not good by foot. I also take my jacket but - as with the umbrella, when one carries it, it doesn't rain - I don't need it at all. There's very little wind and the air is pleasant. The evening is another big success. I begin to understand more and more while Patricia Gonzalez is so popular. She has a great voice and distinct way to interpret the music she sings. She also is very funny. She sings every song and has invited only a few of the international group to sing with her now and then. This is a little disappointing to me because some of these international performers like Vives and Izcaray really appealed to me and I would have liked to hear them just by themselves again.

The crowd is the largest ever. People keep coming and coming and chairs have to be added; in fact, they ran out of tickets and just have the people pay and walk in. It's a huge success and I'm so glad I'm here in Guayaquil to enjoy this wonderful experience in this unbelievable setting providing the background for this extraordinary performance.

Sunday, 9/7/03

Over breakfast I learn from Angela that Elena complained to her about Marco who sleeps outside Amelia's room while Elena sleeps in the same room with her. When Elena returned from a trip to the bathroom last night being half asleep, she saw something dark in her bed scaring her very much. On looking closer after the first shock, she recognized Marco and began yelling: "Get out of my bed; what are you doing here?"

The story doesn't surprise me; inquiring last night about the sleeping arrangement, the idea of Marco being so close to Elena, who is very pretty and young, didn't sound good to me. Angela spoke to him now saying that if she heard one more complaint of that nature he would be out. Like in any big family there's always something going on here - I don't have to make anything up at all.

By the time I go downstairs to buy a newspaper Segundo has left for the day. He's only there for so many hours on Sunday. I walk down the street a little further and luckily see another person selling newspapers.

Angela and Ivanovich drive to Milagro in the afternoon while I stay here. I want to do a few things and read the news. I find a ten-page insert in the paper today regarding the Human and Natural Heritage of Humanity of Quito and the Galápagos Islands. The spot where the capital Quito is located today, the old historic center dating back to 1534, was previously occupied by indigenous people, the Quitus, the Caras and the Incas. The Plaza Mayor with its historic government buildings and church is the nucleus around which the city developed and enlarged. There are many old and narrow streets and plazas dating back to the early colonial days and even though almost five hundred years doesn't seem much time when looking at architectural achievements worldwide, it is considerable time for buildings in the New World being constructed by the people of the Old World at an altitude of around nine thousand feet in the high Andes surrounded by volcanoes. There is much historic background of Quito, the full name being 'San Francisco de Quito,' in this insert with various black and white photos depicting the history of this beautiful city situated on various hills. The landing strip of the airport is on an elevation in the center of the city and not too long ago a plane overshot it. I've been told that it takes an experienced pilot to take off from and land in Quito. Once in a while there's a mishap and I remember reading years ago already about moving the airport; the only question is whereto in these Andes.

The Natural Heritage, the Galápagos, also are described in detail. Situated about 650 miles from the coast of Ecuador in the Pacific, they were originally discovered by a Spaniard, Tomas de Berlanga in 1535. They were not permanently settled till Ecuador claimed them in 1832. In 1835 Charles Darwin visited the islands and was intrigued by its fauna and flora. His book on "The Evolution of Species" theory was a result of his studies and observations in the Galápagos. The Charles Darwin station in Puerto Ayora with some of the remaining giant tortoises, who can weigh more than 300 pounds and can live for 400 years, was named in honor of his extensive work on natural evolution.

Monday, 9/8/03

Amelia looks better today but doesn't have her old appetite back. From being always hungry, she now is hardly eating at all. Angela has to coax her into having just a little food asking all the time what she would like to have. Once she gets the food, Amelia takes a bite or two and says she is full.

"You will not be getting well if you don't eat. You need your strength back," Angela tells her mother who only shakes her head. It's hopeless right now. Perhaps she'll regain her appetite in a few days.

As far as my red blisters in the face are concerned, they are almost gone. I'm so glad that this cream helped. I've had no new ones and the old ones are drying up. How strange, I had them only in my face and nowhere else. Well, another experience. I'll buy a few tubes of this wonderful cream before I return. No doubt in the States it would cost me fifty or sixty dollars whereas here a tube is about three-fifty.

Rosa and I discuss the latest happenings in the country. I appreciate her knowledge and sense of humor more and more and find many situations, or things she does, extremely funny. It's amazing how much humor one can find if one looks for it. I mean to keep only my laughing eyes open, hopefully.

It's almost lunch time which means I've to fix the salad. After looking in the refrigerator and finding rotten vegetables some time ago we had to throw out, I make a big salad almost every day. Rosa tells me she loves my salads.

"I cannot cook at all," she says.

"Rosa, that's not cooking, it's just cutting up a few vegetables and lettuce."

"But you mix all the right things and I just love your salads."

Ursula B. Borck

"I'm glad you do because it's more fun to prepare food if people enjoy it."

Tuesday, 9/9/03

The sky is overcast in the morning. It's a perfect day to walk and walk I do - from one end of the Malecón to the other and then up el *cerro Santa Ana* for my cardio-vascular exercise. The view is wonderful from the top of the hill; with the tide out the growing sandbanks in the river are very visible. If these sandbanks keep growing like that, considerable dredging will be necessary to keep the ever smaller channel open so the ships can pass. Even from last year, the islands seem larger and I don't remember if they were there when I first came to Ecuador.

Segundo has saved me a paper when I return and hands it to me with a smile. There's an unpleasant odor around here from all the digging up of the streets with all kinds of pipes draining 'liquids.' I have to balance over boards close to the house because very dark looking water is being siphoned out of the ditch and running down the street. A narrow plank over the ditch allows people to cross. The odors emitted are not pleasant but Segundo doesn't want a mask, shaking his head, smiling.

Skimming over the headlines of the paper, I wonder if the threatened transportation strike will be happening or if it has been averted by the government by coming to terms with the conductors of the buses and trucks. Ivanovich expressed his concern about this strike looming over the country the day before, because the truck drivers threatened to also block the roads which would, of course, hinder the flow of goods throughout the country. I'm so glad to see that it won't happen because the government and transportation representatives are talking and the original high additional toll to be imposed as of today will be lowered. However, a picture shows that a highway had been blocked and the police have detained about 119 persons.

Then there is a sad article on the children of AIDS who are often homeless because either their parents have died of the disease or their families don't want these children around and desert them. This is a major problem and there is no real home for these orphans or abandoned children, nor are there enough organizations to care

160

for them with money lacking as well. One foundation from the United States maintains a home for about fifteen minors and this is all they can take at the moment. As in other developing countries, the resources simply are missing and children usually do not protest, complain or anything - they have no voice.

Yesterday EL UNIVERSO also featured President Gutierrez and his wife jointly after half a year of not appearing together for official functions. Today, there is a small article regarding a comment the first lady made regarding her marriage: "I didn't marry a presidential band (group) I married Edwin Gutierrez, not President Lucio." She said that they had met and that she loved her husband very much. Another courageous first lady who faces the world!

Soccer players are on the front page because today Ecuador plays against Brazil in Manaus, Brazil, combined with high hopes here. Soccer is big in Ecuador as in all of South America and Europe. Ecuador hopes to be part of the games in 2006 in Germany.

Wednesday, 9/10/03

Well, this hope was dimmed today when Ecuador lost in Brazil as shown on the evening news on all the channels. Everybody played well; the Brazilian team won only 1:0.

I try to take my daily walk during the morning hours before the sun comes out and before it gets too hot. I enjoy these walks where I can observe the world around me, all the hustle and bustle of this city so alive which feels more and more like home People going about their business, police keeping eyes open, vendors trying to make a sale, mothers walking with their children prettily dressed or watching them on the playground at the Malecón. The artists are there painting or sketching the faces of people which they do amazingly well. The Rio Guayas is rushing at its usual fast current carrying water lilies along. Here and there a fishing boat trying to make a catch - everything is as it should be.

When I come back we eat lunch. Ivanovich and his cousin Mario are also present which means I have to make a big salad because everybody has taken to eating salad now, even Ida, Elena and Marco. I wonder if they'll keep it up when I'm gone.

We discuss our trip to Zaruma in the south of the country. We saw a wonderful program on TV regarding places of interest in the country and Zaruma looked enticing, just the place a tourist like me would want to see. We had talked about it and Angela said we should go and see it. Unfortunately, Ivanovich can't come along, Angela can't drive so far anymore and I can't drive a shift car, so Angela announces: "We'll go by bus."

"Good. That's fine with me."

Thursday, 9/11/03

We wake up early this morning and turn on the news. They show some scenes of Memorial Services from New York for the victims of the terrorist attack two years ago. I remember this morning two years ago distinctly wondering, while driving to work, what would happen today this being a number five day for me - expect the unexpected! In my mind I went over various office matters. Never in my wildest dreams did I think of an occurrence of this nature, although I had thought for a long time before that *something* would happen due to many political factors, one of which being that our present administration in particular, has not learned yet that it would be better to live *with* the world rather than *against* it!

Angela is already on the phone trying to find out when the bus leaves for Zaruma only to hear that the office doesn't open till nine in the morning. When we reach the office later, we see that there are many buses and that an express leaves at twelve-thirty. The company is T.A.C. a well-established bus line. We purchase our tickets for an unbelievable reasonable price. While standing at the platform waiting for the bus to arrive we see two tall, sleek and very well dressed young men, hair neatly combed, pass by giving us the once over. They literally look us up and down without hiding it, an unfriendly expression on their faces. Once they are past, Angela and I look at each other and she whispers in my ear: "*Ladrones* - thieves. These are two of this type who will hold up a bus and rob the people."

"You have the same impression then," I answer following them with my eyes as they are with their backs to us.

"Oh yes, they are bad these two."

"They certainly looked us over without any shame."

"This is what they do - sizing us up."

There is every so often a report in the paper where a bus has been held up and the passengers relieved of all their money, jewelry and watches. This can happen on a city bus or a cross-country trip. We are aware of this problem and have nothing valuable with us, but we do have dollars in cash and credit cards and hide most of it as well as we can later on. Meanwhile, these two young men return after having lingered some time at the other end, again staring bluntly at us while passing. I stare right back. Then we see them walking off between two buses further down and are very happy not to have them with us.

We have the front seats with a good view and settle in. This bus line is not of the quality of Ormeño in Peru, but then Ormeño goes international while T.A.C. doesn't. We travel south on highway 25 via Naranjal, Machala and Santa Rosa closer to the Pacific, the same route I had come up from Peru a year earlier with banana plantations to both sides of the road for miles and miles. Also there are many patches of cocoa beans laid out neatly on the side of the highway to dry as is the custom of small farmers here. Nobody seems to steal them and drivers don't run over them either.

From Santa Rosa on we head inland and begin to climb into the mountains on a winding but very good road. We now travel via Piñas, Portovelo to Zaruma, high in the Cordillera. The scenery is beautiful. With every turn in the road, a new vista more spectacular than the previous opens up. The other thing which opens up - or I should say is no longer closed - is the bus door. This means whenever the bus stops or has to slow down because of road bumps, we are being invaded by herds of young boys and men, carrying various packets and baskets trying to sell us their goods. They have everything, from sweets to ice cream to fruit and even cooked meat on sticks and soft drinks. They walk through the bus announcing their goods, sometimes selling quite a bit. Some leave again at the back door of the bus while others will come along to the next stop. Our express bus has basically become a shuttle bus. I now understand much better what passengers mean when I read in the paper they are afraid of this vendor invasion, never knowing who enters the bus. I can't say I am afraid; none of the people strike me as mean or dangerous, but it takes some getting used to and is also very noisy. Much more bothersome are the people who enter the bus and then begin preaching belonging to one sect or another or the ones who try to sell their latest remedies for guaranteed cures of various maladies. They may talk for a long time.

Evening is slowly approaching and with it the long shadows of the setting sun bathing the mountains and the valleys in its golden, mysterious glow. We seem to travel often on top of the world allowing a view into the valleys below and mountain ranges further back in various hues of gray and blue. Here and there are houses emitting a spiral of smoke indicating preparation of the evening meal and by the time we arrive in Zaruma, it's around seven in the evening and quite dark. The terminal is at the main street and we hear that there is a hotel just a little up the street. Everything here is up or down the street with the houses clinging to the side of hills. The street is very steep as we find out right now and numbers or names are hard to see. We pass right by the hotel because the narrow door, behind a big open double door of a pharmacy, is not visible. Once inside, the entrance also is narrow so that one has to squeeze in and by each other. The young boy at the reception is very nice and shows us to a neat, clean room with hot and cold water - our own shower and a color T.V. What more can one possibly want?

Then he directs us to a restaurant across the street at an angle from the hotel saying their food is good. It's fine with Angela who isn't willing to play mountain goat much longer. The restaurant is not too busy, we are being served relatively quickly and we have the benefit of the owner coming over to our table and answering many questions. Zaruma was discovered in 1549 by one Alonso de Mercadillo. The area was part of the Inca Empire inhabited by Indians before the Spaniards came and gold was mined. The official founding of Zaruma took place in 1595 by the order of King Philip II of Spain in the province of El Oro. A tourist pamphlet contains this information.

The mines were worked and produced considerable amounts of gold for the next centuries until production fell off. In 1871 President Garcia Moreno sent experts to Zaruma to see what needed to be done to make the area more productive and bring it up to date if warranted. In 1879 the *Great Zaruma Gold Mining Co. Limited* was formed in London which operated till 1896 when, due to not paying taxes, it signed all rights over to the North American company called *South American Development Company* which operated till

1950. The mines are still producing to this day, although agriculture is the main source of income. There are various other businesses and now there is more tourism since Zaruma is on the list of Patrimonio Cultural de la Humanidad. After all, its architecture dates back about four hundred years. The restaurant owner thinks there are perhaps three thousand inhabitants in Zaruma today. He's a native himself and his three children are all living here as well.

I was surprised to hear that the gold mines are still operating and producing because I thought that since the Americans pulled out, there was no more gold.

We were told that there was nothing going on here at this hour and so we returned to our hotel after dinner to watch a little TV before we fell asleep. Our sleep came to a sudden end in the middle of the night when a group of people decided to party below our window in the street, laughing and talking loudly while others were fighting in a room not far from ours. There was no end to noise and rowdiness; one certainly couldn't speak of 'the silence of the night!'

Friday 9/12/03

Unfortunately the restaurant of last night doesn't serve breakfast so we ask a taxi to take us to another restaurant. We crawl up the steep, cobble-stoned and winding street until we get to the main plaza where the driver lets us out in front of a restaurant which I would not exactly count among the better experiences of my life. In fact, just to look at the fried eggs swimming in butter is enough to take one's appetite away. The lady owner is nice, however, and seems to have her local group of customers. Well, I don't waste much time and leave to look around the main plaza with its old buildings beautifully painted and with carved adornments looking exactly as I had seen it on TV. There are government buildings, a church and the tourist office around the beautifully groomed park, the plaza. A friendly policeman tells me to take the stairs in a certain building to have a better view over the whole plaza and could take a much better photo from there. I follow his advice and he's right. The tourist office is also right there and provides some pamphlets.

Looking down, I see Angela talking with a taxi driver. She hires him to take us to a place where orchids are grown and sold because this region is famous for orchids and Angela wants to add to her collection in *La Granja*. We travel some very steep and rocky roads before we come to a place with orchids, some of them even blooming and very beautiful, but they are not for sale. They mention another place where we can buy and we leave again but not before I've taken some photos of orchids and bromeliads hanging everywhere. I see some boys busy with something and approaching I see that they are panning for gold. They have a little dish standing there which sparkles in a few rays of the sun breaking through the clouds and the trees. I ask them if they find much and they tell me it is so, so - some days are better than others.

At the next place - I don't know how the driver finds them because they are not visible from the road - he climbs up a very narrow little road, actually only two tracks in the dirt. Again, we have to be mountain goats to get around here. Angela finds three orchids she likes, one even blooming, and buys them. Nevertheless, we are told that the best place for orchids is Piñas.

The taxi driver suggests we go and see Malvas further down the road. It is a very little village with a very old beautiful wooden church. The ceiling is entirely of wooden boards with hand-painted religious scenes. The altar is of wood with ornate carvings while most the windows are plain glass, only the ones close to the altar are painted. We look and admire and I cannot help but think how these old churches are so much more solemn than the contemporary ones and how this old church has held up over the centuries. It was well worth the trip and Angela thanks the driver for taking us here.

Then we go back to Zaruma where I walk and explore on my own. Angela stays in the car and the driver will take her around a little longer. The air is pleasant and cool as I walk up and down steep streets to see as much as I can, admiring the architecture of these old buildings clinging to the side of the road or mountain, most beautifully decorated and very well kept up. Some homes are sitting on top of sturdy, high stone walls reminding me instantly of Kronberg, Germany, a very picturesque old town at the foot of the Taunus Mountains, where I had seen this type of construction also. I take photos here and there often stopping to get a view from a different angle. Three school children come towards me and I ask the girl and two boys if I can take their photo because they look so nice in their school uniform, black pants/skirt and white shirts. Readily they pose for me, big smiles on their faces

I'm looking for a restaurant but don't see much that I find really appealing here in the center. In fact, after the breakfast disaster Angela and I talked about what this main plaza needed is a nice restaurant with a big patio where people can sit down and eat or just relax and enjoy the beautiful surrounding. It would be big business. Well, I'm not so hungry anyway and buy a bottle of water and a chocolate bar for lunch and eat while I walk looking in on some of the old churches admiring the ornate decorations

The bus back to Guayaquil leaves early but is no express. People come and go every five minutes it seems to me. Then there are all the vendors again snaking their way through the bus balancing their goods high over their heads at times. We arrive safely in Guayaquil around seven in the evening and say from now on we'll travel by bus, as it's comfortable, easy, interesting and inexpensive.

Saturday, 9/13/03

First of all I find out from Ivanovich that the tour company from Salinas called two days ago to let us know they were going out whale watching yesterday. He told them we were in Zaruma but to let us know again when the next occasion comes up.

After looking in on Amelia who is doing as well as can be expected, we have breakfast before I go on my walk in the cool morning air. I buy EL UNIVERSO and one of the first things I read is that John Ritter passed away on Thursday. I can't believe it! That's really sad because he and his show *Three Is Company* was definitely a part of my TV fare in my younger years as probably of most of our generation. I looked forward to their show and they no doubt added years to my life if the old adage 'laughter prolongs life' is true. Now he's dead at age 55. Just doesn't seem fair.

Ivan's wife comes to visit and to discuss our planned outing to the Jazz Concert tonight at the Malecón. My timing this year is really lucky - there is one presentation after the other going on at the Malecón and I mean to take advantage of this. Now they have a music festival and both of us are planning to attend quite a few of these performances. I'm glad that Ivan's wife likes all these cultural offerings as much as I do so I have company. Angela says she has seen it all.

The Classical Jazz Concert by a group of three from France, two guitarists and one percussionist, turns out to be good. However, it's in the Auditorium at the Malecón which holds about four hundred forty people and so we have to be there early and wait in line. While in line, we have an interesting conversation with a very knowledgeable man who appears to know everything about music but when I ask him if he belongs to the music field, he says no, he's an audiologist and sound is what his ear is tuned to. He knew much more than sounds, however. The concert has been arranged through the Societé Francaise and is offered free to the public. Culturally much is being offered in Guayaquil - either for free or for a very small price.

A cold wind is blowing when we walk home after the concert. I've managed to get Ivan's wife to walk rather than take a taxi. We both walk fast because we didn't bring jackets thinking we wouldn't need them after such a hot day. The temperature changes quickly here; I really have to keep this in mind.

Sunday, 9/14/03

After a late breakfast, I look in on Amelia again as all of us do many times a day. She looks better and smiles. She also seems to be in less pain when she moves her leg but she is in bed so Elena is also stuck in the room with her. She hasn't been out at all and is very patient and gentle with Amelia which is admirable. The only times she comes out is to eat her meals with Ida and Marco on our side. I wonder sometimes how she does it, being so young and sitting in a room taking care of an old lady - no matter how nice - who needs much attention. Angela is there every day to make sure she is clean and changed, checking on her in every way possible, listening to her pulse and checking her blood sugar. She has learned much.

Marco is gone quite a bit. He likes to spend time downstairs with Ivan's sons and plays games with them or he is out in the streets and nobody knows where to find him. Angela wants to fire him almost daily because he is so lazy.

After a delicious meal, we leave for *La Granja*. Marta comes up to open the gate for us. I almost don't recognize her in her short little skirt. She always wears pants. I've never seen her in a skirt. Seems to me she's putting on some weight and Pedro, dressed only in pants with a bare upper torso, isn't getting any slimmer either. We talk a little while Angela checks on a few things before we leave again.

There is a new Festival de Artes starting today at the Malecón, but I won't go tonight. This goes on for a whole week and I think I have a touch of a cold and want to just relax at home. We watch the news on CNN and hear that the Israeli government is considering - among other things - to have Arafat assassinated; what a strange idea for a road to peace! Sometimes I think the Third World War has begun. I remember how happy I was when the Berlin wall came down thinking the world would be a better place to live in. Now here we are surrounded by wars, destruction and hatred - ego, greed and incompetence ruling the world. In two thousand years we haven't learned a thing and yet we call ourselves civilized and wonder why other people and cultures don't want to be like us.

Monday, 9/15/03

After a very inactive morning, everybody suddenly jumps into action. A group of people called and wanted to stay at *La Granja* for two nights, even without the pool. Angela with Ivanovich and Ida depart for *La Granja* to set everything up.

Ivan's wife has asked me to go to another concert, this time at the Politecnic School. Well, the concert and play are as these types of entertainment go. Some talk and sing better, others are inaudible. Luckily the performance doesn't last too long either and we are on our way home where we talk until Angela and Ivanovich return to say the group will not be there after all because they couldn't get the lights going and had told them not to come. They'll have to get the generator going to be independent of the electric company.

On top of it Marco, who was to watch over Amelia, had disappeared and when I return and look in on Amelia, she says: "Ursula, I'm so glad you are here. I called for Ida, Elena, Marco and you and nobody came."

"Where is Marco? He has not been with you?"

"No sé, no sé."

Later Marco returns and we all give him a good talking-to. How much good it will do, heaven knows.

Tuesday, 9/16/03

"I went to see my mother and she was up already," Angela says early in the morning.

"What do you mean *up*? Up, up?"

"Sí. I told her not to get up till at least the end of the week."

"I can't believe it! She didn't complain about pain?"

"No, no pain. However, she needs to rest longer."

"Well yes. She probably is tired of being in bed all the time."

"This is what it is. There's nothing I can do about that either."

Amelia is amazing at her age. Whenever we think she won't pull out of something anymore, there she is full speed ahead, so to say. We are all glad to see her progress and hope she'll be able to walk again.

During my walk in the afternoon, I go to the Malecón 2000 to buy my ticket for this evening's performance of the Ballet of Ecuador. I'll be on my own as Ivan's wife has another obligation.

The attendance is small tonight. In fact, there are quite a few empty seats. Of course, it is the middle of the week and this Festival de Artes follows very close on the heels of the previous four-day event.

I sit close to the stage. Next to me is another lady by herself and we start a conversation. She is very nice and apparently also glad to have somebody to talk with, especially a Gringa with whom she can converse in her own language. I learn that she is a profesora of literature which I find very interesting and tell her that I'm impressed by the many cultural events offered to the public here.

"Sí, these cultural presentations are often free or are offered for very little money because the government wants to educate the people and make them familiar with the fine arts. Many people in this country are not very cultured," she responds apologetically.

"It's probably like anywhere in the world. The ones who are interested attend cultural events, while others' niveau doesn't go past a football game. It's the same in the States."

"Exactly; it is like that here," she answers laughing at my comparison.

"At the French Jazz Trio, I talked with a man who definitely knew much about music and last year at *La Misa Criolla* I overheard people talking about this piece with great knowledge."

"Sí, much depends on the parents and what they expose their children to," adding "You speak Spanish very well."

"Gracias, this is very kind of you, but I speak only a little. I have a hard time understanding some people here in Ecuador who drop endings and speak fast."

"Exactamente," she nods her head knowingly and says: "At the coast they do not pronounce the words so well. It's much better in Quito."

We talk about the children and how they do in school. She tells me that some do not learn so well and that they are at a disadvantage not only because of a possible lower social status of their parents, but for the food they eat or should I say, do not eat. They don't get the proper nutrition they need early on in life and that leaves its mark for the rest of their lives. She says often they don't get enough milk and meat and are simply lacking nutrition needed for proper development.

"Is muy triste," I nod my head.

"Sí, it is sad and many children are affected by this lack of food."

After the announcer opens up the evening, I tell her, "I understood every word he said and I also understand you perfectly well." She smiles and thanks me. Of course, she is a teacher.

The performance is interesting and well choreographed and presented. I enjoy it very much. When it's over, the profesora and I walk together to the parking garage where she left her car. We discuss the improvements in Guayaquil. She tells me it's totally safe here at the Malecón but is still a little surprised to hear I'm walking home all the way. We say our good-bye at the parking garage, hoping we'll meet again.

Once back in the house, I hear that Angela has bought a generator and will open *La Granja* to the public again.

Wednesday, 9/17/03

Like most every day, Ivanovich and his cousin eat lunch with us. I like our meals together because we always have the best conversations going and many laughs as well because Ivanovich can be extremely funny. Cousin Mario and I had a, for me, informative discussion regarding presidents Lucio Gutierrez of Ecuador and Luis Inacio Lula da Silva of Brazil. Even though perhaps the upper crust of Ecuador was not so pleased to have Lucio as president, there seems to be little opposition to him now. Giving him the most trouble are his own indigenous people. As Segundo had said to me, "He doesn't do what he promised to."

As to President Lula da Silva of Brazil, he's genuinely liked and respected here and, apparently in much of South America. As the head of the largest country of this continent, he reaches out to the other leaders of the South American countries to work together to fight certain problems they all face. He visited Colombia yesterday to meet with Alvaro Uribe to discuss problems regarding the Revolutionary Army of Colombia kidnapping eight tourists, which they deny. When I see Lula on TV he comes across as very personable, one who can laugh heartily - somehow like Bill Clinton - not stiff or stilted in any way but the same infectious laugh and when he speaks, he makes sense.

Amelia needed a lot of attention this morning but by noon she is taking some steps supported by Ida and Nellie, the former nurse who has the orange drink stand below. She came to our aid last year when Amelia was in much pain and needed a shot which neither Ida nor I could give. I like Nellie very much. She aids when she can without any demands and is always friendly. I'm sure she was an excellent nurse but prefers her present life of more freedom and more money. Who can blame her; she's probably in her early fortieth with a family.

That brings Berto back to mind. He had a little shop below in the house and I ran into him all the time. He always knew where everybody was and warned me of the *ladrones* lurking everywhere when I went out walking by myself. He also visited with Amelia either downstairs when she could still walk, or upstairs to chat with her in her kitchen. I haven't seen Berto this time and ask Ivanovich about this.

"Oh, you know, I told him to leave because I wasn't sure how much he could be trusted. I became aware of certain things while taking over the management of this building."

Strangely enough I don't find this surprising because this man knew everything and was everywhere all the time. Anyway, this explains his absence from here.

"I gave the shop to Segundo's daughter who sells electronic items. She asked me for space earlier and so it works out just fine."

"I see. Now tell me about Segundo. He says he has to move from his spot downstairs."

"Yes, he wants a space in the house below, but I don't have one anymore."

"What about the yogurt shop your son used to have years ago?"

"This has become part of the pharmacy. They needed more room and asked me if they could have this space so I gave it to them."

"I understand. Too bad, because Segundo is such a nice person."

In the evening, Ivan's wife and I leave for the Malecón again to attend another *Ballet del Teatro del Centro de Arte* performance as part of the International Festival de Artes taking place. The first part of this performance is beautiful, real ballet as one knows it. They receive much applause. When I think of ballet, I think of pirouetting ballerinas, gracious movements and elegant leaps. Therefore, I don't even think that the second part can be called ballet, perhaps not even dance, because it consists mostly of rolling around on the floor resembling physical exercise - in my eyes. Of course, I'm no expert in the field, but I've seen enough ballet and dance in my life to know what I like. Ivan's wife doesn't like the second part either while she loved the first one. Next day I read in EL UNIVERSO that the second part was a performance against war and for peace in the world. Well, that explains all the people rolling around on the floor, dead and wounded people falling. How horrible! Young lives snuffed out just like that.

We are walking home as usual for exercise after sitting so long during the performance without intermission. These days, however, I take my jacket because the evenings are rather cool and often there is a strong wind blowing

Thursday, 9/18/03

Angela says we'll eat breakfast early. I know what that means by now – there's a big difference between her early and my early because she is often sidetracked by having to take care of this and that or busy with her mother so I'm going for a quick walk and when I return we eat breakfast around ten in the morning. EL UNIVERSO presents a fantastic photo of the eye of hurricane Isabel with an article saying it has arrived at the east coast of the United States. The photo is amazingly clear, a close-up, definitely looking like an eye. Isabel is expected to be powerful and destructive.

Another article on bus reduction in Guayaquil catches my eye. Finally! I do think this is overdue because there are fleets of buses in the streets by different companies following and trying to overtake each other, heading in the same direction and having perhaps two or three people on board. They congest the busy streets even more and increase the air pollution. About 160 buses will be withdrawn from traffic because there are far too many and some are too old.

There is another article and accompanying photo of six truly beautiful girls in the paper today representing their countries for a benefit performance here to raise money for social and medical needs of the poor of Ecuador. Miss Universe and twelve others will be participating. It's always encouraging to see the young use their fame and energy not only for personal gain but for the benefit of others.

Something else catches my eye, an offer to the citizens of Ecuador to fly to the Galápagos for a very low price, namely two hundred nineteen dollars, which also includes three nights at a hotel - economy class, breakfast, a welcome drink and a farewell dinner. The article says that it's often difficult for Ecuadorians to visit the Galápagos as prices there are high. This special offer is valid from the first of September to the fifteenth of November and, hopefully, will enable many people to visit this Natural World Treasure of Humanity of their own country.

Right after lunch we look for another generator for *La Granja* because Ivanovich thinks it's better to have two to run the place. Then we drive to Milagro and straight to Maestro Gutierrez' house to take him with us. He's the electrician Angela goes to most of the time and the same man who accompanied us a year ago on a Saturday night late in his pajamas!

Indeed, it doesn't take long and the generator starts up with ear deafening noise which sends the three cats scattering in all directions. Even the birds take off. To everyone's delight the water starts flowing and every single light comes on. Hurrah, it works! The generator is sitting close to the kitchen house outside to try it out first. This is actually a shame, because now arrangements will have to be made to move it. The empty storage house close to the wall and out of sight and reach of people is to be the final location. Gutierrez says some modification will have to be made for it to be less noisy plus it will be inside and is far away from the pool and cabaña where the people spend most the time. We hope that it will all work out well because with this tranquility shattering noise it's doubtful anybody will stay.

Milagro is celebrating its ninetieth birthday with different parades, festivities and vendors of every imaginable type of wares. The streets are so busy and it is extremely difficult to get through by car. Finally Angela finds some spot to park so we look at a few of the stands where she buys some items for the kitchen and I buy a little sleeveless top of the kind I see Elena wear. I had brought some gifts for the others and when I hand Elena the top, she's so obviously happy about this unexpected gift that she gets up and gives me a hug and a kiss on the cheek. Such a little gift causes so much happiness!

Another thing happened this morning at breakfast. Angela and I, for the past few weeks, had been talking about another trip and considered various options. This morning out of the blue she suggests, "Let's go to El Oriente." In Ecuador they refer to the eastern part of the country as El Oriente which means the Rain Forest, the jungle of the Amazon. We have talked about going to El Oriente for at least the past ten to twelve years without ever doing it. I'm surprised at this news and ask her if she really means it.

"Yes," she answers. "I have seen much of Ecuador but I've never been to El Oriente, so let's go."

"By all means, I'm ready. There isn't much time left for me anymore before I have to return to the States. When do you have in mind?"

"Let's go to the bus terminal today and find out when the buses leave. I think this bus travel is not bad at all. Ivan and Mario have no time to drive us. What do you think?"

"Okay, let's do it. I'd love to go and the bus is great because we'll see more and we won't have to worry about the road."

"Yes, that's another consideration I have, the roads and what condition they'll be in once we get to the jungle area where it rains a lot."

I announced this happy news the moment I saw Ivanovich. He also thought it was a great idea. So now on our way home, we stop by the enormous bus terminal where Ivanovich goes to collect all the information for us, saying we should take at least a week to see as much as we can. Buses leave daily. Angela suggests we leave Monday and reminds Ivan that he and his wife will have to look after Amelia while we are gone. Amelia is doing better and with Elena there looking after her and Ida cooking, it should all work out.

Ivanovich also called the whale watching tour people but was told they didn't have anybody for this week-end and would need at least five people to make it worth while for them with the boat.

Friday, 9/19/03

"We'll leave early for Milagro today," Angela says at breakfast.

"Okay, fine with me."

By now it is one fifteen in the afternoon, Ida is almost done with lunch and I fixed a big salad so probably we'll eat pretty soon. Ivanovich comes up for lunch and asks me if I heard something from the Tour Company in Salinas. I haven't and so he calls them to ask what's happening and why they haven't called us. They tell him that they have but nobody answered and they got the fax machine. What a shame because I heard the phone ringing but thought Angela would pick it up which she did, but too late. I ran to the roll-over phone and also got the fax machine. They had a boat go out with five people. This tour is jinxed.

Nobody goes to Milagro anymore today. It's too late and very hot. I haven't even gone for a walk because of the heat, but I'll catch up tonight when I go to attend a musical performance, called *Son*

Caribe. This is a group of nine musicians, most of them from México who entertain us with this type of music which I like so much. How lucky for me to be here at this time when so much is offered, especially this type of music which I seldom hear at home. For almost two hours the band plays to a large, very appreciative audience not sparing with applause. The result is that the band honors us with two encores which is very much the custom in South America as in Europe. It's a beautiful evening and I'm totally happy.

Once home, Angela informs me that Ivan's wife had asked her if she would help with preparations for the christening of her second son, who is twenty-one, which will be taking place when we are away. Now what? Well, says Angela, she'll prepare a dish ahead of time.

Saturday, 9/20/03

The phone rings early and Angela goes down to let Rosa in. We have a nice breakfast together after a quick wash, because this morning there is no water so early. We have fallen into the habit of saving a bucket full the night before for just such a surprise.

Elena is going home today and will be back tomorrow. Finally, after having been with us for four weeks, three of which she spent mostly in a room with Amelia, the girl gets a day off. I feel sorry for her and am glad she'll have some time for herself. Hopefully she'll also come back.

As I sit here pondering life's injustices Elena comes in to tell me she is going home.

"Yes, I heard; I'm so glad for you. What will you do tonight?"

"I'll go out dancing with my friends."

"Of course; I hope you'll have a truly wonderful time."

"I'll also buy some clothes," she adds having received her pay.

"Don't spend all your money today the way I did when I received my first paycheck being a little younger than you. Never occurred to me I'd have to wait four more weeks until we were paid again."

"I will not do that," she answers smiling, shaking her head.

"Ciao!"

Rosa accompanies us to Milagro. We visit the market first and Angela buys fruit and vegetables as well as meat to take to *La Granja.*

Then, to my surprise, we pick up three men from the street to take to *La Granja* to move the generator into the building where it's to be located permanently. The three men pile into the backseat with Rosa. I feel sorry for her but luckily we don't have far to go. I wished we could wait to have this expensive piece of equipment moved by people who know what they're doing but Angela thinks it can't wait. I watch the men straining under the weight trying to move the generator.

"It is very heavy," they say, while they push and pull and roll the generator along on three wooden poles, taking the end pole and putting it in front again and again, dripping oil all over the place from the oil pan underneath. It doesn't look good to me and I hope the generator hasn't been damaged.

Our Pedro, who is the strongest of all the men and whom I expected to be the leader of the group, isn't that at all. One of the other three men says what needs to be done and gives the orders when to drag and shove. Finally they have it inside and put it in a place that looks good to me also. Then Angela pays them and takes them back to town. Rosa goes with her while I stay behind. They haven't gone long, when maestro Gutierrez arrives per bike with another man.

"Maestro, we would have needed you so badly a little earlier," I greet him saying what just happened here. He greets me and then goes into the small building where the generator is. After checking it all out, he finds a few things were loose on the machine and would need tightening but no major damage.

By the time we are finally in Guayaquil, it is eight-thirty in the evening. I'm glad we arrived safely because Angela really doesn't see well at night, hitting the curb in one spot. Once home, Rosa has had it. She doesn't even come up anymore but goes straight home. Angela still needs to talk with the man she purchased the generator from so she and Ivanovich leave again.

I stay behind look in on Amelia, who is improving daily. Then I fix myself a nice big salad and watch a movie on TV. As my daughter-in-law would say, "Life is good!"

Sunday, 9/21/03

We have a very leisurely day today around the house. I wash and iron my clothes to get them ready for our trip tomorrow. I read EL UNIVERSO in detail; I didn't get through it all yesterday and finish up today. I'm in shock when I see a photo of Fells Point in Baltimore totally under water and a man wading through water almost reaching his arm pits.

"I stood here only two months ago, almost to the day," I point out to Angela showing her the exact spot on the photo. "Look at it now! This is a very beautiful old area with red brick buildings, stores, boutiques and restaurants. All this is now under water."

"You were in Baltimore also?" asks Angela.

"Yes. I visited my room mate from my China trip two years ago. Carolyn had invited me to come when she learned I was visiting Pennsylvania. I wonder how she's doing. Baltimore is a beautiful city and I had perfect weather there. I must call her when I get home."

Another headline reads how Wesley Clark, the new democratic presidential contender, asks Bush to tell the truth about Iraq. Ha, wishful thinking!

In today's EL UNIVERSO, there is an extra inlay called DOMINGO - Sunday - which, under the heading of *Overweight, the Enemy of Public Health,* devotes three pages to overweight people and the hazards they face daily, starting with many illnesses which limit their enjoyment of life, shortens their life span, makes it difficult for them to find clothes in their size not to speak of the problems they face finding employment, insurance, a doctor who will treat them and the jokes they have to listen to from family, friends and strangers. This new phenomenon is largely blamed on fast food and a sedentary society which needs to be educated. Sounds familiar - I've read and heard the same back home.

Another heading catches my eye, namely that the Amazon area was home to an advanced civilization before Christopher Columbus reached the new world. Through Satellite images and follow-up excavations in the Xingu zone of the upper Amazon by the University of Florida, together with other scientists and indigenous people, a net of well planned out villages has been discovered complete with plazas, bridges and ditches, connected with pathways, displaying advanced engineering abilities. It further shows that fields were cultivated and that the area was not at all *primitive*. It's believed that between two thousand five hundred and five thousand people lived in each village before the arrival of the Europeans. The carbon 14 method dates the peak of these villages to about one thousand two hundred fifty and fourteen hundred. After the arrival of Europeans, the population declined. From two photos accompanying the article, showing refined designs of clay pot artifacts, it's evident that they don't represent the very beginning of pottery anywhere. And here we thought for so long that the jungle was only inhabited by the simplest of tribes.

Then I walk to the Malecón to the ticket office to get some tickets for tonight's performance, the last one of the eight of the International Art Festival.

A large crowd is present for this performance from India, called *Astad Debbo*, consisting of two parts. Five men from northern India perform a dance which is about body and muscle control. The performance lasts over an hour and is amazing, alone in its physical endurance and accomplishments.

Right after that, two *old* men march up to the stage in the middle isle right through the crowd and start entertaining by satirical conversations and comments about every day life in Ecuador. I could understand most everything as they spoke very clearly and reading the paper daily, I get the political jokes as well and truly enjoy this. They receive much laughter and applause with people still laughing all the way out.

Monday 9/22/03

Amazonia here we come! Angela and I are actually on the bus to go to El Oriente; till the last minute I was wondering if it would happen but here we are.

The bus is comfortable, our bags are right above us. We packed lightly but also have a sandwich, an apple, a bottle of water along for the bus ride. At first we travel through banana plantations on both sides of the road. Then we are climbing up to the high Sierra which is absolutely beautiful with picturesque villages and small towns here and there. Everything looks very clean, much cleaner than in the warmer, more humid climate at the coast. Angela dozes off and on while I enjoy the view. Heading to Riobamba, Ambato & Baños is like new country for me as I haven't been here for many years.

"Tell me when we are in Riobamba," I say to her because sometimes the signs are easy to miss or not even present. "All my life I've wanted to see Riobamba. When I was very young, I had read a book by somebody who talked about his travels in South America and mentioned Riobamba in particular. Ri-o-bam-ba - the sound of it still fascinates me. Is it beautiful?"

"Oh yes, it is. I have a girl-friend there and over the years have been in Riobamba many times. This time, however, we can't stop here because we have far to go. This will have to be a future trip."

Then we see it - *Bienvenido a la Sultana de los Andes - Riobamba* - the large, very visible, welcome sign announces. For me a dream fulfilled! Riobamba is the capital of Chimborazo Province, situated at an elevation of nine thousand feet in a basin of the Andes. This Riobamba was relocated to the east in 1797 after an earthquake and landslide destroyed the original Riobamba founded in 1534. Ecuador, having so many active volcanoes, one or two of which are forever spewing at least ashes and rumbling, has suffered many destructions by eruption or earthquake and landslide. People are used to it and unless directly affected by an eruption, don't dwell on the ever-present danger.

The bus takes us through the city into the center and I'm excited to be here and see with my own eyes a large part of Riobamba, craning my neck in every direction trying to see as much as possible. The divided main street, planted with trees in the middle, is flanked by some beautiful architecture and looks very clean. Indian women in their colorful skirts and dark hats, babies on their backs, are everywhere. It comes to me there are not many women without a baby slung on their back. They all walk slightly bent over, due to carrying either a baby or some other load on their backs. Another reason is, of course, that they are forever climbing up, sometimes enormous hills, on small narrow paths. Too bad we don't have enough time now to stay here.

All too soon we leave Riobamba again and watch the Indian woman across the isle from us. She has a baby of about one year in her arms which is presently sleeping. Four more children, two boys and two girls, cleanly dressed and very nice looking are around her.

The girls in their white, lacy gowns, squeezed in beside her while the two boys are now in the seats behind us. We don't even hear them. There is no shuffling and fighting, no noise. They are extremely well behaved, something I have noticed many times on my travels.

Then the baby wakes up again feeling for her mother's breast and starts feeding.

"This is what they do here," Angela whispers in my ear; "where ever these women are, public place or not, they breastfeed their babies."

The little girl is very cute - she doesn't cry either - Angela and I watch her off and on during our trip. Finally we start talking with the mother, slender and nice looking herself, and this after five children. I ask her if I could take a picture of her and the baby which she doesn't mind. The baby is feeding most of the rest of the way; the mother unperturbed doesn't even try to cover up. The woman tells us they are visiting family in Ambato, probably some grandparents they left behind. We have a pleasant little conversation with her and admire the cute baby with its big dark eyes until they leave the bus in Ambato, another clean city with many stores carrying everything which we noticed in Riobamba as well. The majority of the population in these Andean cities is indigenous. The very steep, green mountains and pastures remind us of Switzerland just like around Otavalo and Ibarra north of Quito close to the Colombian border. It's beautiful here.

At the entrance of these towns of the high Sierra there is often a monument displaying huge fruit and vegetables showing the fertility of the land, the mother earth supporting its grateful people. Due to the fertility of the soil caused by the erupting volcanoes, the vegetables grow so much larger in this elevation than anywhere else. Sometimes the monument includes a person.

On this beautiful clear day, while coming to Riobamba and Ambato, we are suddenly face to face with the volcano Chimborazo in all its might and glory to our left. It towers over the land, a wisp of a cloud - or is it smoke - topping off its peak. I wished I could take a photo, but the bus hurries along having to keep a schedule.

Finally we are on the last leg of our trip for today, approaching Baños where we arrive around seven in the evening. A taxi takes us to the Sangay Hotel Ivanovich had recommended because of its hot and mineral rich healing waters coming from the volcano Tungurahua. There are many hot springs and spas here as the name, Baños, indicates.

"This is something you have to do. That is what Baños is all about," Ivan had told me. "Otherwise why go there."

Right, I thought listening carefully to all he had to say. I took my notes to make sure we would see - if not all - at least most of what there was to see. He had been this way years ago and passed on much valuable information to me.

Angela does all the talking and reserving of the room, because the rates are often different for Ecuadorians than for Gringos. We end up with a suite, two rooms with enough beds to sleep five people for thirty dollars. Arrangements like these come in handy for families who come here for a little spa vacation. We drop our bags in our rooms and head towards the dining rooms. There are two; one holds a large group of Dutch tourists, while the smaller and nicer dining room has a few Ecuadorians enjoying a drink and dinner. We have a most delicious dinner, starting with a big salad, trout with potatoes and vegetables. After all, this is trout country and the best potatoes grow here and in Peru. We wash everything down with some excellent wine - even Angela joins me in a glass of wine - ending the day in a most agreeable way.

Tuesday, 9/23/03

We wake up early and I put on my bathing suit to go across the street into the hot pools. Angela doesn't want to come so I take a towel and walk to the spa where I find many already enjoying the hot pools. Some of the Dutch people from last night are there, some French, some Ecuadorians and I. The hot water, I find out, is really hot in some pools and high in sulfide and salt with many other minerals. The pool I am in has a bearable temperature, while another one I try out later is awfully hot. I ease in and down but can't bear it long while some people, in there already before I came, are still sitting there up to their armpits in hot water. I don't know how they do it - I surely can't but when I hear them speak, I realize they are locals and come here all the time. In fact one man tells another that this is how his every day starts out. No wonder - they are used to it!

I spend a good hour in there enjoying every minute, regretting the fact that we can't stay longer. I make a mental note that I'll come back some other time because right now we want to still see so much more and it's a long way to go.

After breakfast I rush out to take a taxi to the Cataracts of Ballion. Angela refuses to come. "I have seen the Iguazu Falls in Brazil and Niagara Falls and these here are just little."

"I have seen them also, but hopefully this is worth seeing also."

Of course, we have been told we have to climb down and up which is something she can't do. The taxi driver is a very nice man called Ramiro and definitely Indian although he tells me that only his mother was Indian and his father Spanish. I don't care either way because I don't judge people by their ancestry, just by the way they are. Besides, I like Indian people and their sense of humor which I've seen many times and never had one bad experience with one yet, neither in Arizona, New Mexico, Central or South America. Ramiro is super, I find out very quickly. He's amiable and talkative, pointing out the surrounding to me. Baños is situated in a narrow valley of the Andes surrounded by very green, steep mountains. Now we are driving in a narrow canyon with towering mountains on our left, seemingly leading straight into the sky. To our right we are looking down into a river hurrying along deep below also flanked on the other side with high mountains. Right now, there are wisps of clouds hanging here and there until Ramiro points out Tungurahua to me saying that the gray cloud, obstructing a clear view of the peak, is neither mist nor clouds but ashes. Hmm!

"Aren't you afraid of this volcano?"

"No."

"But there is much destruction all the time and there could be a big eruption or explosion. You know about Mt. Rainier in the State of Washington. People never thought of anything like that happening."

"Sí, es possible," he nods his head. "We have been fortunate here. The wind usually blows the ashes the other way towards Ambato and Riobamba. We have very little fallout if any at all in Baños."

"Oh, I see. Of course, this could change."

"Sí. Then we clean up and all is well again. These volcanoes support our lives. The fertile soil is giving us big, good vegetables and potatoes, the hot springs in Baños are attracting tourists from all over the world who want to see what is around here, like you are doing right now," he answers smiling at me.

"Sí," I return the smile. "What else is there to do here? Not much, I think."

"Mucho," Ramiro answers. "We have horseback riding and tours as well. Whole families come and spend a week or more here to enjoy what we have to offer."

I'm indeed beginning to see. Ramiro stops here and there so I can admire the many waterfalls of various sizes slamming down the side of the canyon along the way. At one stop a man comes up a path with his mule. The mule looks sad to me as most mules do and some horses also. Here and there a single house peaks down at us from across the river and sometimes there is even a cluster of homes seemingly glued to the side of the mountains. We pass two suspension bridges crossing the Río Pastaza we are presently following. Rio Pastaza seems to spring from the volcano Chimborazo and is one of the main tributaries flowing into the Río Marañon which is later called Rio Amazonas. Of course, where we are traveling now, it doesn't at all resemble the mighty river it's becoming later.

The road along the river isn't paved either once we are out of Baños. There are many pot holes and rocks in our path which make Ramiro maneuver the car slowly to avoid big problems. Finally the road crosses the Río Verde and looking down I see a few women sitting on some rocks, little colorful specks, washing their clothes in the cold clear waters of the river.

We have arrived. Ramiro stops the car and we start descending down a hair needle shaped path in good condition and about two yards wide. I wear the perfect footwear for this occasion, my platform sandals - very comfortable - not so good for the way down, better for the way up. Ramiro said they would be okay to get down and he was right. It was certainly easier than walking on my platform high heels on a glacier in Alaska some years ago.

The path is well maintained with some stairs here and there where it's a little steeper. We are in the Rain Forest displaying an amazing variety of plants which Ramiro points out to me, especially bromeliads and orchids. He also has me taste a grass that has lemon flavor. It's quite warm and humid and rather misty. We are nearing the waterfall and walk out on the little suspension bridge below we had seen from above. While on the bridge and looking back I notice a steep rock wall to one side, an uplift formation, which looks as if sheet after sheet of gray rock had been neatly stacked on top of each other. One part of it looks like a honeycomb where erosion has apparently eaten away at the flat sheets. It's a most unusual formation which fascinates me; ever since I've taken a class in geology at college, I look at the world around me with different eyes. It would be nice to get closer to check the rock out - could be limestone - but that's impossible with all the growth and my sandals!

Stepping off the bridge again we now have to climb. The last part is steep. A restaurant is perched on a rock platform among all the trees and plants but we have to climb even higher to get to the waterfall called *Pailón del Diablo*. I feel the mist around me as I get closer to take a photo of the cataract, a huge cascade of water falling down the steep side of the cliff, surrounded by a giant cloud of mist. I wipe my camera carefully afterwards and do not linger in this wetness. Well, perhaps the waterfall is very little compared to the others Angela and I had seen but the whole trip was well worth it.

We walk back down again to where the restaurant is. Ramiro points out all the orchids around us. The flora is amazing with plant growth shooting out of the limbs of the trees. Then we climb up again walking at a crisp pace and once on top, Ramiro admiringly comments: "You are in very good physical condition."

"Gracias! Walking and swimming almost daily and eating relatively healthy helps I suppose." Ramiro nods his head repeating again that I'm in very good physical condition.

We walk back to the car to start our return trip. Ramiro suggests we go here and there, but I make it clear to him that my friend is waiting and I've to get back to Baños. Once back in the car another interesting conversation develops. In the morning driving out Ramiro had, of course, asked where I came from and where I learned Spanish so well, etc. the usual conversation with people one meets for the first time. Hearing that I'm from the States he tells me that quite a few Americans are coming to Baños, especially women by themselves. And, according to Ramiro, they are coming for a reason: Indigenous people are very strong and the men are in better condition than their American counterparts and perform better in bed.

"Really!" I answered laughing. "I never heard that before and can't comment since I have no comparison." I've been propositioned before by a very young man who wanted to follow me to the end of the earth and a taxi driver in Punta Arenas - at the end of the earth - on the way to the airport; I just laugh it off.

"At least," adds Ramiro, "this is what they say. Quite a few American women come here to have affairs with the men."

"Perhaps, I wouldn't know."

Then I remembered the trip on the Amazon so many years ago. Our bartender told me one night that he was engaged to an American woman, a lawyer. He said he would be going to New York in about ten days to be married. He was very excited about this upcoming change and could hardly wait. I found this revelation most interesting, because this relationship would certainly not be based on intellectual or cultural equality. All I could think was 'poor man,' as I looked out at the most spectacular sunset over the Amazon, wondering how he would feel after a while having exchanged this beautiful Amazonian jungle for the asphalt jungle of New York. He said he was born here and lived all his life here. What a rough awakening would be in store for him!

Ramiro brought me back to the present pointing out another waterfall. This was on the way out. Now returning, our conversation goes as follows:

"Ramiro, the families here have many children; how many brothers and sisters do you have?"

"My mother had twenty-three children."

"She had twenty-three children - your poor mother!"

"She was very happy."

"She was a baby factory."

"Sí, es la verdad. Today, fourteen of us are still alive."

"Fourteen? Are you one of the older or younger ones?"

"I am one of the youngest. My father died when he was eighty-three and my mother when she was sixty."

He shows me the little village across the river he came from saying how driving a taxi is so much better. "Most of the people here work from seven in the morning to four or five in the afternoon and all they get paid is four or five dollars. You can't do anything or go anywhere with that."

"No, you certainly can't."

"With this taxi I earn so much more each day, even if I only have one person like you today. This money will be enough for me and I'll stay home in the afternoon. Sometimes I have two tours a day, one in the morning and one in the afternoon." I paid fourteen dollars.

"Are you married and do you have children?" I ask.

"Sí, I have two daughters. One is three and a half and the other is six months.

"How nice; do you want more children?"

"No, two children, that's it for me."

"Good for you, children are expensive. This way you'll be able to afford a good education for your daughters and they can work their way up."

"Exactamente. No quiero más que dos."

Ramiro is nice to talk with. He regrets that I don't have more time to stay longer because he was thinking to call a friend to introduce me to and go out with. "He's very nice and I'm sure you would have a good time with him."

"That will have to wait for another time," I tell him with a laugh. Taxi service doesn't seem to be Ramiro's only business.

"Ciao, Ramiro, y muchas gracias por todo."

"Ciao y que te vayas bien!"

Back at the hotel Angela is curious about my trip. I tell her that it wasn't Iguazu Cataracts we had visited together on our *Around South America Trip* years ago, but it was a nice tour in the area. She had also taken a little taxi tour in Baños and ended up in a place where they had many snakes which was not to her liking. I'm glad she did something. We take a taxi to the terminal and leave in a very short time for Tena, closer to Amazonia.

We travel the same road of the morning, passing Tungurahua, barely visible now. Then we suddenly have the jungle to both sides of the road which is not in good condition either, unpaved and often very narrow so that I wonder how two big vehicles can ever pass by each other. I find out shortly, they make it all the time, even if one vehicle has to wait at a slightly wider spot for the other to pass. Nothing to worry about!

The road is full of potholes and rocks so that the bus moves slowly. Then there is constant coming and going of people. Whenever people wait at the roadside the bus will stop and pick them up. When somebody wants to get off, they will say "Gracias" and the bus driver stops while the passenger will hand a coin or two to the assistant responsible to collect the fare. The school children don't pay. I think we both paid about eight dollars total or so for this stretch of the trip.

The bus picks up the school children from their homes hidden in the jungle and takes them to school and back to their homes again along the road. I see quite a few children get off in the middle of the jungle, so to speak, with no house visible.

Again, I cannot stress enough how well these children are behaved and how nice they look in their school uniforms worn by all school children in Ecuador. Not to mention how beautiful they are. I don't see any fat children here at all. They look like children are supposed to look, slender, alert and quite tall. They'll probably be taller than their parents one day.

We travel a very winding up and down road. The jungle looks ever thicker - even right from the edge of the road it appears impenetrable to me. Ramiro had told me that there are many poisonous snakes here. One has to be very careful.

"What do you do when you walk up to your houses and you suddenly come upon a snake?" I had asked him.

"We kill it; we always carry a stick with us and we beat it to death so it can't harm our children. One has to do that, you know."

I had observed that all the Indians have a walking stick, more like a pole, to help them walk up and down hill and over all terrain. This stick serves for other purposes as well.

A young student sits next to me going home on vacation. Angela and I prefer to sit up front if possible. There were two seats left, one on each side of the isle, so we sit across from each other. Jorge and I start talking - no better way of getting information - and he tells me he is twenty years old and in his third semester at the university in Ambato where he studies engineering. His father and only sister are also on the bus, in the seat behind us, I find out. He has four more brothers, so there are six children in the family. Tena is their home and he will have to be back in school by October first. That's not a long vacation. Jorge points out certain landmarks along the way and we both look at my map to find out exactly where we are. Out in nowhere, it seems, there is a very modern glass and steel building which Jorge identifies as part of the University. He's a very pleasant traveling companion.

Arriving in Puyo, we have a little stopover to eat. I use the time to look around town but there isn't much to see. The sky is overcast and the streets are wet. During my short walk it starts raining again rather heavily and I quickly dart for shelter under an overhang where some people are already assembled to wait out the shower which doesn't last long but the rain comes down in sheets.

Once back at the bus, we start rolling again. The road now is quite bad in parts, washed out at times, a sign of much rain in the area. We pass road building equipment and crews in many places where the road has been widened and graded. All that's needed is the hard top. We are both glad we took the bus and didn't go by car. The driver does an excellent job as he eases the bus around curves, past other vehicles trying to avoid pot holes, rocks and the road falling off. He's crawling along at a snail's pace.

"This is the Rio Mulato," Jorge points to the large river we are just crossing. "It's joining the Rio Napo here. Now we are almost in Tena."

"Do you like living here?"

"Sí," he tells me as the outskirts of the little town become visible.

"It doesn't look as though there is much to do for young people."

"Oh yes. We have a movie theatre and we have some discos where we can go dancing."

"I see."

"Sometimes we have parties with our friends. There is much to do here. I also play soccer on the soccer team which I really enjoy."

"I see! Do you also play soccer in Ambato?"

"Sí. I'm on a team there as well."

The bus stops somewhere on what looks like the main street and Jorge says good-bye. I tell him what a nice travel companion he has been and wish him a good vacation. His face lights up with a smile. "Gracias," he says waving his hand before he follows his father and sister off the bus.

We go a little further to the terminal. Angela makes some inquiries on how best to get to the Anaconda Hotel at the Napo River which Ivanovich had recommended to us. We take a taxi and the long way to the Rio Napo because we are unfamiliar with the area. It's quite a ride, not cheap either, which takes us to Misahualli, a most picturesque little town with an interesting plaza. I would have loved to spend some time here but Angela wants to get to the hotel. She's right, of course, because it's evening and we have no idea how far we still have to go. The taxi driver takes us to the bank of the river where various long and slender boats are waiting for passengers. He calls out to the men standing around there that we would like to go to the Anaconda Hotel. Yes, he can take us for fifty dollars which we both find extremely high. Angela asks if he can't come down a little. "No, I can't because it takes forty-five minutes to go there."

Another man walks over followed by one very unpleasant looking guy saying he can take us at his best discounted price which is only seventy dollars. Really! We are haggling a little almost considering not going at all.

"Well, let's leave," Angela says as we both walk back to the taxi. Now what? She talks with the driver and he wants to know, do we go back to Tena or do we stay here. Back and forth we discuss the matter and then think maybe this young Indian boy we talked with before this unpleasant man interrupted with the much higher price, would be willing to take us for less. So the taxi takes us back down to the river where the driver and Angela talk directly with the young man again. He agrees to make an exception and take us for forty dollars to the Anaconda Hotel, saying he wasn't going to make any money because it was a long ride. Besides it's late by now and we really need to hurry.

We grab our bags and set them down in the boat, the bottom of which is covered by a wooden grate. It doesn't take long either and I know why. I manage to take one photo of Angela standing in the canoe with our bags - the other men in the background are not looking happy - when the Indian boy pushes away from the bank. Clumsily we climb into the boat and move to the middle of the canoe, where the Indian boy wants us to sit side by side. Light-footed and sure the boy walks from one end of the boat to the other to start the electric motor. We are on our way on the turbulent Rio Napo riding the waves into the sunset. The Rio Napo is one of the major tributaries to the Rio Amazonas. It flows into the Rio Marañón, as it is called here, which later becomes the Rio Amazonas somewhere around Iquitos, Peru. There are a few more rather large rivers, the Rio Tigre, Rio Morona and Rio Santiago, but the Rio Pastaza and Rio Napo are definitely the two largest ones. I don't think I ever consciously realized before, that both these rivers have their beginnings in Ecuador.

The young Indian guides the boat expertly from side to side or down the middle through this very fast moving river avoiding large rocks or outcrops or sandbanks, actually rock banks, dispersed throughout the Rio Napo. I see rocks everywhere. Still, we move at considerable speed with the boat leaning into the waves more and more. The rim of the boat is hardly above the water to begin with and sure enough, another sharp left turn in the turbulent waters creates a big wave and much spray with a swash of water smashing over the edge soaking my left side from the waist all the way down to the leg. For a moment I fear we would capsize right here and now. After all, I had witnessed a capsizing just like that on the Amazon during my four-day trip from Iquitos some years ago. A narrow long boat, just like ours, lying low in the water, was hit by the wave from our larger boat and next thing I saw all three people in the river trying to catch and hang on to the boat. So these things do happen. I'm also wondering if the Indian did this purposely. Well, what am I thinking? This is our adventure!

"I was almost afraid we would end up in the water and have to swim with the Anaconda," says Angela.

"Same here; look at me, I'm all soaked and I feel cold now." The air is rather cool because we move at such speed, but I control this sense of cold as best I can. What the fast moving speed does also, it dries my pants and blouse fast.

Meanwhile the sun is setting rapidly and the jungle to both sides of the river becomes ever darker. Some very tall trees tower above the rest of the jungle, perfectly outlined against the colorful evening sky. Here and there we see some people along the edge of the Rio Napo taking their evening baths. Another late boat is hurrying along to somewhere because I don't see houses. While I take all this in, the scenery, the setting sun, the beauty and wonder of actually traveling on this powerful river in Amazonia, old memories come back to me from years ago while traveling on the Amazon.

We were about thirty tourists on this boat, most of them travel agents from Australia and a few of us from the States. We enjoyed sitting along the boat in the deck chairs, feet propped up on the reeling, looking out over the river and the jungle - sometimes far away depending on the width of the river. I always loved this evening time on the Amazon when the green jungle became dark and the blue sky would turn into a spectrum of color. A lone bird might streak across the sky hurrying to his favorite tree or a cry would break the silence. Best of all was one night when we went in small boats to see alligators and were surrounded by a symphony of sound created by thousands of frogs and toads the like of which I've never heard before or since.

But here we are now on the Rio Napo and, coming around a bend in the river, we look directly at a big house standing high up on the banks. Thinking we've arrived Angela asks the Indian if this is it but he answers it's the Swiss Hotel, very nice and very expensive owned by somebody from Switzerland. The Anaconda is further down the river. We travel for some more time on the fierce, unpredictable river until suddenly stopping somewhere along the river bank covered with huge rocks. The Indian tells us that we have arrived.

"Are you sure?" I ask in disbelief.

"Sí, es el Anaconda Hotel."

"Where are the steps?" Angela asks looking around at the steep bank covered with nothing but topsy-turvy big rocks to protect the river bank from being washed away.

"No hay casa," I throw in, seeing no building whatsoever.

"Sí, hay," he answers suggesting I climb up. I get out and climb up the side of the bank, hanging on to the rocks hoping I won't break a leg and wondering how Angela is going to get up here. What was Ivanovich thinking recommending this place to us?

Sure enough, once on top of the bank, I can see beautiful landscaping and buildings.

"Angela, come up. There are really buildings here but not a soul in sight."

With the Indian pushing and me holding out my hand, Angela stumbles up but not without looking for and admiring beautiful rocks until the Indian says he really needs to leave as it's getting dark. He brings up her bag; I had taken mine along. Standing on top of the bank, we look down at the fast moving river and the erosion around us. There had been some steps here before but the currents had eventually taken them out as the banks are retreating ever further.

"Angela, we have to pay him," I say turning around and looking at the young boat man in front of us. She usually pays up front when we travel.

She pulls out some money and hands it to him thanking him for getting us here safely but also asking where the people are.

"Gracias," he answers calling out for whoever is living here. It takes a while before a young Indian woman walks up. The boat man talks with her briefly and then is on his way with our eyes following him.

"Hola! Cómo estás?" I greet the young, pretty woman.

"Hola!" she answers obviously surprised to see us here so unexpectedly. She exchanges a few words with Angela before she leaves again and then returns after some time with a baby in her arms and a man pushing a wheel barrow loaded with bananas for the monkeys he tells us. They want to know who we are and what brought us here and do we have reservations. No, we have no reservations. So how do we know about the Anaconda Hotel? We tell him that Angela's son had been here years ago and recommended the Anaconda for its uniqueness. Fernando, he introduced himself to us, wants to know when he was here because he says he's been here for more than twelve years and with his wife manages the place. They stay for twenty-two days and then are off for eight days, Fernando informs us. Then another couple fills in for them for these eight days. We are impressed because the gardens look very well kept but we don't know exactly when Ivanovich was here with his family. Probably more than ten years ago. Do they have a room, we ask. Yes, they have plenty of rooms; we are the only guests here. A group of fifteen Dutch people had left the day before. He tells us that the young woman is his wife, called Melia and this is their daughter, Angela, who is two years old. Melia is a very nice looking young woman and little Angela is as cute as can be. I already made friends with her by stepping over and talking with her and her mother. A nice young family, I can't help but think.

We ask if we could have some dinner and are told Melia will prepare it for us. Then Fernando takes us to our little house because this particular hotel consists of individual huts of one room, containing two beds for two people and a bathroom with shower. There is a real door that can be locked and huge windows on two sides covered with screens to keep the bugs out and allow the air to pass through. A veranda in front with hammocks, a table and chairs is most inviting. A few steps lead up to it. The houses are entirely of wood with metal roofs, the room inside is also all natural stained wood and very clean and neat with a functioning bathroom. We put our bags down and then go outside to follow Fernando to look at the animals he keeps and admire the beautifully manicured property.

There is a rather long Anaconda, not fat yet, in a fenced-in cage with pool. Fernando tells us that he caught this one right here in the Rio Napo. I'm so glad our boat didn't turn over! There are some small monkeys, a toucan, a lorry, a deer, a pig, etc. We walk around admiring everything before we go to the big open platform made entirely of wood and beautifully polished used for dinner and parties. Many tables and chairs await large groups with one table in the middle nicely set up with table cloth, flowers and a candle ready for us. Electricity is produced by generators lighting up the platform and the kitchen area. Otherwise the world around us by now is pitch dark. While we walked around with Fernando, Melia has prepared a very nice dinner for us consisting of salad, vegetables and chicken, everything very tasty and very nice. Yet, for some unknown reason, Angela expresses a concern about the cleanliness of the meal.

"Angela, why shouldn't the meal be good and clean; they have tourists here all the time and I'm sure Melia knows how to prepare everything properly."

As for me, I enjoy every bite and the whole atmosphere of *la selva en la noche*, very quiet so far. Fernando walks up to us holding the tiniest of monkeys on his arm with a very cute face and alert eyes. We admire it and take a photo. When Fernando returns, I ask him if we can't have a drink. He regrets that there's nothing left because the Dutch group finished every drop and he needs to go shopping tomorrow for supplies before the next group comes the day after. But, he adds, he has some homemade chicha which the Indian people make for themselves for special occasions and would I like to have a cup of this? Yes, I would. It's made from sugar corn and served with Guayaba juice and hot water.

He brings a little coffee pot with this drink and some cups and starts pouring. Angela refuses to have any, even after I tell her that it's very good and she should try a cup. Fernando joins me in a drink and because it's really good, I have a little more while he tells us that they are from Tena but that they love to be here in the Anaconda Hotel and meet people from all over the world. They will go back and visit their families tomorrow when they have to go to town to make their purchases.

By now it's around nine in the evening and time to go to bed. Fernando hands us two candles, one lit to walk back to our little cabin and one for the room. We wonder aloud if we'll find the way back in this darkness, but Fernando tells us how to walk and says we should have no problem; it's easy to find. Well, having our doubts already, Angela and I start walking. We walk very slowly holding on to each other with the one lit candle, stepping carefully and peering into the absolute darkness ahead of us. We follow a path, take a slight turn and walk on when suddenly it appears to end.

"I think we are wrong," I say to Angela.

"No we are right. I see the house right there."

"Where? I see nothing but what appears to be jungle. Fernando should have come with us and not let us walk by ourselves."

"No. I see the house already!"

"There is no house. Let's go back and get Fernando. We are lost. I see nothing but what looks like trees."

"Okay," she replies.

Carefully we walk back towards the light from the kitchen because the dining platform is dark by now as well.

"Fernando," we call, "we need help."

Fernando accompanies us. The first thing he does is to wrap a big leaf loosely around the candle turning it into an instant lamp giving out much more light to our surprise because the glare is gone. Sure enough, we were headed into the wrong direction - straight into the jungle. We say good night again and walk up the steps into our little cabaña. Once inside, we light the other candle also and put one in the bedroom and one in the bathroom. Perfect! We are all set and happy to go to bed after this long full and wonderful day. I'm just so lucky to be here and see all this.

I cannot sleep quickly and look up at the sky through the glass windows at the very top of the cabin. Millions and millions of the brightest stars I've ever seen are sparkling and blinking above, appearing far more brilliant because of the darkness of the jungle Fernando had told us. How lucky we can marvel at the universe from this unspoiled part of the world.

Wednesday, 9/24/03

Waking up early, I see Angela moving around.

"Are you okay? What are you doing up so early?"

"I have diarrhea and soiled the bed. Can you believe this?" she answers turning around completely disgusted.

"You have diarrhea just like that? Listen, this is supposed to happen to me; I'm the Gringa, not you!" I look at her standing there with all these sheets.

"I told you last night I didn't trust the dinner and now this. You can put this in your book: I soiled the bed," she spouts furiously.

"We ate the same food. It was very tasty. I noticed no bad taste at all."

"Neither did I, but I had this strange feeling."

"What did you buy from the vendors on the bus?"

"Nothing."

"We ate the same - the only difference being I had the chicha afterwards, the medicine, which kills many germs."

Ursula B. Borck

"That's true. I should have had some also. There is no water here for me to wash out the sheets a little. Can you please go and tell Fernando we need water?"

Instead of a night gown, I wear this little house/beach shirt I bought at the Indian Market in Guayaquil thinking this might come in handy on the trip - just in case - and here we are. I find Fernando, Melia and little Angela up and busy already. They are obviously surprised to hear the news and Fernando promises he'll get *la bomba* going at once so that the water should be flowing shortly. I walk back slowly to our cabaña enjoying the silence of the early morning in the jungle, interrupted only by a bird call here or there. Once back at the cabin, Angela turns the faucet on but no water. I head back again to the kitchen and tell Melia, who says that Fernando is working on it right now and there should be water by the time I get back.

I hear some pounding and walking in the direction of the river, I see Fernando working on the water pump right at the sloping bank between some big rocks. Erosion moving inland! He is pounding away at the pump; no need to talk to Fernando again. I turn around once more, slowly meandering back to our little cabin. Departing I suddenly hear the motor humming. Good, it's working.

Angela turns on the faucet and the water is indeed flowing. She cleans up and washes and we both take our showers, a short one for me because the water is cold, before we walk to the dining platform for breakfast. Angela is determined to eat only a piece of bread, definitely no fruit which means I have two pieces of fruit. Fernando and Melia can't believe what happened and Melia agrees to wash her pants and dry them by ironing. Angela had washed her underwear now decoratively spread over some bushes waiting to be dried by the sun.

Every ten minutes she has to run to the bathroom and each time she emerges wearing another pair of shorts until she runs out of shorts and appears with a towel wrapped around her, walking in her usual composed way as if this were the most natural way to appear. She also has a great sense of humor and laughs when I comment on her latest fashion. Luckily the towel appearance is her last trip to the bathroom. If this had to happen, how good it happened here and we were the only guests.

Melia is so nice and takes care of all of Angela's laundry, while we follow Fernando around feeding all the animals. He opens the cage of the Anaconda to walk in, sticks in his hands, and pulls her more into the light so we can see her better. Little Angela follows him right inside. I lift her up so she can look in from the top because the sides are covered and she can't see. The Anaconda looks a lot larger today than she had appeared to me last night but her head is relatively small. She doesn't really like to be moved around and rears her head slightly, eyeing us suspiciously.

Fernando has offered to take us along in their hotel boat and says we won't have to leave till eleven in the morning, because our bus is not leaving until about noon. So we are back at the dining veranda when little Angela comes looking for me dressed in only a T-shirt, holding out her pants. We had become friends fast. She's totally toilet trained at the age of two Melia told me yesterday.

"Come, I'll help you dress," I say, putting on her pants.

It doesn't take long before she brings me her socks, shoes and shoelaces. I get her all dressed, knowing her mother has no time being busy with Angela's clothes. She is too cute and follows us around everywhere. I'll miss her I know that already and won't forget her.

Angela is feeling much better by now which makes both of us very happy. If the diarrhea were not so serious, the whole episode would be extremely funny.

Another very young Indian girl comes up towards us, greeting us friendly, carrying a baby on her back. She looks no older than fourteen or so, very pretty face and very slender - just a little girl. I find out that the baby on her back is not her brother but her son and is about ten months. An older man, slightly limping, thin and not very tall walks ahead of her. I take them for father and daughter until Angela tells me that this is her husband and they are the people to fill in now for Fernando and his wife. He has to be at least forty years older than she and she is so beautiful and so young.

"This is what they do here", Angela fills me in. "The young girls often have no say in these things as long as the husband provides for them." I feel sorry for her.

We leave around eleven in one of these long, narrow boats being the only means of transportation here. Everybody uses the boats for visits, shopping or transfer of goods and tourists. We are looking forward to this boat trip because we love being on the Rio Napo again. It looks different this morning. The jungle on both sides is not so dark and forbidding in the morning sun, but the water still rushes along with the same urgency, skillfully navigated by the people who call the jungle their home. They know how to avoid all the big rocks, above and below the water and all the rock banks popping up here and there. Their navigational skills are something to behold. We both feel we can trust our boats man completely.

There is more traffic on the Rio Napo as other boats hurry along up and down stream. The temperature is a little higher, but speeding down the river, a nice breeze keeps us cool. I wished we could just travel on and on but we do arrive at the landing from where the bus will take us to Puerto Francisco de Orellana simply called El Coca because it is located at the point where the Rio Coca joins the Rio Napo.

Fernando and his family are along to go to Tena to buy supplies for the new group of tourists arriving on Friday. After the bus ride together we say good-bye in Tena with big hugs all around. I'll miss this family, especially little Angela.

Once again we are on the bus surrounded by dense jungle on both sides of the road. Sometimes the road is so narrow that the crowns of the trees from both sides of the road touch in the middle providing a natural roof giving the impression we are driving through a tunnel. Then again we appear to be driving through a gorge with banks on both sides of the narrow road rising high, making it extremely dark. It's not an easy stretch to drive as the road is only partially paved and looks much more like an obstacle course than even the attempt of a highway. I admire the bus driver how he tries his best to circumvent rocks, big holes or huge puddles which can be very deep and dangerous. Yet again he stops to take people on where ever they are waiting on the side of the road or to let people off after hearing their *Gracias*. Also, there is all the dust from the road if a vehicle comes toward us or if we pass. We cannot close the windows. We need the air to keep comfortable because these buses have no air conditioning.

We are not going fast and it's easy for the many vendors to jump on or off the bus as is convenient for them. They offer everything from cooked meats to fruit, candy and *pan de yucca* which is very good but neither Angela nor I buy anything from them other than a bottled drink or ice cream. These vendors are all men of varying ages trying to make a living.

Then I see a tall mountain in the distance throughout this part of the journey which is popping up now and then as we drive through the terrain. It has to be a volcano by the shape of it. Out comes my map and sure enough, I see that three thousand nine hundred meters high Sumaco is to the left of our road. As the road climbs or dives the volcano appears or disappears until finally it reappears in front of us in all its might and glory against the red sunset of the approaching evening. A view to behold! There is truly nothing more beautiful or grander than nature. Trying to take a photo is impossible and when I finally ask the bus driver to stop, the bright red has turned into a grayish hue and doesn't look as beautiful anymore.

Something else is following the road and snaking along - the oil pipeline. Close to Tena we had noticed a refinery on the left side of the road and a big pipeline, slightly raised above ground. Sometimes it's below ground, then it jumps across little rivers and currents of which there are many here. This pipeline, however, doesn't have the circumference of the one in Alaska which I had seen many years ago. We are definitely in Amazonia - El Oriente - rich in oil and close to the Colombian border. People had warned us about the *bad* Colombians but I told them that I didn't think all Colombians were bad and I would just not worry. Neither is Angela a person who is afraid of her own shadow as so many people are. It appears to me that the people who have not been anywhere or done anything, always know all the horror stories.

Just as it's beginning to get dark, we arrive in El Coca. A taxi takes us to the hotel Ivanovich had recommended but we don't like it much. The room is hot and stuffy and the air conditioning doesn't appear to work well. Angela takes one look at the situation and suggests we leave again because she doesn't want to spend the night in a hot room. The taxi driver had mentioned another hotel to us, *La Misión,* and is now taking us there. El Coca is not a very big town but it does have more than one hotel.

We like *La Misión* immediately. The grounds are well kept, the room is much better with an air conditioning that works and they have a dining room which the other hotel didn't have either. We settle in quickly as it's eight in the evening by now and we were told the dining room closes by nine. Angela also talks with the receptionist, a very nice lady, about a tour for us tomorrow into the Rain Forest of Amazonia before we go to eat. While eating our dinner somebody called Patricio telephones us to say we have to go a minimum of three days and he mentions one price to Angela and another one to me which I don't find out till after the conversation. He also says we'll be doing a lot of walking in the Rain Forest which is fine with me but anathema to Angela who stresses she can't walk much. We end up discussing a day-tour for tomorrow.

Thursday, 9/25/03

After breakfast in the morning, Patricio appears and asks us to walk with him to the tour office to pay before we start the tour. Angela is not happy.

"What kind of a tour is this that makes you walk to their office? They are supposed to come and take us by taxi," she says.

"Oh, the office is so close and that's why we walk," Patricio replies.

It really isn't far but Angela has a point. Once at the office she tells me she isn't going, saying I can go if I want to, but she would not. Pointing to one of the typical colorful Ecuadorian buses which are open all around, she tells me this is what we'll be traveling in and she doesn't like it at all. For some reason I don't feel so excited about this tour either anymore, particularly since Angela would be left here with nothing to do. We tell Patricio, who doesn't look happy, and walk back to the hotel. *La Misión* is beautifully situated at the Rio Napo and offers a wonderful view over the river and the surrounding area. We stroll along, admiring the beautiful tropical garden and a colorful toucan who eyes us curiously as we pass.

"We should try to get another river tour," Angela suggests.

"That's a good idea. I would like that also."

However, this turns out to be no easy undertaking. Nobody is available, although there are boats and people standing around. We have to go to the harbor authority, we are told, if we want a tour. A taxi takes us there and we actually find somebody willing to take us. After some haggling about the price once again, three young men take us out in a little launch that even has a roof over the middle to protect us from the sun. We travel from the Rio Napo into the smaller Rio Coca which, the young men tell us, is more interesting. I think they are right because huts on both sides of the river can be seen, many on stilts to protect against wild animals and flooding. People are bathing and washing their clothes with laughing, happy children swimming in the water. Scenes like this fascinate me.

The three young men, one an Indian named Carlos, the driver a Colombian and the young man in charge, an Ecuadorian of German background with the name of Fritz are very friendly and entertaining. In fact Fritz is outright amusing. He wears a T-shirt which says *Chiemsee* in front. He tells me he has cousins in Germany but when I ask him where, he answers he doesn't know.

"Well, where does this T-shirt come from?"

"My cousins sent it to me!"

"Then they live in Southern Germany because the Chiemsee is located in the Alps."

"That's right. They live in the mountains," Fritz answers asking "Have you been there?"

"Yes, I was there when I was very young. It's beautiful and if you can you should go and visit your cousins."

"Perhaps one day. It's expensive and I have to save the money first."

Next the conversation turns to the giant Anaconda. Neither Angela nor I are very fond of snakes and as Fernando had told us, there are plenty of Anacondas in the area.

"Sí, they are here," we are told by the young men.

"Yet people are swimming in the river all the time. Aren't they afraid?" I ask.

"No, the Anaconda isn't everywhere," he replies.

Then Carlos tells me that he has been attacked by one while swimming in this very river.

"You have been attacked!" I exclaim. "What did you do? Did the snake coil around you and were you able to free yourself all by yourself?"

"No, I wasn't able to do it by myself; I had a friend with me who helped me to get free."

"You were lucky! Are you now afraid to swim in the river?"

"No."

"No? When did this happen?"

"It happened within the last year."

"You see," says Angela. "I tell you, there are Anaconda here and they do attack people."

"There was also a story in the paper within the last year, I believe, where a man had been attacked in his boat, killed and swallowed by a giant Anaconda," Fritz interjects.

"He was attacked in the boat!" I exclaim.

"Yes. He was out alone on the Rio Napo fishing. His wife became worried when he didn't return after some time had passed and turned to the authorities for help. They went looking and found the boat with his fishing gear, but not the man," Fritz tells us.

"Didn't anybody see the attack?" I asked.

"No," Fritz answers, "but they also found the snake a little later and noticed her unusual body shape telling them that she had eaten something big recently. They caught her, killed and opened the snake up and found the missing man inside with every bone in his body crushed."

"That is absolutely terrible," I answer shocked while Angela nods her head in agreement.

All the things we learn on this trip. Sebastian, the Colombian, tells us he, like so many of his fellow countrymen, came to live here because there are too many problems in his home country. He likes it here and the three are a team who work together all the time. The time with the young men in the boat passes by quickly and we enjoy this excursion with them and all their stories immensely.

Returning, Fritz asks me suddenly how old I am. I tell him he will have to guess and he comes up with fifty. We let him believe that he's close. Then he says they would like to take us out to a disco in the evening. We just laugh saying that we are grandmothers. He thinks this doesn't matter at all but we are leaving this afternoon. We pay and thank them for the wonderful tour which we enjoyed tremendously.

Angela is still determined to go further into Amazonia. I'm delighted that she actually wants to continue since this trip - the bus travel that is – isn't always a joy ride on these bad roads - not to mention the diarrhea episode. Besides, there is Amelia at home but she says that she talked with Ivanovich who told her all was well, not to worry and to go on and have a good time. We continue to Lago Agrio at the Río Aguarico close to the Colombian border. Perhaps we can get a tour into the jungle from there. Great!

We check out of the hotel and the taxi driver from earlier takes us around the town on a little sightseeing tour, but there really isn't that much to see. We are looking for a gift shop and find one which has mainly Indian headdresses, spears and a few masks - all things a little difficult to take along. The taxi driver takes us to the bus station and before we know it, we are on the road again to Lago Agrio.

Parts of the road are also in bad shape and the driver has his job cut out for him. The pipeline follows us again and we also pass by another refinery. One thing I notice is that the houses here are better built and larger. Even the typical wooden houses on stilts are larger and in better shape than we had seen in other parts of the country. These rectangular houses, also on stilts, usually have a closed-in room at each end while the middle platform is left open where the whole family congregates to eat, spend time with guests and enjoy the cool evening breeze passing through. I had observed this same type of house in the Amazon Rain Forest many years ago when I traveled by boat down the river with daily excursions into the jungle; families sitting on the large open middle platform, enjoying talking with friends who passed by below. It's ideal to visit with others and the equivalent to the open verandas of the early houses here in the States.

Besides the old style houses, there are new houses built of cement and bricks showing that the people here enjoyed a better income from the oil industry. Prosperity is on the way. We constantly take many people on board along the way and let them off again. Quite a few come with various tools like shovels, saws and machetes. I smile to myself thinking what fear that would cause in the States and how such a person would be quickly removed from the bus, retained and questioned. Nobody pays any attention to them here; it's just part of daily life. Others bring sacks of potatoes and vegetables into the bus and place them wherever there is some room. Usually the driver assistant helps them heave these heavy sacks up into the bus and then down again when the people leave somewhere into the dusty jungle. The women usually have their hands full with children anyway, beautiful children with large brown, curious eyes.

We arrive at the Rio Aguarico and have to wait for the ferry to take us across. There is no bridge. It's hot and I find a shady place to look out onto the river and watch the people selling drinks, fruit and ice cream from their little stands. Then we walk onto the ferry while the bus drives on and enjoy the quick trip across.

In late afternoon we arrive in Lago Agrio, get a taxi and find ourselves a very nice hotel surrounded by a beautifully kept tropical garden with most unusual plants and blooming bushes which even Angela had never seen. A taxi takes us to the center of town where we walk around a little to take in the scene. It is a larger town with busy streets. Stores everywhere and goods are also placed on the sidewalk on racks and stands. There are many Colombians here and goods from Colombia, like shoes, boots, belts and handbags, etc. while some shoe stores sell mostly Brazilian shoes and goods. We also see restaurants galore.

Eventually we manage to find a travel agency and arrange a two-day trip into the jungle at a cost of sixty dollars per person. We'll be picked up tomorrow morning at eight-thirty. Happily we return to the hotel, have a drink and buffet style dinner which is very tasty. We see many *Gringos* in the dining room this being oil country. Later back in our room we turn on TV and find various channels with news and movies in English due to the large foreign oil community but the movies are all of the violent type. Always the same thing!

Friday, 9/26/03

We are both up early and off to breakfast outside on the terrace where, so it seems, every hotel guest is already there. After breakfast we walk around the beautiful grounds once more and then wait outside to be picked up for the tour. A *Gringo* sits next to us and it doesn't take long before we are talking with him. Turns out he's an oilman from Louisiana who, for the past five years, comes down here whenever needed. He is an engineer and comes when problems show up which the people here can't fix. He stays as long as needed, telling us that last time he was here for forty-one days. We ask him if he has ever run into any problems with the narco people (drug cartels) or any of the bad elements supposed to be around here so close to Colombia, but he says nothing has ever happened to him.

"You don't have to worry," he tells us, "they only kidnap oil people for ransom money. What would they get from you?"

"Exactly," we agree laughing telling him about Angela's friend who is afraid of everything.

"There are people like that," he replies smiling.

He also says that not only American but Canadian oil companies are involved here which I didn't know. The presence of the foreign oil companies is also responsible for the higher prices in the area for hotel and food. He just arrived yesterday and does not know how long he'll be needed this time. Just then his ride arrives and he says good-bye wishing us a good trip.

Finally we also are on our way - late - but the travel lady of last night told us that there had been some confusion with the hotel because there is another one here that has a very similar name. That explains it. At the bus station we meet our Indian guide, Luis, who has worked for this particular company for twelve years he tells us. He is a senior guide and utterly trustworthy. He sits away from us in the bus, so we don't get to find out till later how fortunate we are to have him.

The bus ride takes about three hours over a bumpy, dusty road. It's so dusty that the grass and bushes - even the trees lining the road - look gray with a heavy layer of dust. My hair by now seems glued together. It's also quite warm because the bus is moving slowly due to the bad road condition which makes for little air movement. Finally we arrive at our destination, Puerto de Putumayo, where we have to pay a fee to enter the nature preserve of the Rio Cuyabeno before we can board a canoe already waiting for us. This canoe has a wider body and better seating for which we are grateful because we have been told we will be following the narrow, winding Rio

Cuyabeno for another two hours before we get to the camp. The river is an obstacle course in itself with bushes in the middle of the river, fallen tree trunks and low-hanging branches obstructing the route and sometimes the vision. The young boy driving the canoe expertly steers it along the winding river around sharp turns and obstacles in the water. He also has to keep tightly to the right side because the river is narrow and has oncoming traffic, tourists who are returning.

It's a tremendous experience to travel through this jungle of Amazonia where trees at the edge of the water are leaning far over with branches hanging wide over the water covered with foliage, orchids and bromeliads and other blooming plants. Luis says November to January all these orchids bloom sprinkling the green jungle with color - a sight to behold. There are lianas working their way up into the tree tops sending shoots down towards the water, which again spread out into ten to fifteen shoots and become a giant root packet before they disappear into the water. With so much foliage and other growth clinging to these trees and branches it's extremely difficult to determine which leaves are of the tree.

We see skinny, spiny palm-like little trees with trunks which bend at a sharp angle over the water and then go straight up so as to catch some sunlight in an empty spot which, if they grew straight up, they wouldn't receive. Nature is a marvel where ever one looks. We see the same very tall trees towering above the jungle we had seen earlier along the Rio Napo with relatively thin stems and very airy crowns of leaves allowing sunlight to pass further down. Luis points out plants and trees to us as well as some monkeys swinging through the crowns of the tall trees which we would never have seen. A blue heron takes off when we come around a bend in the river. We take all this in with joy and excitement on our faces.

Finally the jungle opens up and in front of us is *La Laguna*, wide like a lake. Bright light hits our eyes and makes us squint after traveling all this time in more or less semi-darkness. Then we see them, the big trees which stand in the middle of the water. Their stems are enormous and not in proportion with the crowns which consist of some heavy, stubbly arms reaching up showing some thinner branches. Coming closer we notice these trees are also covered with different types of bromeliads as well as orchids and other growth. Some of the bromeliad leaves show up red and yellowish sprinkling the trees with color. There are quite a few of these trees in this huge *Laguna*, but they are distributed more around the edges while the middle of the rather large lake is free of any growth. The whole *Laguna* is hugged by the never ending jungle under a blue sky in which some white clouds play catch.

"We have arrived," Luis announces

"Where is the camp?" I ask.

"It's on the other side. You can't see it from here because of the jungle."

Our boatman is indeed aiming straight across the lagoon. We see a few boats in the distance while Luis tells us that there are actually thirteen lagoons connected by water and one can travel from one into the other. Some wooden houses become visible and the boatman heads directly towards them. A few more boats sway in the water as well as some wooden planks over which we have to balance to go ashore. The boatman and another young Indian are carrying the supply bags and go ashore with me right behind them. The edge of the water is muddy so a wooden staircase has been built to walk up the slope on which the camp is located. On top we are being greeted by Hairo of the camp personnel.

First of all we see a house consisting of a wooden open platform for cooking and eating and gathering of the group much like at the Anaconda Hotel. The kitchen is in the back separated by a counter; all the sides are open with some poles supporting the roof. A railing encloses the platform with tables, benches and some hammocks. Angela swings herself into one hammock and I into another. How wonderful it is! Luis announces that lunch will be ready within the hour and offers us some water which we accept gratefully.

Another young man shows up when lunch is being served and introduces himself as Everisto from Barcelona, Spain. He is a very nice young man, slender with dark long curls any girl would envy him. He wears glasses, is a botanist and very interested in the local flora, especially healing plants. Everisto is very well educated and, like most Europeans, very aware of what goes on in the world which makes for a lively conversation. When he finds out I'm from the States, he wonders how the American people can put up with this "disaster" as he puts it. He is totally anti-Bush. He's aware that world knowledge is not the strong side of the average American and thinks this is the only reason we have this president and his team. Everisto tells us that their own president, Aznar, is also not liked because most people in Spain are against the Iraq war and demonstrated for peace which was ignored by Aznar just like by Bush who said he doesn't care how many peace demonstrations there are. Everisto is fully aware of everything and doesn't hold back. All these young people are the future of their countries; how sad they have become so anti-American. Hopefully this will change again in the future.

After lunch Luis says he'll take us to the lagoon so that we can take a closer look at the trees and can go swimming.

"Swimming," I ask, "with the Anaconda, the crocodiles and the poisonous snakes. I'm not so sure of that. We came to see more than swim."

"The water is very nice and we have never experienced a problem in the middle of the lake and this is where we'll swim," Luis answers.

"The Anaconda can be anywhere and so can other snakes," I respond.

"The Anaconda is closer to the edge of the water and so are other snakes. We never had a problem."

"We really came to see the pink dolphins. The lady in the travel agency told us that there are pink dolphins here and this is what we want to see," says Angela.

"There are no pink dolphins here now, they are white or grey because they change color with the temperature of the water. Lately I haven't seen any dolphins at all," Luis informs us.

"No pink dolphins?" Angela is really disappointed and so am I. "If there are no pink dolphins, I'm not coming because I'm not going into the water with the Anaconda. I'll stay right here in this hammock," swinging herself back into it, "but you go on, Ursula, go on the tour if you like."

"Yes, I will. I don't want to sit here all day," taking my bag and following Luis to show me where our cabin is, we are passing by a few other cabins with little porches in front until we come to ours at the far end of the camp. Arriving at our little wooden house, I almost can't believe my eyes. A sheet is hung where the door should be, moving it aside, I step into one large room containing three sets of bunk beds, two of them covered with netting to protect from the bugs. The windows to the back are cut-outs and totally open with tree branches reaching almost into the room. The walls of the room do not reach entirely up to the roof either; there is an open area over which the aluminum roof is suspended on posts.

"We have to sleep here? No door, no windows, everything open. The monkeys can practically swing in here and any snake can slither in."

"There are no snakes here," Luis answers. We have never had a problem."

"There's always a first time; where are the bathrooms?"

"They are outside in a separate building. I'll show you."

I follow Luis on a boardwalk up to another building with three bathrooms and showers. Again, sheets serve as doors in front of the showers while the toilets have actually wooden doors one can close from inside with a hook.

"I always have to go to the bathroom at night. You expect me to walk outside in the dark?"

"Don't you have a flashlight?" asks Luis.

"No. The lady in the travel agency generously forgot to mention that. She said all we needed was some bug repellant which we bought."

"I'll lend you my flashlight."

"And where are the towels?"

"There are none. Didn't you bring one?"

"No, it has been a very long time since I traveled with a towel."

"I'll give you one of mine," Luis offers immediately.

"Thank you," I say resigned. Luis is very nice and all this is not his fault.

I change into my bathing suit, put a blouse on over it and walk back to the dining platform where Angela swings in the hammock.

"Am I glad we are only spending one night here and not two as we had originally planned," I announce to Angela.

"Why?" Angela looks at me questioningly. She isn't used to complaints from me regarding travel situations.

"Wait until you see the room. No door, no windows, everything is open and the bathrooms are outside."

"They are outside?"

"Yes outside. I'm just glad we didn't take the three-day tour."

Hairo walks over to us asking what the problem is. We had spoken English and find out now that Hairo understands and speaks English also. He assures us that all will be well and not to worry. Hmm, that's easier said than done.

Luis walks over and asks Angela to join in the boat ride but she absolutely refuses, saying: "There is nothing new for me to see now that you have told me there are no pink dolphins which I really wanted to see. I've already seen all the trees and bushes. I'm Ecuadorian, you know."

"The dolphins turn white, maybe gray when the water is warm like right now. They are only pink when the water is cool," Luis repeats again.

We are both disappointed to hear this but I'm hoping we'll see at least a gray dolphin or whatever their color is right now. I follow Luis down to the canoe, a very small one this time, with paddles.

"We are going in this canoe? How can we see all the lakes? We should take the one with the motor."

"This is not permitted. We can use the big canoe only to take people in or out. To go sightseeing we have to use the paddles. This area is ecologically protected," Luis informs us.

"Okay; this travel agency lady forgot to mention a lot of things to us."

We shove off and Luis takes me around to various spots to look at the big trees closely covered with plants and to take photos. We also look for the dolphins - after all the *Lagunas* are all connected - but in vain. Luis tells me that sometimes they go through one of the channels into another lagoon and do not return for a long time which must have happened right now because he hasn't seen them in a while. Still, to go into another lagoon with this boat would have meant a lot of rowing for Luis with the sun burning down on us.

Approaching one big tree causes sudden fluttering when a flock of what looks like birds takes off in a semi-circle heading for the next tree where they are hiding in the branches.

"Birds," I say.

"No, they are bats."

"Bats, I've seen bats fly at day time at *La Granja* many years ago. They had chosen to hang from the ceiling of a bathroom with a broken window. Whenever somebody entered they rushed out the hole with precision."

We approach the other tree. Immediately the bats take off again with considerable noise heading back to the first tree. I admire the growth on the trees. A broken branch hanging in the water is covered with the most beautiful bromeliads and orchids.

It's getting warmer and warmer and Luis is rowing towards the middle of the lagoon and says this is where we can swim. I look at the black water which looks dirty but is not as Luis shows me, then at the small boat and wonder if this is a good idea.

"I'll never get into the water from this small canoe and even worse, how am I going to get back into the boat again?"

"Sí, you can do it; "I'll hold the boat."

I still have my doubts, but I'm so hot by now and as Luis glides into the water hanging on to one end steadying the canoe and encouraging me to come in also, I crawl over the side into the cooling water which feels wonderful and we both swim for a long time. I don't even worry about Anaconda, snakes or anything else that may be looming below because the water is so pleasant. I can see nothing under me, the water is definitely dark and I certainly don't know if anything lurks below. Finally I want to get back into the boat so Luis hangs on to one end on the other side of the boat while I struggle heaving myself back up and in. I don't know how many grandmothers have tried to heave themselves up and into a shaky canoe; I do that - three times - because we are swimming some more! Let me just say it was neither easy, nor fast nor elegant or with élan but it was an act and a half struggling to pull myself back up and in. I know I'll sport a big blue spot on my right thigh which I swing over the side of the boat first.

What looks like an empty boat comes towards us, but coming closer we see Hairo lying inside and relaxing.

"You're working hard, I can see," I greet him laughing.

"Sí, I'm working because we are also watching the lagoon that people don't throw anything into the water. Just now I had to tell a man that he can't wash his clothes here."

"Oh, you do that also. That's good."

We all go swimming again and are soon joined by Everisto and his guide in another boat. They have been on a nature walk and feel like cooling off now. So here we are enjoying the lagoon, monsters or not. Luis was certainly right, it's most enjoyable. We are having so much fun in the water - swimming close around the boats - that we don't even notice how the sky turns all shades of yellow, orange and red being bathed in the setting sun. It's beautiful. I love sunsets and want to take some photos. Therefore, I hurry - this is a laugh - crawl back into the boat to get my camera ready. We also pay no attention that Hairo's canoe is drifting farther and farther away which he is now trying to retrieve by swimming furiously towards it while I shout to him to be in a certain position with the setting sun's light floating on the water for me to take a photo. Hairo indulges me. Luis then rows our boat towards the side so I can take the big trees in the water against the beautiful evening sky but by the time we are in the right position, the sunset is almost gone. Too bad!

It's getting darker fast by now while Luis rows us back to the camp. I climb out of the boat and walk up the steps where Angela is still swinging in her hammock and being obviously relieved to see me.

"I was ready to send a search party out for you," she greets me. "I was really worried when you didn't come back for so long."

"I had such a good time and it's too bad you didn't come also."

"I would never have gotten back into the boat. I'm surprised you did."

"I'm surprised myself and look what I got," showing her the big bruise on my thigh. "By the way, have you been up to our cabin?"

"No, I haven't left the hammock from after lunch."

There are meanwhile three young women present who have returned from a more extended trip to an Indian village further away. So we are six around the dinner table and each one of us is from a different country which makes for a lively dinner conversation. Dinner, by the way, is very good. Luis had asked me during our boat trip what I liked and I told him a nice big salad would be great and when he mentioned chicken I told him I like that also. So we have a very good salad, chicken, potatoes and vegetables. Excellent! There isn't much light, one little candle burning on the counter separating the dining area from the kitchen and one little candle on our table. We are surrounded by stark darkness.

One other person has arrived, an older Ecuadorian who is a volunteer guide helping out as needed. His name is Ricardo but they all call him *Platón* because he reads so much making him wise like Plato. Angela says she had a nice conversation with *Platón* before we returned and that he is very knowledgeable. He is tall and slender and tells me this is the life for him. Mostly he doesn't get paid but helps out with various things in return for meals and a bed for the night which is really all he needs living here in paradise. Hairo, who is actually from Guayaquil but moved with his parents to Lago Agrio about four years ago, says he isn't going back to Guayaquil either but will stay right here. Well, the air is certainly cleaner and life freer. Spending his time here at *La Laguna* with people from all over the world isn't so bad either.

Luis told me earlier that the lagoon is dry in November and December and is no more than three meters deep and will gradually fill up when the rains start in January. During the dry season they have to carry all supplies in on their backs. Walking across the lagoon area takes them one hour. It's hard to believe this lagoon is totally dry at a certain time of the year.

I also ask Luis how many different tribes there are in the area and am told about seven, the largest being the Huaorani.

"The Huaorani are also in Paraguay but called Guarani if I remember correctly. "

"Sí, they are a very large tribe covering a huge area and different countries these days."

"Sí; and Paraguay is completely bilingual with Guarani being taught in schools so that every person speaks Spanish and Guarani."

"That is correct," Luis replies. "The Guarani in Paraguay are more civilized and their lifestyle has changed largely."

I remembered the couple I saw daily in Asunción, the capital of Paraguay, when I was there in nineteen hundred and eighty-seven. They are tall, good-looking Indians and very friendly. They weave very colorful shawls, belts and little bags, head dresses, headbands and make seed necklaces. I bought one of their beautiful little bags and then asked somebody to take a photo of the three of us. Another great memory!

Platón and two of the other girls go out on the lagoon for a night canoe ride. Upon their return, *Platón* said he was the only one swimming. Well, I suppose it makes no difference whether one swims at day or at night because with the dark water, one can't see anything anyway. Everisto involves Luis in a big botanical conversation being so glad to have him available to answer all his questions. Hairo, Angela and I are swinging in the hammocks. Eventually Luis joins us and Everisto takes over Angela's when she wants to go to bed. I have no desire to go up to the cabin any sooner than is absolutely necessary, having seen this open door, open window, open everything concept. Angela says good night and Luis walks with her, candle in hand, in this pitch black night. I actually expect her to be right down again after seeing our accommodations, but Luis returns alone.

"What did Señora Angela say about the room?"

"Muy bien," he answers with a grin on his face.

"Yeah, really!"

I have some whiskey left which we all share. Enjoying the pleasant evening, we talk and relax in our hammocks. Finally it's time for bed for all of us. Luis gives me a towel and his flashlight to walk up the hill in the cool evening air. I push the curtain aside, crawl under the mosquito net into bed and fall asleep quickly.

Saturday, 9/27/03

An enormous noise wakes me up in the middle of the night. Drowsily I sit up and look around before my brain registers where I am and what is happening. Horrendous thunder scares me to death while the entire cabin is bathed in red by lightening shining through the open space between the walls and the roof all around. Not just one thunderstorm but many seem to be hovering above us. Continuous lightening is turning the sky red creating earthshaking thunder. Rain is coming down in sheets or buckets on the metal roof of the cabin adding to the noise. Never in my life have I experienced anything like this. It seems all hell has broken loose. I'm afraid and looking at my watch in the brightness of the lightening it shows three in the morning.

"Surely it must stop soon," I think. But no such luck. Whenever one thunderstorm seems to move away a little, others come closer. We are surrounded by storms on all sides which then appear to stand right above us. There's no end to noise as the rain keeps on thundering on the metal roof. I hear Angela moving in the bed next to me.

"Have you ever seen anything like this?"

"No," she answers.

Looking over to her bed her head is at the foot end of the bed without it really registering with me because more thunder and lightening scares me to death. The sky is constantly red and I wish it would be over. I don't like thunderstorms and lightening and this is a particularly bad one. I don't know how much longer I am awake, an eternity it seems, but eventually I fall asleep and when I wake up next it is six thirty in the morning and still pouring. No lightening nor thunder but rain, rain and more rain.

"We won't get out today if this doesn't stop." This thought pops into my mind and doesn't make me happy thinking we'll have to spend another night here.

Angela's head is still at the wrong end of the bed.

"I got up during the night," she says raising her head, "and I didn't even know anymore where I was. I slept the other way around. It's raining in and half my bed is wet."

"It is? Oh my goodness! Why didn't you say something? If this doesn't stop, we'll be here another night. Did you think of that?"

"Yes, it occurred to me also."

We listen to the rain falling and doze off again. When next I wake it's about eight in the morning which, we had been told last night, is when breakfast would be ready. Well, I see no activity anywhere but take my shower anyway.

"Go ahead," says Angela, "I'm not taking one with this lake water."

"Why not; the water is filtered anyway."

"No, I won't take one."

Walking on the boardwalk - I can see now why they needed these steps and walkways everywhere - I enter the shower which consists of one heavy stream of water but it works and is actually much warmer than the very cold water at the Anaconda Hotel. It's still raining but not so heavy anymore. Around nine we all show up at the dining platform for breakfast.

"I love this weather," *Platón* tells us happily while we look at him with mixed emotions.

"I don't," I answer, "because if it doesn't stop soon, we'll have to spend another night here. The area is beautiful but the accommodations leave a lot to be desired. I like at least a real door and a screen on the windows and the bathroom close and not outside, an endurance walk away in the middle of the night."

"I understand," *Platón* nods smiling swinging in a hammock, a book by Gabriel García Márquez in his hand.

"Oh, I know this author also," I tell him. "I have one of his books, *One Hundred Years of Solitud* which I loved very much."

"Sí, this is perhaps his most famous one. He is an excellent writer," *Platón* answers. "This book is very good also. García Márquez is a Colombian writer, but lived most of his life in Mexico and Europe - Spain I believe."

Platón is a very interesting man. No wonder the others consider him knowledgeable and wise. To encounter such a learned man and philosopher in the Amazon jungle is truly unexpected and a wonderful extra benefit. As I say, the people one meets along the way... He isn't always here but visits other camps as well, helping out wherever needed which makes life more interesting, he says, because a change of surrounding is always good. So true, so true! I contemplate the fact that we have two such knowledgeable Ecuadorian men, *Platón* and Luis, with us and gain much from them.

By the time we are finished with breakfast consisting of a big fruit salad, scrambled eggs with bacon and potatoes, the rain has almost stopped. The canoes, half sunk and full of water, are sitting at the edge of the lagoon. Everything is wet and muddy. Suddenly Luis gets our attention pointing to the trees where a troupe of little monkeys is swinging by high up in the tall tree tops. We all try to catch a few glimpses of them before they disappear from our eyes completely, moving at a very fast pace. Then Hairo gets us to come over to the side of the veranda pointing down to the water's edge where two *caimanes* are feeding. They are a good size - two to three meters long - and enjoying whatever our camp guides throw down for them. I can't believe my eyes thinking I swam in this lagoon yesterday.

"This is what you swam with," says Angela as if she were reading my thoughts.

"They are not out there," interjects Luis. "They're really only around the edges."

We all watch their feeding with fascination, opening their giant snouts wide, shaking their heads and turning them up as they swallow. I get my camera, but my battery decides to die right now. That ends the photo session.

Luis announces that we'll be leaving about eleven in the morning. Another boat will come and take us to the bus.

This is good news. We had a wonderful day yesterday and the rain stopped after more than six hours. *Platón* had said it could rain for a day or more so we are in luck and won't have to spend another night in this open, jump-in, slither-through cabin. *Platón* and Luis tell us that there are other camps nearby which do have doors and windows and inside facilities. Apparently it was meant for us to have this experience. Well the people certainly are great, the area beautiful and it's an unusual adventure. As Angela always says one has to have an adventure; what else would one talk about?

We walk down to the boat, all six tourists with Luis, Hairo and the boat driver. *Platón* and one other young guide are staying behind. They load bags and bags of garbage into the boat because this is an ecological area and everything has to be taken out again, Luis says. We even stop at another camp across the lagoon and pick up garbage from them. Angela thinks they'll dump it all in the water, but they don't.

The sky is still dark and it is pleasantly cool. Soon we enter the Rio Guayabeno which seems even darker than before without sun. Still we enjoy the boat ride again and even see a bird diving for fish which looks like a kingfisher and immediately dives under water when we turn up. I wished the boat ride wouldn't end.

Two hours later we are back at the entrance of the park where we started out. The bus is not there yet and so we all get some lunch in a little restaurant. Walking around the area I notice a tall tree with many weaver bird nests hanging from the branches looking like giant pears against the sky. Then we meet up with a very young girl from Germany who is on her way in. She wants to know what the camp is like and how we liked it. We give her some information and mention that she'll probably be the only tourist there for the night but not to worry, the people are nice. Angela and I feel sorry for her having to be there without other tourists. She does speak some Spanish and will be able to communicate.

Soon we are on the bus again which takes us back to Lago Agrio. The sky has cleared somewhat and the sun is peeking through. The first thing I really notice is how green everything is. After the heavy rain of the night there is no dust and the grassy sides of the road, the leaves on the bushes and trees, everything seems to be light green just like in the spring when the first new leaves come out. The difference from yesterday is so amazing that it literally jumps into my eyes. The world is new and clean again and millions of water droplets sparkle in the light.

In Lago Agrio we say our good-byes and give Luis a good tip for looking after us so well. Hairo gets something, too, and I don't think I'll ever forget the two of them - nor *Platón*, the *wise* man. Then we are back on an express bus straight to Guayaquil because Angela is anxious to get home and see how her mother is doing. I would like to go to Quito from here being closer, but she says we don't have the right clothes for Quito and she needs to present the proper image there. Better to go home first and then take a separate trip to Quito. She's right, we don't have the proper clothes and what we have isn't clean anymore either.

Sunday, 9/28/03

It's a very long bus ride; in fact it lasts seventeen hours. We sleep off and on which surprises me because usually I have a hard time sleeping on planes or buses. There is a stop occasionally until the last five hours or so when our express turns once again into a shuttle service picking up and dropping off people along the way. Once in Guyaquil, a taxi takes us home and what a homecoming this turns out to be.

Ivanovich is upset and so is his wife because Elena had left suddenly Saturday morning. Angela heard bad things from all sides except Elena who had come back Saturday night to talk with Angela but we weren't back. Somehow Ida, although Angela had told her specifically not to let anyone into the apartment, allowed Elena and her so called cousin she had brought along the day we left and who Angela should have sent right back home again, as well as Ivan's youngest son into her apartment. They bought wine and had a party which wouldn't have been so bad but there were other considerations. Elena's cousin, the girl with an unpleasant, angry face, seemed to be right in the middle of it all. The moment I saw her before our departure I didn't like her face; it wasn't a good face. There was also talk that Ida had not given food to Elena and the girl, although Angela had told her to cook the meals for them. It seems that Ida was quite a bit at fault in Ivanovich's eyes as well as his wife's. Too bad, Elena was very good to Amelia and very patient with her. Angela is quite upset by this turn of events saying again how difficult it is for her to get away these days.

Amelia, however, is better and very happy to see us back safely. She's always worried that something will happen to us. She still doesn't eat much but she seems to have less pain. We spend some time with her and Angela takes her blood pressure and checks on her diabetes, the things she does every day when home. She wants to know from Ivanovich if Amelia has taken all her medications while I tell him in detail about our trip since we had followed most of his directions. He's happy to hear that we had such a good time and all worked out. Then, after everything and everybody has settled down, we rest most of Sunday afternoon. I take a walk to the Malecón and then go to bed early sleeping very well.

Monday, 9/29/03

"Let's take the night bus to Quito today," says Angela.

"Do you want to leave with all these happenings here?"

"Sure. We'll go spend two days and come back because you are already leaving on Saturday."

Yes time is always going too fast here. She and Ivanovich are going to Milagro to see how things are at *La Granja* while I stay in town and take care of a few things like reconfirming my return flight with American Airlines in their nice office conveniently located at the Malecón, get the latest photos developed, buy some gifts, etc.

After my walk at seven in the evening I pack the few things I'll need for the trip and watch TV until Angela and Ivanovich return at ten-thirty. I'm really looking forward to seeing Quito again because it's been a few years since I was there last. After Angela is packed, Ivanovich takes us to the bus terminal and by eleven-thirty we are on the bus to Quito.

Tuesday, 9/30/03

"Ursula, wake up," I hear Angela saying without it really sinking in.

"Why? What's going on?" I answer sleepily.

"We have to leave the bus. There is a military control. This is Babahoyo and we all have to leave the bus."

That's a first! All the years I've traveled in Ecuador, I've never experienced this. Seems the whole world is going crazy. A look at my watch shows one-thirty in the morning. Too bad, I had been sleeping so well. One soldier looks into our handbags while another one opens every bag and goes through it. Once finished, we are allowed back on the bus and continue our trip.

We arrive in Quito before seven in the morning but until we get to our more centrally located terminal another hour passes during rush hour in this heavy traffic. My eyes are glued to the window as I look at all the new sky scrapers, beautiful highways and overpasses and the continuing construction. A taxi takes us to a nice little hotel in the center of town. After freshening up and eating breakfast I can hardly wait to explore Quito again. It's so exciting being back in Quito, the capital of Ecuador, situated only fifteen miles from the equator - which has given Ecuador its name - at an altitude of nine thousand three hundred fifty feet keeping temperatures pleasantly cool year round. A considerable indigenous population in and around Quito gives the city such a colorful, vibrant atmosphere. I fell in love with this city from my first encounter with Quito.

Quito was founded in 1534 by a lieutenant of conquistador Francisco Pizarro and even prior to the Spanish settlement, the site served as the northern capital of the Inca Empire at one time. Quito functioned as a major cultural center during the colonial period attracting many outstanding artists and sculptors of its period. To this day Quito preserved much of its colonial architecture with its low buildings and overhanging roofs and balconies - despite earthquakes. The cobble-stoned, narrow streets in the center of the city go back to the colonial beginning with a central plaza in the old city surrounded by the cathedral and government buildings. Spanish rule ended in eighteen hundred and twenty-two and in eighteen hundred and thirty Quito became the capital of an independent Ecuador.

Under a blue, sunny sky we walk along Wilson Street towards Avenida Amazonas, the main street of the city, being approached many times by Indians walking toward us selling their beautiful crafts. It doesn't take long before we make our first purchases despite my thinking that I shouldn't buy anything but seeing all the beautiful weavings, folklore paintings, pottery, carvings, leather goods etc. my resistance breaks down. One Indian lady selling folklore oil paintings follows us around and wants for me to buy more. With a big smile on her face she shows me more paintings. It's like a game and they don't give up. Stopping here and there, looking and buying a few items, we eventually arrive at the Hotel Colón to eat lunch in their beautiful dining room where the food is good for an international clientele.

Afterwards we hire a taxi for a city tour into the old town with its colonial government buildings and churches. I remember that on my first visit here, I walked much of this old town - in high heels - surprising Angela how I could do that. Well, I don't do it anymore and my shoes have very low heels these days. We get back to the hotel in late afternoon under a much darker sky by now because in Quito it usually rains in the afternoon. We are both tired from walking around at this high altitude and take a little nap. At dinner time Angela says she doesn't feel like going out anymore so I go by myself remembering the little fish restaurant I had seen which looked very nice and, according to the hotel owner, also has good food As I step outside, however, it's raining heavily. What now? The owner offers me his big umbrella and off I go. It's raining steadily but the restaurant isn't far away. Only a few people are seated in *La Rede* and I pick a nice table on a higher level. The restaurant is rather rustic in décor with fishing nets, fish and other ocean ornaments displayed. I like the atmosphere and have a most enjoyable trout dinner in this little place. Next to me, two young ladies are in a lively conversation until one turns around and I learn that they have been traveling for three months with three more months to go. One is from Massachusetts, the other from England. The young woman from England says she started out in Mexico, then to Central America and is working her way down through South America. The two had met along the way and decided to travel together. We have a nice conversation with me enjoying their company and learning about their adventures.

Leaving the restaurant, it rains even heavier now. I'm glad for my big umbrella. At the corner of Amazonas and Wilson, a young man stops me asking: "Do you speak English?"

"Yes," I answer immediately suspicious.

"I'm sorry to ask you, I've never done this before, but I've been robbed. My shirt, my wallet and everything has been taken. I went to the American Embassy but they were closed already. Could you give me four or five dollars?" My alarm bell goes off.

"Your story may or may not be true," I answer turning to walk away. "I'm sorry I can't help you."

"Sorry to have bothered you," he says politely.

I walk on, not knowing what to think. Should I help him out or is this a ruse and dangerous, especially late at night and by myself. Back at the hotel, Angela says, "Good you didn't give him anything because you know what they do? You pull out your wallet and they grab it and run off."

"Exactly! If he really had this misfortune I wouldn't have minded but how does one know? This could be his way of making a living. Still, I feel unsure about this."

"You did the right thing! Lucky he didn't attack you."

Wednesday, 10/1/03

We want to have breakfast somewhere else today and walk down Avenida Amazonas where we saw what looked like a nice café upstairs in a corner building. Well, we are out on a veranda with a great view of the street below but the breakfast is nothing to write home about. Only the coffee is excellent. Afterwards we separate for a few hours because Angela has to take care of a few things while I want to look at some stores. Meandering down Avenida Amazonas, I stop here and there and look at the many stands and some stores selling Indian goods, take a few photos and talk with some of the Indians who manage to sell me a few more items. Finally I take all my purchases back to the hotel and return to Avenida Amazonas where I had noticed this nice outside café yesterday and a group of grandfathers apparently meeting there daily. I saw them earlier again.

I find myself a nice table close to the building with a good view over the broad sidewalk busy with well-dressed ladies and men in business suits interlaced with Indians in their colorful dresses displaying their goods. Around me are mostly business men negotiating deals. I watch the world go by and the people around me savoring the whole scene when two young men sit down at the table next to mine. Working on my notes, at first I pay no attention to them whatsoever until I believe to hear them speak German. After listening a little more I address them and get involved in a lengthy conversation about many things.

First of all they are no tourists. They are two young Germans who, instead of fulfilling their military duty, are here to provide one year of social services to save street children. Apparently this can be done either twelve months abroad without pay or ten months at home with some pay. They have to pay their own way receiving only free food and accommodation in the same building with the children. They teach the boys and try to get them on a normal path and turn their lives around by guiding them and setting examples. They see to it that they have medical and dental care and clothing, they play ball and go on excursions with them but on outings quite a few of the boys use the opportunity to disappear

"If a boy has spent most of his seventeen years in the street he's not likely going to change. He likes his freedom too much," I'm being told.

"They take off, ha?"

"Yes. However, there are also the others who really do want to change their lives. That's what makes it worth while. If only one or two are saved, it's worth it."

"Do you enjoy your work?"

"Very much," answers the one who has been in Ecuador for thirteen months and could actually return home but has elected to stay until just before Christmas.

"I think this is a wonderful thing you are doing. I had no idea that Germany gave its young people this option. After all not everybody wants to be a soldier in this day and age."

"Exactly," they both answer nodding their heads. "We can do something good by helping other young people and, at the same time, broaden our own horizon by getting to know another country and culture. I understand that the United States has something similar, the Peace Corps. The only thing is - so I've been told - very few people want to join these days because of the political situation the US has managed to get itself into."

I nod my head.

"As a matter of fact," the young man continues, "I've been told by some Americans who traveled in Costa Rica and also in Chile that they put 'Canadian' stickers on their luggage because they didn't want to be recognized immediately as Americans."

"Really; that's so sad," I answer thinking the supposedly freest country in the world is no longer so free with many people afraid to travel - especially abroad - and then trying to hide their nationality.

"Yes, in some parts of the world it's really bad. No wonder, of course, the war with Afghanistan and especially now Iraq and the ongoing Palestinian situation doesn't help the US at all," I'm being told.

"I know," nodding my head, "it's absolutely terrible. All this fighting everywhere is intolerable and I feel so sorry for our soldiers and the people of Iraq, especially for the children. I know what they are going through because there was a time in my life when I went through all these horrors myself and had nightmares for years after. I don't even know how I survived it. Our country is so divided because of this war and we certainly set an extremely bad example for the rest of the world. This administration doesn't seem to understand that you don't lead with weapons alone but by setting examples. Respect has to be earned because fear alone doesn't work in the long run."

"You know, all the Americans I've run into here in Ecuador - even the twenty Stanford and Harvard students who came down here to work with us, say the same things. None of them approve of this war with Iraq or of the foreign policy of their country."

"I've always said that people who travel have a different mindset and realize that it's definitely preferable to have an open world and freedom. Now we have neither. After all, people everywhere want the same thing: a decent job, a roof over their heads, food on the table, an education and a better life for their children and some happiness."

"That's right. I'm so glad we don't send troops into Iraq but we'll have to give some other help. Bush went and bombed the country into rubble and now he wants the world to fix his mess. I don't understand why the Americans don't speak up and go along with all this craziness."

"There are some people who speak up, but their voices are overshadowed by the ruling political machine which tries to drown them out. Everything has become very political, the country is really divided and one can only hope that more people are waking up eventually to all the problems we face in the United States. There is no money for social programs at home, but when it comes to Iraq, there is all the money in the world. The state of affairs is sad."

"Oh sure, the economic damage to your country and the whole world is great. Of course, it takes brains to think things through and plan ahead and that just isn't there."

What is one to say to these observations? Nothing! Pretty soon we'll be total prisoners of our own fear and idiosyncrasy. We talk for a long time about world affairs and then the conversation switches to what to do and see in Ecuador.

One young man came only a month ago and is being taught the ropes by the one who has been here for thirteen months. He says his parents had also been here to visit and that he actually was in the Cuyabeno area where we just came from but in a better lodge with facilities inside. I further learn that just before he arrived at the lagoon a few months ago, it was forbidden to swim for two weeks because one Anaconda crossed the lagoon often.

"Wonderful! I'm glad I didn't know that before. What happened to that Anaconda?"

"It was caught and brought to the river. I have to tell you, however, I was thinking about the Anaconda all the time while I was swimming there. Like you, I couldn't resist the wonderful water and swam quite a few times. I'm so glad I didn't take my parents along. I would never have heard the end of it."

"Right," I answer laughing thinking of the sermon I got from Angela.

"I'm so glad nothing happened when we were there. I told Luis, our guide, that there was no guarantee a snake or a caiman wouldn't turn up just because it hadn't happened before. Luis generously forgot to mention this particular adventurous Anaconda altogether. I might not have gone into the water after all."

It's time for me to leave for the Marriott Hotel to meet Angela for lunch. They point me in the right direction - along Avenida Amazonas - and we say our good-byes. I learned a lot from these young men and am always interested to hear other people's opinion. Angela and I arrive at about the same time. This hotel is relatively new with an ultra modern entrance/lobby area open and bright, with a wonderful dining room a few steps down. We have the buffet lunch which is good but not as fancy as yesterday in the Colón. Finally, early evening, we pick up our bags at our hotel and take a taxi to the bus terminal.

Thursday, 10/2/03

We arrive in Guayaquil around two-thirty in the morning, take a taxi and are back home around three with enough time left to sleep. This time there is no particular disaster. Amelia is fine; Ivanovich and his wife have looked after her and are with her when I go in to see her in the morning. Ida and Marco generally get on well and Elena hasn't come back so far. Amelia looks much better and even walks a little supported by Angela and Ida. Later that day we drive out to *La Granja* in Milagro after picking up some chemicals for the pool. The tourist center will be open to the public again very shortly because so far no buyer has turned up. Pedro tells us the generator works, the pump is pumping water but the water is yellow. They are pumping from another well and may have to go back to the original well.

Pedro is the only one present. Unfortunately Marta is in Guayaquil to take care of a few personal things so I will not be able to say good-bye to her personally. I have not seen much of her or *La Granja* during this visit. I take one last walk around the property regretting that it isn't open already. Thinking of my visit a year ago and how different everything was then, I wonder if I'll be back again or if it will be sold soon. It's such a beautiful place.

Stalin hasn't returned but Angela heard he has moved with his family to Quito. Well, I hope things are going well for him there.

Friday, 10/3/03

This is my last day here. I still have to say good-bye to my Indian friends at the Mercado on the Malecón. By now it's about noon and quite warm outside but at the Malecón a fresh breeze from the Río Guayas is a welcome change. The sisters are happy to see me but sad to hear that my visit is ending. So am I. I buy a few items before we say good-bye and they remind me not to forget them. How can I? They are a very positive memory of my visits to Ecuador having spent much more time these last few weeks visiting and talking with them.

I buy one more EL UNIVERSO from Segundo who is still here with his stand and the streets around the house still torn up. He is waiting to be officially told that he has to move before he'll leave. I don't blame him. He has been in this spot for many years with a steady clientele. He says he's sorry to see me go and I'll miss Segundo also. He is always friendly and we talked more during this visit. Altogether, during my lengthy visits these last two years, I've become much better acquainted with everybody and life in Ecuador. He and all the others will be forever imprinted on my mind. Even the security guard at the corner by the pharmacy has always had a friendly greeting for me and thinks I should not leave.

The area around Parque Centenario is one giant rubble pile right now as every single street is torn up. There is much dirt and dust and I still have to skip over various obstacles every time I leave the house. I tell Angela I'm not coming back until all this construction is finished. It should be completed by Christmas - not too soon for all the people living and working here because it's difficult to keep the houses clean. Even with windows closed the dust penetrates somehow. I'm always amazed how much dirt Marco sweeps up. Of course, to breathe the air filled with dust particles is not too healthy either.

Then it's packing time. I've definitely bought too much again. My suitcase is very full. Amazing how things accumulate.

Angela had Ida fix a *little* salad for us which turns out to be a huge meal with lettuce, potatoes, vegetables and camerones, soup and wine. Ivanovich joins us with his wife and daughter. Once again we are all around the table enjoying a wonderful meal and each other's company accompanied by a lively conversation. I don't even want to think about leaving and regret that the time always passes so quickly. Originally we planned on going out to dinner but these plans changed somewhat. Angela had called the employment agency leaving word with them that she had liked Elena's work and wanted to talk with her. She had heard from Segundo and his wife downstairs that Elena had told them she was leaving because the other two made life too difficult for her and that she wanted to talk with Angela. So right now we only have Marco and Ida and because Ida is going home tonight to visit her family, Angela wants to stay here with her mother and not leave her alone with Marco, who cannot always be counted on. I hope Elena will come back to talk with Angela so all this can be cleared up.

Ivanovich, his wife and I want to go out and have a drink somewhere intending to be back by ten in the evening but since the word *puntualidad,* about which much noise is being made in the country right now, isn't well known here, we leave at about ten to go to the Planet Universo where one of Ivan's sons is working. In Ecuador one doesn't come back by ten, one leaves by ten. Like all sports bars and restaurants this one is also very noisy but the food is good. We have a wonderful time take some photos, enjoy a few drinks and are back home around midnight - an improvement over last year.

To come back to *puntualidad,* two articles in EL UNIVERSO yesterday supported by photos of people setting their wrist watches - one even of el Presidente Lucio Gutierrez and some dignitaries - stress the necessity of being punctual and ask Ecuadorians to synchronize not only their clocks but change their attitudes as well. Wonderful intentions and very necessary but will they succeed? Probably not immediately but if properly reinforced, especially at the schools, the next generation should be up to the challenge. In fact, Ivan's daughter was not allowed in at school yesterday because she was a few minutes late. She and her mother were upset but both will make more of an effort to get there in time.

Angela has no doubt she'll wake up at five in the morning, yet it's I who actually wake up about four-thirty. After my shower I get the coffee ready and wake up Angela who says she was actually awake already. We arrive at the Simon Bolivar Airport in plenty of time but the airport is under construction and no car can enter. Angela and I say our good-bye here once again and I thank her for the wonderful time I've had with her and her family who really feel like my family by now as well. The many visits before and especially the last two lengthy stays have brought us all so much closer that it becomes harder and harder for me to leave.

"Come back soon!" Angela still shouts after me. I turn around and wave a smile back to her then walk the long way to the airport building showing my ticket and passport at the door before passing from counter to counter. Finally in the plane, I read EL UNIVERSO one last time. A little article on the front page catches my eyes, the Huaorani Indians of Ecuadorian Amazonia demand that the lumbermen who have come to cut down valuable trees retreat from their area, namely the Pastaza and Orellana area, the very place Angela and I had visited because they found the bodies of three Indians whose death, they said, was caused by these lumbermen. These are their forests and they don't want any outside lumbermen there. I can't blame them. This Rain Forest is not only important to the indigenous people who live there but it's important to the world climate and grows many medicinal plants. My mind wanders back to Luis, Hairo and the Indian boy who maneuvered the boat on the Guayabeno and especially *Platón*, the man who knows much and who loves this part of the world so much with or without lightening and thunderstorms. Why is it, I wonder, that we 'civilized' and technically advanced nations have to destroy so much and infringe on other people's rights? Are the improvements worth the destruction, in particular if we are not welcome? People's cultures and lifestyles are the direct result of their environment and should be respected as such without forever trying to convert them to our way of thinking and living, particularly in view of the ebb of morality in most of the western world. These are some of my thoughts as the plane lifts off to take me home and I'm wondering what lies ahead for myself and the world.

EPILOGUE

I have continued to travel to Ecuador every year since I wrote this book to see the country and all my friends; unfortunately, some of the latter are no longer with us. Henry Schaefer, who arranged the tours for me in the Galápagos, has passed away but I've met his wife Angie while he was still alive and become good friends with her since and we get together frequently when I'm in Guayaquil and stay in contact.

One American friend is no longer with us either and neither is Mario who passed away just before Christmas.

And Amelia, Angela's mother, the kindest lady I've ever met left us recently. She was 96 and we all miss her terribly because she was always there, always. They will be in our hearts forever and may they all rest in peace.

The tourist center we refer to as *La Granja* is still in Angela's hands and operating. Problems have been cleared up and people come to enjoy the tranquility or celebrate big parties like weddings and other events there. Angela is following more and more in her mother's footsteps by helping people where she can which I became aware of years ago already.

All the street reconstruction in Guayaquil has been completed so that it is a real pleasure to walk along my familiar routes. The Malecón and cerro Santa Ana are maintained beautifully and very clean. I make it a point to climb the four hundred forty-four steps up cerro Santa Ana various times a week for my cardio-vascular exercise, not only for the view which I enjoy also.

Segundo is back at the corner where he's always been selling his newspapers, magazines and candies and I continue buying my daily newspaper from him when in town.

President Lucio Gutierrez didn't last but unlike the presidents before him, he didn't have to leave the country. An interim president filled in the remainder of his term until Rafael Correa was elected President of Ecuador. He is still in office making many changes.